vSphere High Performance Cookbook

Second Edition

Tune your vSphere to maximize its performance

Kevin Elder
Christopher Kusek
Prasenjit Sarkar

BIRMINGHAM - MUMBAI

vSphere High Performance Cookbook

Second Edition

First published: July 2013

Second edition: June 2017

Production reference: 1290617

Published by Packt Publishing Ltd.
Livery Place
35 Livery Street
Birmingham
B3 2PB, UK.
ISBN 978-1-78646-462-0

www.packtpub.com

Credits

Authors
Kevin Elder
Christopher Kusek
Prasenjit Sarkar

Reviewer
Luca Mattana

ProofReader
Safis Editing

Indexer
Aishwarya Gangawane

Production Coordinator
Arvindkumar Gupta

Technical Editors
Bharat Patil
Joel Wilfred D'souza

Project Coordinator
Kinjal Bari

Acquisition Editor
Vijin Boricha

Content Development Editor
Monika Sangwan

Copy Editor
Gladson Monteiro

About the Authors

Kevin Elder lives in Portland, Oregon, and is a Principal Architect and Engineer at Xiologix LLC. With over 15 years of experience in IT, focused on selling, installing, and supporting virtualization and storage technologies, Kevin is responsible for customer success from initial design through implementation. He has been installing, managing, and selling VMware products for over 10 years. Kevin holds a VCP 6 and is a Dell EMC Elect for 2017.

Kevin was a technical reviewer for *Learning VMware vSphere*, published by *Packt Publishing*. This is his first publication as an author.

> *I would like to thank my wife, Ellen, for her support and encouragement throughout this process. I would also like to thank Christopher for his assistance and guidance. Thank you also to our editors at Packt for their guidance and to the technical reviewers for their invaluable assistance.*

Christopher Kusek lives in Portland, Oregon where he is Chief Technology Officer and Executive VP of Engineering at Xiologix. With over 20 years of experience in IT as a technology evangelist and industry leader, Christopher plays a key role in Xiologix's growth, leading its storage and engineering practice to evaluate and architect solutions that meet the client's tactical and strategic goals.

He has over 20 years of experience in the industry with virtualization experience running back to the pre-1.0 days of VMware. He has shared his expertise with many far and wide through conferences, presentations, CXIParty, and sponsoring or presenting at community events and outings, whether it is focused on artificial intelligence, cloud, machine learning, networking, security, storage, or virtualization.

He is the coauthor of the following books:

- *VMware vSphere 5 Administration Instant Reference* by *Sybex* (localized in English, German, and Russian)
- *VMware vSphere Performance: Designing CPU, Memory, Storage and Networking for Performance-Intensive Workloads* by *Sybex*
- *vSphere Design Best Practices* by *Packt Publishing*

Christopher has also written an EMC whitepaper: *Ten ways to reduce cost while modernizing your IT*, and many more. He has been a frequent contributor to VMware communities, vBrownBag, Twitter, and YouTube, and has been an active blogger for over a decade.

Christopher is a proud VMware vExpert and a huge supporter of the program since its inception. He continues to help drive the growth of the virtualization community. He was named EMC Elect in 2013, 2014, 2015, and 2016, and continues with the renamed program of Dell EMC Elect in 2017. Christopher is a Cisco Champion 2016 and 2017, and has been a member of the VMware vExpert Program for nearly 10 years. Christopher is a vExpert specialist in the breakout designations of vExpert VSAN and vExpert NSX, and he's been a frequent contributor to VMware communities such as vBrownBag. Christopher shares his expertise online in the Thwack community as a SolarWinds ambassador, and he's a regular contributor and delegate to the Gestalt IT Tech Field Day series. You'll find Christopher directly through his Twitter handle, `@cxi`, and on his YouTube channel, CXI.

You can find him dressing up like a cat, cosplaying some obscure anime or game character, tweeting pictures of his cats, or spending time with his family taking #DevOps and #DadOps to the next level!

I'd like to acknowledge some friends, family, and colleagues. This book would not have been possible if not for the meticulous attention and determination of my coauthor Kevin Elder so to him, hats off! I'd like to thank my dear friend Chad Sakac who continues to rock at every single opportunity. A special shout out to both Pat Gelsinger and Michael Dell who I've met on many an occasion and I know quite intimately the struggle you face to help make our future a possibility. Community leaders such as Stephen Foskett, Cody Bunch, Josh De Jong, and Dave Henry are the very execution of rock stardom and a special shout out to fellow vExpert Thom Greene, who coined the term DadOps.

Lastly, I would like to thank my cats, Taylor, Asher, and Snow, and my actual human family, Alexander, Chris, Emily, Erehwon, and Isabelle!

Keep on catting on! Err, something-something virtualization!

Prasenjit Sarkar is a product manager at Oracle for their public cloud, with a focus on cloud strategy, Oracle Ravello, cloud-native applications, and the API platform. His primary focus is driving Oracle's cloud computing business with commercial and public sector customers, helping to shape and deliver a strategy to build broad use of Oracle's Infrastructure as a Service offerings, such as Compute, Storage, and Database as a Service. He is also responsible for developing public/private cloud integration strategies, customers' cloud computing architecture visions, future state architectures, and implementable architecture roadmaps in the context of the public, private, and hybrid cloud computing solutions that Oracle can offer.

He has also authored six industry-leading books on virtualization, SDN, and physical compute, among others.

He has six successful patents and six more patents pending at the US PTO. He has also authored numerous research articles.

About the Reviewer

Luca Mattana is a VMware certified IT professional with over 15 years of experience. For the past 9 years, he has worked at ING Bank N.V., Italian branch, as senior system administrator. His work has been mainly focused on virtualization in enterprise solutions, especially on VMware products, designing, deploying, and maintaining, as main referent, production and disaster recovery infrastructure.

Before his ING Bank experience, he worked with the Sanpaolo group (now Intesa Sanpaolo), as Windows system administrator, and there he had his first encounter with virtualization technology, working on projects in Italy and in the Irish branch.

Starting from 2017, Luca has been working as a Cloud Architect and Senior System Engineer for Blueit, specializing in IT technology infrastructure management processes for enterprise companies.

Luca was also the reviewer for the following video courses by Packt Publishing:

- *Mastering VMware vSphere 6.5*
- *VCP6-DCV(6.5) Examination Preparation Guide*

www.PacktPub.com

For support files and downloads related to your book, please visit `www.PacktPub.com`. Did you know that Packt offers eBook versions of every book published, with PDF and ePub files available? You can upgrade to the eBook version at `www.PacktPub.com` and as a print book customer, you are entitled to a discount on the eBook copy. Get in touch with us at `service@packtpub.com` for more details. At `www.PacktPub.com`, you can also read a collection of free technical articles, sign up for a range of free newsletters and receive exclusive discounts and offers on Packt books and eBooks.

`https://www.packtpub.com/mapt`

Get the most in-demand software skills with Mapt. Mapt gives you full access to all Packt books and video courses, as well as industry-leading tools to help you plan your personal development and advance your career.

Why subscribe?

- Fully searchable across every book published by Packt
- Copy and paste, print, and bookmark content
- On demand and accessible via a web browser

Customer Feedback

Thanks for purchasing this Packt book. At Packt, quality is at the heart of our editorial process. To help us improve, please leave us an honest review on this book's Amazon page at `https://www.amazon.com/dp/1786464624`.

If you'd like to join our team of regular reviewers, you can e-mail us at `customerreviews@packtpub.com`. We award our regular reviewers with free eBooks and videos in exchange for their valuable feedback. Help us be relentless in improving our products!

Table of Contents

Preface

Welcome to *vSphere High Performance Cookbook, Second Edition*. The authors here are focused on providing a cookbook of resources and recipes, so you can go from understanding your environment to optimizing your infrastructure characteristics to achieve optimal performance. As you take in each chapter, they will provide you with independent insights into different aspects of design that can be treated independently, but when utilized together will make for a more performance-ready and optimized virtual infrastructure. Central to this book is the leveraging of the VMware vSphere suite.

VMware vSphere 6.5 is a sophisticated suite of software. Although it is straightforward to initially set up, the default options may not result in the best performance in your environment. This book focuses on tuning the parts of vSphere that can result in a better-performing environment. The recipes in this book walk through the major components of a VMware environment and highlight where potential performance issues are and how to address them. As vSphere has matured over the years, many third-party software companies have been created to complement vSphere. This book also has recipes dedicated to third-party software and their benefits, where appropriate.

The book has been written for VMware administrators running vSphere 6.5. Administrators running earlier versions of vSphere will find most of the ideas and suggestions relevant to their versions; however, the specific steps in the recipes will be different.

What this book covers

Chapter 1, *CPU Performance Design*, contains a background on CPU performance in a virtualized environment. It also talks about how to monitor CPU performance and takes you through CPU performance best practices.

Chapter 2, *Memory Performance Design*, explains the memory management techniques that VMware uses and how to optimize memory performance.

Chapter 3, *Networking Performance Design*, covers performance considerations for vSphere Standard and Distributed switching.

Chapter 4, *DRS, SDRS, and Resource Control Design*, covers DRS, SDRS, and related performance topics.

Chapter 5, *vSphere Cluster Design*, discusses the various options in vSphere cluster design, as vSphere cluster design is critical to a performant vSphere environment.

Chapter 6, *Storage Performance Design*, discusses the performance of various types of storage, including VSAN and VVols.

Chapter 7, *Designing vCenter on Windows for Best Performance*, discusses one of the options for installing vCenter: vCenter on Windows. The benefits, drawbacks, and performance considerations of this method are covered in this chapter.

Chapter 8, *Designing VCSA for Best Performance*, discusses another method of vCenter deployment: the vCenter appliance. This chapter also covers this method's benefits, drawbacks, and performance.

Chapter 9, *Virtual Machine and Virtual Environment Performance Design*, covers the performance considerations for virtual machines to help them perform their best.

Chapter 10, *Performance Tools*, covers PowerCLI and third-party tools to provide insight into the performance of your vSphere environment.

What you need for this book

Readers of this book will need a working vSphere environment with ESXi 6.5 already installed. A minimum of three ESXi hosts is recommended. Some recipes in this book require a vSphere Enterprise Plus license. If you do not have access to an Enterprise Plus license, the 60-day temporary license that comes with ESXi 6.5 will work.

Who this book is for

This book is designed for vSphere administrators who already have an understanding of the way vSphere operates and are looking to improve the performance of their environment. This book does not cover vSphere installation or initial configuration instructions.

Sections

In this book, you will find several headings that appear frequently (Getting ready, How to do it..., How it works..., There's more..., and See also).

To give clear instructions on how to complete a recipe, we use these sections as follows:

Getting ready

This section tells you what to expect in the recipe, and describes how to set up any software or any preliminary settings required for the recipe.

How to do it...

This section contains the steps required to follow the recipe.

How it works...

This section usually consists of a detailed explanation of what happened in the previous section.

There's more...

This section consists of additional information about the recipe in order to make the reader more knowledgeable about the recipe.

See also

This section provides helpful links to other useful information for the recipe.

Conventions

In this book, you will find a number of text styles that distinguish between different kinds of information. Here are some examples of these styles and an explanation of their meaning.

Code words in text, database table names, folder names, filenames, file extensions, pathnames, dummy URLs, user input, and Twitter handles are shown as follows: "We can include other contexts through the use of the `include` directive."

A block of code is set as follows:

```
foreach ($myHost in get-VMHost)
 {
  Write-Host '$myHost = ' $myHost
  $esxcli = Get-EsxCli -VMHost $myHost
  $esxcli.storage.core.device.partition.list() |
  Where {$_.StartSector -eq "128"} |
  Select Device, StartSector
 }
```

Any command-line input or output is written as follows:

```
~ # esxcli system settings kernel set --setting=" netNetqueueEnabled" --
value="TRUE"
```

New terms and important words are shown in bold. Words that you see on the screen, for example, in menus or dialog boxes, appear in the text like this: "Clicking on the **Next** button moves you to the next screen."

 Warnings or important notes appear in a box like this.

 Tips and tricks appear like this.

Reader feedback

Feedback from our readers is always welcome. Let us know what you think about this book—what you liked or disliked. Reader feedback is important for us as it helps us develop titles that you will really get the most out of.

To send us general feedback, simply email feedback@packtpub.com, and mention the book's title in the subject of your message.

If there is a topic that you have expertise in and you are interested in either writing or contributing to a book, see our author guide at www.packtpub.com/authors.

Customer support

Now that you are the proud owner of a Packt book, we have a number of things to help you to get the most from your purchase.

Downloading the color images of this book

We also provide you with a PDF file that has color images of the screenshots/diagrams used in this book. The color images will help you better understand the changes in the output. You can download this file from `https://www.packtpub.com/sites/default/files/downloads/vSphereHighPerformanceCookbook_ColorImages.pdf`

Errata

Although we have taken every care to ensure the accuracy of our content, mistakes do happen. If you find a mistake in one of our books—maybe a mistake in the text or the code—we would be grateful if you could report this to us. By doing so, you can save other readers from frustration and help us improve subsequent versions of this book. If you find any errata, please report them by visiting `http://www.packtpub.com/submit-errata`, selecting your book, clicking on the Errata Submission Form link, and entering the details of your errata. Once your errata are verified, your submission will be accepted and the errata will be uploaded to our website or added to any list of existing errata under the Errata section of that title.

To view the previously submitted errata, go to `https://www.packtpub.com/books/content/support` and enter the name of the book in the search field. The required information will appear under the Errata section.

Piracy

Piracy of copyrighted material on the Internet is an ongoing problem across all media. At Packt, we take the protection of our copyright and licenses very seriously. If you come across any illegal copies of our works in any form on the Internet, please provide us with the location address or website name immediately so that we can pursue a remedy.

Please contact us at `copyright@packtpub.com` with a link to the suspected pirated material.

We appreciate your help in protecting our authors and our ability to bring you valuable content.

Questions

If you have a problem with any aspect of this book, you can contact us at `questions@packtpub.com`, and we will do our best to address the problem.

1
CPU Performance Design

In this chapter, we will cover the tasks related to CPU performance design. You will learn the following aspects of CPU performance design:

- Critical performance consideration - VMM scheduler
- CPU scheduler - processor topology/cache-aware
- Ready time - warning sign
- Spotting CPU overcommitment
- Fighting guest CPU saturation in SMP VMs
- Controlling CPU resources using resource settings
- What is most important to monitor in CPU performance
- CPU performance best practices

Introduction

Ideally, a performance problem should be defined within the context of an ongoing performance management process. Performance management refers to the process of establishing performance requirements for applications in the form of a **service-level agreement** (**SLA**) and then tracking and analyzing the achieved performance to ensure that those requirements are met. A complete performance management methodology includes collecting and maintaining baseline performance data for applications, systems, and subsystems, for example, storage and network.

In the context of performance management, a performance problem exists when an application fails to meet its predetermined SLA. Depending on the specific SLA, the failure might be in the form of excessively long response times or throughput below some defined threshold.

ESXi and **virtual machine (VM)** performance tuning are complicated because VMs share the underlying physical resources, in particular, the CPU.

Finally, configuration issues or inadvertent user errors might lead to poor performance. For example, a user might use a **symmetric multiprocessing (SMP)** VM when a single processor VM would work well. You might also see a situation where a user sets shares but then forgets about resetting them, resulting in poor performance because of the changing characteristics of other VMs in the system.

If you overcommit any of these resources, you might see performance bottlenecks. For example, if too many VMs are CPU-intensive, you might experience slow performance because all the VMs need to share the underlying physical CPU.

Critical performance consideration - VMM scheduler

A **Virtual machine monitor (VMM)** is a thin layer that provides a virtual x86 hardware environment to the guest operating system on a VM. This hardware includes a virtual CPU, virtual I/O devices, and timers. A VMM leverages key technologies in **VMkernel**, such as scheduling, memory management, and the network and storage stacks.

Each VMM is devoted to one VM. To run multiple VMs, VMkernel starts multiple VMM instances, also known as worlds. Each VMM instance partitions and shares the CPU, memory, and I/O devices to successfully virtualize the system. A VMM can be implemented using hardware virtualization, software virtualization (binary translation), or paravirtualization (which is deprecated) techniques.

Paravirtualization refers to the communication between the guest operating system and the hypervisor to improve performance and efficiency. The value proposition of paravirtualization is in lower virtualization overhead, but the performance advantage of paravirtualization over hardware or software virtualization can vary greatly depending on the workload. Because paravirtualization cannot support unmodified operating systems (for example, Windows 2000/XP), its compatibility and portability are poor.

Paravirtualization can also introduce significant support and maintainability issues in production environments because it requires deep modifications to the operating system kernel, and for this reason, it was most widely deployed on Linux-based operating systems.

Getting ready

To step through this recipe, you need a running ESXi Server, a VM, a vCenter Server, and vSphere Web Client. No other prerequisites are required.

How to do it...

Perform the following steps to get started:

1. Open up vSphere Web Client.
2. On the home screen, navigate to **Hosts and Clusters.**
3. Expand the left-hand navigation list.
4. In the VM inventory, right-click on **virtual machine**, then click on **Edit Settings**. The **Virtual Machine Edit Settings** dialog box appears.
5. On the **Virtual Hardware** tab, expand the **CPU** section.

6. Change the **CPU/MMU Virtualization** option under **Advanced** to one of the following options:

- **Automatic**
- **Software CPU and MMU**
- **Hardware CPU, Software MMU**
- **Hardware CPU and MMU**

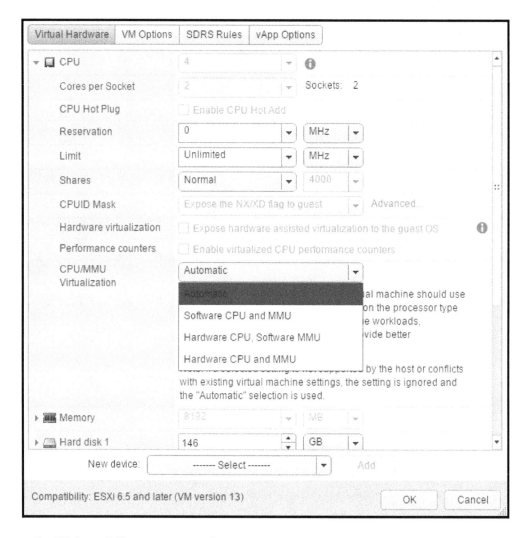

7. Click on **OK** to save your changes.

8. For the change to take effect, perform one of these actions:

- Power cycle or reset the VM
- Suspend and then resume the VM
- vMotion the VM

How it works...

The VMM determines a set of possible monitor modes to use and then picks one to use as the default monitor mode unless something other than **Automatic** has been specified. The decision is based on:

- The physical CPU's features and guest operating system type
- Configuration file settings

There are three valid combinations for the monitor mode, as follows:

- **BT**: Binary translation and shadow page tables
- **HV**: AMD-V or Intel VT-x and shadow page tables
- **HWMMU**: AMD-V with RVI or Intel VT-x with EPT (RVI is inseparable from AMD-V, and EPT is inseparable from Intel VT-x)

BT, HV, and HWMMU are abbreviations used by ESXi to identify each combination.

When a VM is powering on, the VMM inspects the physical CPU's features and the guest operating system type to determine the set of possible execution modes. It first finds the set of modes allowed. Then it restricts the allowed modes by configuring file settings. Finally, among the remaining candidates, it chooses the preferred mode, which is the default monitor mode. This default mode is then used if you have **Automatic** selected.

For the majority of workloads, the default monitor mode chosen by the VMM works best. The default monitor mode for each guest operating system on each CPU has been carefully selected after a performance evaluation of the available choices. However, some applications have special characteristics that can result in better performance when using a non-default monitor mode. These should be treated as exceptions, not rules.

The chosen settings are honored by the VMM only if the settings are supported on the intended hardware. For example, if you select **Software CPU and MMU** for a 64-bit guest operating system running on a 64-bit Intel processor, the VMM will choose Intel VT-x for CPU virtualization instead of BT. This is because BT is not supported by the 64-bit guest operating system on this processor.

There's more…

The virtual CPU consists of the virtual instruction set and the virtual **memory management unit** (**MMU**). An instruction set is a list of instructions that a CPU executes. MMU is the hardware that maintains the mapping between the virtual addresses and physical addresses in the memory.

The combination of techniques used to virtualize the instruction set and memory determines the monitor execution mode (also called the monitor mode). The VMM identifies the VMware ESXi hardware platform and its available CPU features and then chooses a monitor mode for a particular guest operating system on that hardware platform. It might choose a monitor mode that uses hardware virtualization techniques, software virtualization techniques, or a combination of hardware and software techniques.

We have always had a challenge in hardware virtualization. x86 operating systems are designed to run directly on bare metal hardware, so they assume that they have full control over the computer hardware. The x86 architecture offers four levels of privileges to operating systems and applications to manage access to the computer hardware: ring 0, ring 1, ring 2, and ring 3. User-level applications typically run in ring 3; the operating system needs to have direct access to the memory and hardware and must execute its privileged instructions in ring 0.

Binary translation allows the VMM to run in ring 0 for isolation and performance while moving the guest operating system to ring 1. Ring 1 is a higher privilege level than ring 3 and a lower privilege level than ring 0.

VMware can virtualize any x86 operating system using a combination of binary translation and direct execution techniques. With binary translation, the VMM dynamically translates all guest operating system instructions and caches the results for future use. The translator in the VMM does not perform a mapping from one architecture to another; that would be emulation, not translation. Instead, it translates from the full unrestricted x86 instruction set issued by the guest operating system to a subset that is safe to execute inside the VMM. In particular, the binary translator replaces privileged instructions with sequences of instructions that perform the privileged operations in the VM rather than on the physical machine. This translation enforces encapsulation of the VM while preserving the x86 semantics as seen from the perspective of the VM.

Meanwhile, user-level code is directly executed on the processor for high-performance virtualization. Each VMM provides each VM with all of the services of the physical system, including a virtual BIOS, virtual devices, and virtualized memory management.

In addition to software virtualization, there is support for hardware virtualization. This allows some of the work of running virtual CPU instructions to be offloaded onto the physical hardware. Intel has the **Intel Virtualization Technology** (**Intel VT-x**) feature. AMD has the **AMD Virtualization** (**AMD-V**) feature. Intel VT-x and AMD-V are similar in aim but different in detail. Both designs aim to simplify virtualization techniques.

CPU scheduler - processor topology/cache-aware

The ESXi Server has an advanced CPU scheduler geared towards providing high performance, fairness, and isolation of VMs running on Intel/AMD x86 architectures.

The ESXi CPU scheduler is designed with the following objectives:

- **Performance isolation**: Multi-VM fairness
- **Coscheduling**: Illusion that all vCPUs are concurrently online
- **Performance**: High throughput, low latency, high scalability, and low overhead
- **Power efficiency**: Saving power without losing performance
- **Wide Adoption**: Enabling all the optimizations on diverse processor architecture

There can be only one active process per CPU at any given instant; for example, multiple vCPUs can run on the same pCPU, just not in one instance--often, there are more processes than CPUs. Therefore, queuing will occur, and the scheduler will become responsible for controlling the queue, handling priorities, and preempting the use of the CPU.

The main tasks of the CPU scheduler are to choose which world is to be scheduled to a processor. In order to give each world a chance to run, the scheduler dedicates a time slice (also known as the duration in which a world can be executed (usually 10-20 ms, 50 for VMkernel by default)) to each process and then migrates the state of the world between run, wait, co-stop, and ready.

ESXi implements the proportional share-based algorithm. It associates each world with a share of CPU resource across all VMs. This is called entitlement and is calculated from the user-provided resource specifications, such as shares, reservations, and limits.

Getting ready

To step through this recipe, you need a running ESXi Server, a VM that is powered off, and vSphere Web Client. No other prerequisites are required.

How to do it...

Let's get started:

1. Open up vSphere Web Client.
2. On the home screen, navigate to **Hosts and Clusters.**
3. Expand the left-hand navigation list.
4. In the VM inventory, right-click on **virtual machine**, and click on **Edit Settings**. The **Virtual Machine Edit Settings** dialog box appears.
5. Click on the **VM Options** tab.
6. Under the **Advanced** section, click on **Edit Configuration**.

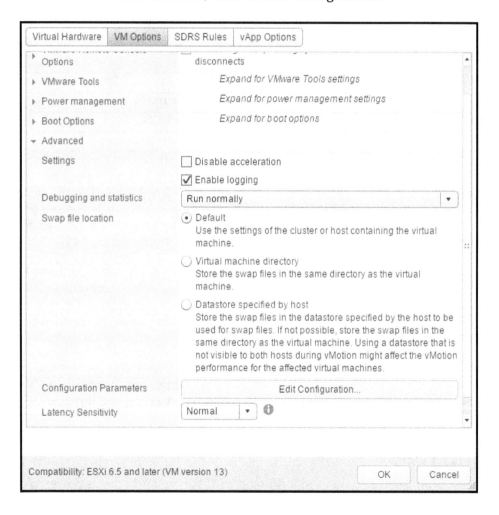

7. At the bottom, enter `sched.cpu.vsmpConsolidate` as **Name**, `True` for **Value**, and click on **Add.**

8. The final screen should like the following screenshot. Once you get this, click on **OK** to save the setting:

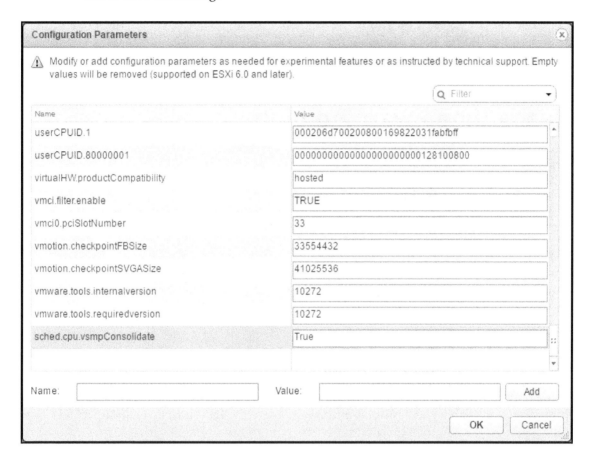

How it works...

The CPU scheduler uses processor topology information to optimize the placement of vCPUs onto different sockets.

Cores within a single socket typically use a shared last-level cache. The use of a shared last-level cache can improve vCPU performance if the CPU is running memory-intensive workloads.

By default, the CPU scheduler spreads the load across all the sockets in under-committed systems. This improves performance by maximizing the aggregate amount of cache available to the running vCPUs. For such workloads, it can be beneficial to schedule all the vCPUs on the same socket, with a shared last-level cache, even when the ESXi host is under committed. In such scenarios, you can override the default behavior of the spreading vCPUs across packages by including the following configuration option in the VM's VMX configuration file: `sched.cpu.vsmpConsolidate=TRUE`. However, it is usually better to stick with the default behavior.

Ready time - warning sign

To achieve the best performance in a consolidated environment, you must consider a ready time.

Ready time is the time during which vCPU waits in the queue for pCPU (or physical core) to be ready to execute its instruction. The scheduler handles the queue and when there is contention and the processing resources are stressed, the queue might become long.

Ready time describes how much of the last observation period a specific world spent waiting in the queue. Ready time for a particular world (for example, a vCPU) indicates how much time during that interval was spent waiting in the queue to get access to a pCPU. It can be expressed in percentage per vCPU over observation time, and statistically, it can't be zero on average.

The value of ready time, therefore, is an indicator of how long a VM is denied access to the pCPU resources that it wanted to use. This makes it a good indicator of performance.

When multiple processes try to use the same physical CPU, that CPU might not be immediately available and a process must wait before the ESXi host can allocate a CPU to it.

The CPU scheduler manages access to the physical CPUs on the host system. A short spike in CPU used or CPU ready indicates that you are making the best use of the host resources. However, if both the values are constantly high, the hosts are probably overloaded and performance is likely poor.

Generally, if the CPU-used value of a VM is above 90 percent and the CPU-ready value is above 20 percent per vCPU (high number of vCPUs), performance is negatively affected.

This latency may impact the performance of the guest operating system and the running of applications within a VM.

Getting ready

To step through this recipe, you need a running ESXi Server, a couple of CPU-hungry VMs, a VMware vCenter Server, and vSphere Web Client. No other prerequisites are required.

How to do it...

Let's get started:

1. Open up vSphere Web Client.
2. On the home screen, navigate to **Hosts and Clusters.**
3. Expand the left-hand navigation list.
4. Navigate to one of the CPU-hungry VMs.
5. Navigate to the **Monitor** tab.
6. Navigate to the **Performance** tab.
7. Navigate to the **Advanced** view.
8. Click on **Chart Options**.
9. Navigate to **CPU** from **Chart metrics**.
10. Navigate to the VM object and only select **Demand**, **Ready**, and **Usage** in **MHz**.

    The key metrics when investigating a potential CPU issue are as follows:

   - **Demand**: The amount of CPU that the VM is trying to use.
   - **Usage**: The amount of CPU that the VM is actually being allowed to use.
   - **Ready**: The amount of time during which the VM is ready to run but (has work it wants to do) is unable to because vSphere could not find physical resources to run the VM on.

11. Click on **Ok**.

In the following screenshot, you will see the high ready time of the VM:

Notice the amount of CPU this VM is demanding and compare that to the amount of CPU usage the VM is actually being able to get (usage in MHz). The VM is demanding more than it is currently being allowed to use.

Notice that the VM is also seeing a large amount of ready time.

> Ready time greater than 10 percent could be a performance concern. However, some less CPU-sensitive applications and VMs can have much higher values of ready time and still perform satisfactorily.

How it works…

A vCPU is in a ready state when the vCPU is ready to run (that is, it has a task it wants to execute). But it is unable to run because the vSphere scheduler is unable to find physical host CPU resources to run the VM on. One potential reason for elevated ready time is that the VM is constrained by a user-set CPU limit or resource pool limit, reported as **max limited** (**MLMTD**). The amount of CPU denied because of a limit is measured as the metric max limited.

Ready time is reported in two different values between `resxtop`/`esxtop` and vCenter Server. In resxtop/esxtop, it is reported in an easily understood percentage format. A figure of 5 percent means that the VM spent 5 percent of its last sample period waiting for the available CPU resources (only true for 1-vCPU VMs). In vCenter Server, ready time is reported as a measurement of time. For example, in vCenter Server's real-time data, which produces sample values every 20,000 milliseconds, a figure of 1,000 milliseconds is reported for 5 percent ready time. A figure of 2,000 milliseconds is reported for 10 percent ready time.

> Since we know that vCenter reports ready time in milliseconds (ms), use the following formula to convert the ms value into a percentage:
>
> $$\text{Metric Value (In Percent)} = \frac{\text{Metric Value (In Millisecond)}}{\text{Total Time of sample period}} \times 100.$$
>
> This refers to the total time of the sample period (by default, this is 20,000 ms in vCenter for real-time graphs)

Although high ready time typically signifies CPU contention, the condition does not always warrant corrective action. If the value of ready time is close in value of the amount of time used on the CPU and if the increased ready time occurs with occasional spikes in CPU activity but does not persist for extended periods of time, this might not indicate a performance problem. The brief performance hit is often within the accepted performance variance and does not require any action on the part of the administrator.

Spotting CPU overcommitment

When we provision CPU resources, which is the number of vCPUs allocated to run the VMs, and if its number is greater than the number of physical cores on a host, it is called CPU overcommitment. CPU overcommitment is a normal practice in many situations as it increases the consolidation ratio. Nevertheless, you need to monitor it closely.

CPU overcommitment is not recommended in order to satisfy or guarantee the workload of a tier-1 application with a tight SLA. It may be successfully leveraged to highly consolidate and reduce the power consumption of light workloads on modern, multicore systems.

Getting ready

To step through this recipe, you need a running ESXi Server with SSH enabled, a couple of running CPU-hungry VMs, an SSH client (Putty), a vCenter Server, and vSphere Web Client. No other prerequisites are required.

The following table elaborates on Esxtop CPU Performance Metrics:

Esxtop Metric	Description	Implication
%RDY	The percentage of time a vCPU in a run queue is waiting for the CPU scheduler to let it run on a physical CPU.	A high **%RDY** time (use 20 percent as the starting point) may indicate the VM is under resource contention. Monitor this; if the application speed is OK, a higher threshold may be tolerated.
%USED	The percentage of possible CPU processing cycles that were actually used for work during this time interval.	The **%USED** value alone does not necessarily indicate that the CPUs are overcommitted. However, high **%RDY** values plus high **%USED** values are a sure indicator that your CPU resources are overcommitted.

How to do it...

To spot CPU overcommitment, there are a few CPU resource parameters that you should monitor closely. They are:

1. Log in to the ESXi Server using an SSH client (Putty).
2. Type `esxtop` and hit *Enter*.

3. Monitor the preceding values to understand CPU overcommitment.

```
8:27:05am up 22:23, 401 worlds, 12 VMs, 24 vCPUs; CPU load average: 0.68, 0.58, 0.44
PCPU USED(%):   52   52 1.5 1.2 2.0 1.1 1.4 1.2 2.1 1.2 3.1 1.0 2.0 1.3 1.7 1.1 AVG: 8.0
PCPU UTIL(%):  100  100 1.9 1.6 2.1 1.3 1.7 1.4 2.6 1.7 3.8 1.5 2.5 1.7 2.2 1.6 AVG:  14
CORE UTIL(%):  100      2.8     3.2     2.7     4.0     5.0     4.0     3.5     AVG:  15

      ID      GID NAME             NWLD   %USED    %RUN   %SYS   %WAIT %VMWAIT    %RDY  %IDLE %OVRLP   %CSTP %MLMTD %SWPWT
       1        1 idle               16  681.25 1600.00   0.00    0.00       - 1600.00   0.00   1.72    0.00   0.00   0.00
   96067    96067 Res-Hungry-4        8   44.60   67.64   0.03  619.52    0.90   98.34  33.69   0.08   15.87   0.00   0.00
   95554    95554 Res-Hungry-3        8   43.80   66.18   0.01  634.87    2.11   84.09  39.86   0.08   16.01   0.00   0.00
   94278    94278 Res-Hungry-2        7   21.96   33.42   0.00  592.44    0.00   75.14   0.00   0.09    0.00   0.00   0.00
   91336    91336 Res-Hungry-1        7   21.76   33.17   0.00  589.64    0.00   78.21   0.00   0.06    0.00   0.00   0.00
   83604    83604 vCenter-VA51        8    3.78    4.21   0.05  796.85    0.19    0.10 196.06   0.02    0.00   0.00   0.00
   83528    83528 ESXi151-B           9    3.75    3.96   0.17  897.08    1.68    0.26 394.83   0.04    0.00   0.00   0.00
   83520    83520 ESXi151-A           9    3.37    4.28   0.10  896.87    1.22    0.15 395.10   0.03    0.00   0.00   0.00
   93942    93942 esxtop.61739        1    2.14    2.13   0.00   98.01       -    0.00   0.00   0.00    0.00   0.00   0.00
   83620    83620 Analytics VM        8    2.06    2.44   0.06  798.66    0.45    0.07 197.60   0.01    0.00   0.00   0.00
   83586    83586 vCloud Director     6    1.57    1.53   0.05  599.28    0.02    0.06  98.66   0.00    0.00   0.00   0.00
   83627    83627 UI VM               8    1.11    1.12   0.04  799.96    0.91    0.09 198.32   0.00    0.00   0.00   0.00
   83611    83611 vShieldManager      7    1.01    0.96   0.04  699.98    0.00    0.07 199.83   0.01    0.00   0.00   0.00
    1743     1743 hostd.2978         20    1.00    1.02   0.01 2000.00       -    0.07   0.00   0.00    0.00   0.00   0.00
    2643     2643 vpxa.3454          19    0.53    0.55   0.02 1900.00       -    0.04   0.00   0.00    0.00   0.00   0.00
   83535    83535 OpenFiler           8    0.50    0.64   0.01  800.00    0.15    0.03  99.42   0.00    0.00   0.00   0.00
```

This example uses `esxtop` to detect CPU overcommitment. Looking at the pCPU line near the top of the screen, you can determine that this host's two CPUs are 100 percent utilized. Four active VMs are shown, **Res-Hungry-1** to **Res-Hungry-4**. These VMs are active because they have relatively high values in the **%USED** column. The values in the **%USED** column alone do not necessarily indicate that the CPUs are overcommitted. In the **%RDY** column, you see that the three active VMs have relatively high values. High **%RDY** values plus high **%USED** values are a sure indicator that your CPU resources are overcommitted.

From the CPU view, navigate to a VM and press the *E* key to expand the view. It will give a detailed vCPU view for the VM. This is important because, at a quick level, CPU that is ready as a metric is best referenced when looking at performance concerns more broadly than a specific VM. If there is high ready percentage noted, contention could be an issue, particularly if other VMs show high utilization when more vCPUs than physical cores are present. In that case, other VMs could lead to high ready time on a low idle VM. So, long story short, if the CPU ready time is high on VMs on a host, it's time to verify that no other VMs are seeing performance issues.

You can also use the vCenter performance chart to spot CPU overcommitment, as follows:

1. Log in to the vCenter Server using vSphere Web Client.
2. On the home screen, navigate to **Hosts and Clusters.**
3. Expand the left-hand navigation list.
4. Navigate to one of the ESXi hosts.
5. Navigate to the **Monitor** tab.
6. Navigate to the **Performance** tab.
7. Navigate to the **Advanced** view.
8. Click on **Chart Options**.
9. Navigate to **CPU** from **Chart metrics**.
10. Select only **Used** and **Ready** in the **Counters** section and click on **OK**:

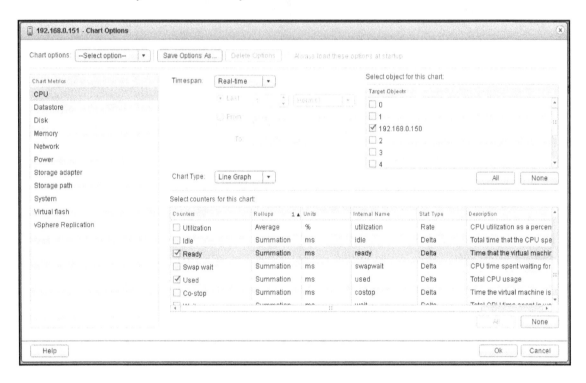

Now you will see the ready time and the used time in the graph and you can spot the overcommitment. The following screenshot is an example output:

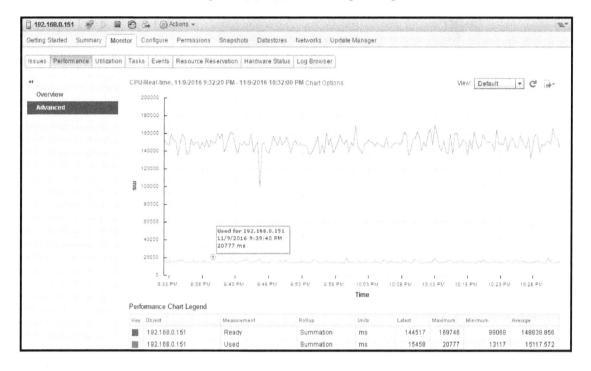

The following example shows that the host has high ready time:

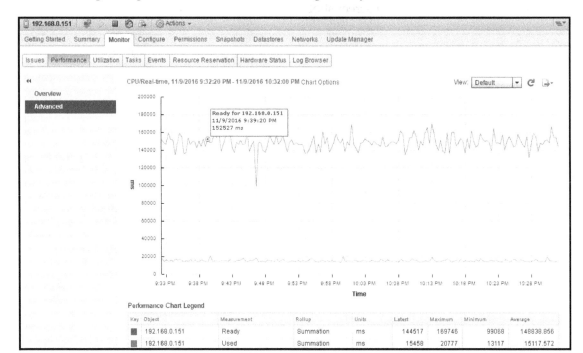

How it works...

Although high ready time typically signifies CPU contention, the condition does not always warrant corrective action. If the value of ready time is also accompanied by high used time, then it might signify that the host is overcommitted.

So the used time and ready time of a host might signal contention. However, the host might not be overcommitted due to workload availability.

There might be periods of activity and periods that are idle. So the CPU is not over-committed all the time. Another very common source of high ready time for VMs, even when pCPU utilization is low, is due to storage being slow. A vCPU, which occupies a pCPU, can issue a storage I/O and then sit in the WAIT state on the pCPU, blocking other vCPUs. Other vCPUs accumulate ready time; this vCPU and pCPU accumulate wait time (which is not part of the used or utilized time).

Fighting guest CPU saturation in SMP VMs

Guest CPU saturation happens when the application and operating system running in a VM use all of the CPU resources that the ESXi host is providing for that VM. However, this guest CPU saturation does not necessarily indicate that a performance problem exists.

Compute-intensive applications commonly use all of the available CPU resources, but this is expected and might be acceptable (as long as the end user thinks that the job is completing quickly enough). Even less-intensive applications might experience periods of high CPU demand without experiencing performance problems. However, if a performance problem exists when guest CPU saturation is occurring, steps should be taken to eliminate the condition.

When a VM is configured with more than one vCPU but actively uses only one of the vCPUs, resources that could be used to perform useful work are being wasted. At this time, you may at least see a potential performance problem from the most active vCPU perspective.

Getting ready

To step through this recipe, you need a running ESXi Server, a couple of running CPU-hungry VMs, a vCenter Server, and vSphere Web Client. No other prerequisites are required.

How to do it...

To spot CPU overcommitment in the guest OS, *ready time* and *usage percentage* are two CPU resource parameters that you should monitor closely:

1. Log in to vCenter Server using vSphere Web Client.
2. On the home screen, navigate to **Hosts and Clusters.**
3. Expand the ESXi host and go to the CPU-hungry VM.
4. Navigate to the **Monitor** tab.
5. Navigate to the **Performance** tab.
6. Navigate to the **Advanced** view.
7. Click on **Chart Options**.

8. Navigate to **CPU** from **Chart metrics**.

9. Navigate to the VM object.

10. Navigate to the **Advanced** tab and click on **Chart Options**.

11. Select only **Usage**, **Ready**, and **Used** in the **Counters** section and click on **OK**:

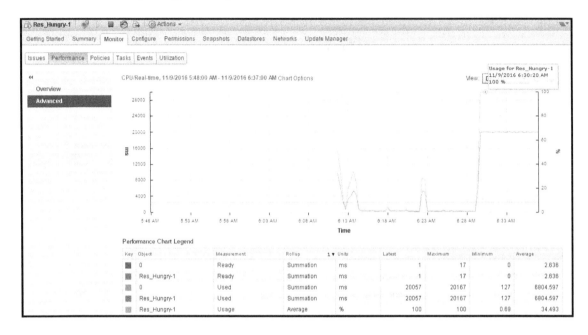

The preceding example shows the high usage and used value on a VM configured with one vCPU. We can see its overall CPU usage is 100 percent:

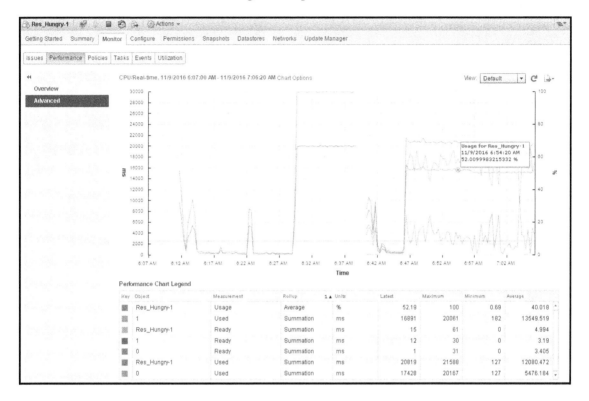

The preceding example shows that after you added a second vCPU to the VM, the percentage of overall CPU usage dropped down to 52 percent.

How it works...

So in the case of an SMP VM, if it demands high CPU resources, it may happen that either the application is single threaded, or the guest operating system is configured with **uniprocessor HAL**.

Many applications are written with only a single thread of control. These applications cannot take advantage of more than one processor core.

In order for a VM to take advantage of multiple vCPUs, the guest operating system running on the VM must be able to recognize and use multiple processor cores. If the VM is doing all of its work on vCPU0, the guest operating system might be configured with a kernel or HAL that can recognize only a single processor core.

In the preceding graph, the OS is sharing the load of the single-threaded application between both the available vCPUs.

You have two possible approaches to solve performance problems related to guest CPU saturation:

- Increase the CPU resources provided to the application
- Increase the efficiency with which the VM uses CPU resources

Adding CPU resources is often the easiest choice, particularly in a virtualized environment. If a VM continues to experience CPU saturation even after adding CPU resources, the tuning and behavior of the application and operating system should be investigated.

Controlling CPU resources using resource settings

If you cannot rebalance CPU load or increase processor efficiency even after all of the recipes discussed earlier, then it might be something else that is keeping the host CPU still saturated.

It could be a resource pool and its allocation of resources toward the VM.

Many applications, such as batch jobs, respond to a lack of CPU resources by taking longer to complete but still produce correct and useful results. Other applications might experience failure or might be unable to meet critical business requirements when denied sufficient CPU resources.

The resource controls available in vSphere can be used to ensure that resource-sensitive applications always get sufficient CPU resources, even when host CPU saturation exists. You need to make sure that you understand how shares, reservations, and limits work when applied to resource pools or to individual VMs. The default values ensure that ESXi will be efficient and fair to all VMs. Change the default settings only when you understand the consequences.

Getting ready

To step through this recipe, you need a running ESXi Server, a couple of running CPU-hungry VMs, a vCenter Server, and vSphere Web Client. No other prerequisites are required.

How to do it...

Let's get started:

1. Log in to vCenter Server using vSphere Web Client.
2. On the home screen, navigate to **Hosts and Clusters.**
3. Expand the ESXi host and go to the CPU-hungry VM.
4. Navigate to the **Monitor** tab.
5. Navigate to the **Performance** tab.
6. Navigate to the **Advanced** view.
7. Click on **Chart Options**.
8. Navigate to **CPU** from **Chart metrics**.
9. Navigate to the VM object.
10. Navigate to the **Advanced** tab and click on the **Chart Options**.
11. Select only **Ready** and **Used** in the **Counters** section and click on **OK**.

Now if there is a lower limit configured on the VM, and at the same time if it is craving for a resource, then you will see high ready time and a low used metric. An example of what it may look like is given in the following image:

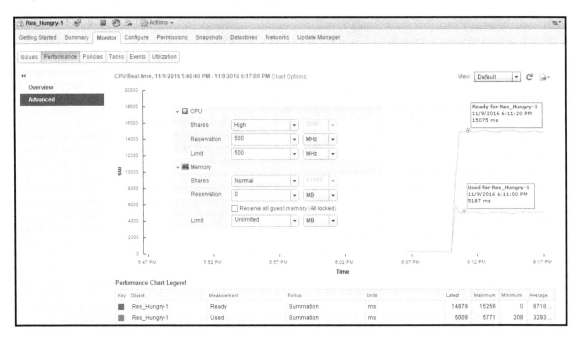

Look at the preceding example and see when the VM is craving for more CPU resource. If you put a limit on top of it, then it will experience high ready time and low used time. Here, in the preceding example, this VM is set with a limit of 500MHz.

Now to rectify this, we can change the limit value and the VM should perform better with low ready time and high used value.

1. Right-click on the CPU-hungry VM and select **Edit Resource Settings**.
2. Under CPU, change the **Shares** value to **High** (2,000 Shares).
3. Change **Reservation** to **2000MHz** and the **Limit** value to **2000MHz**.
4. Click on **OK**.

Now the VM should look and perform as shown in the following screenshot:

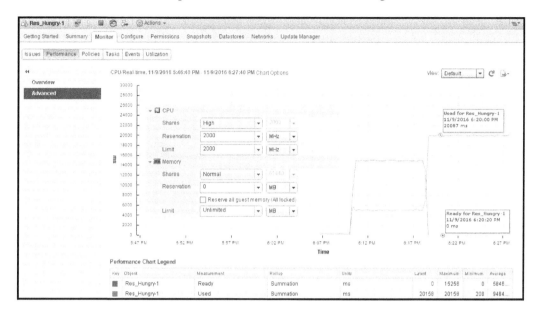

What is most important to monitor in CPU performance

Before you jump to conclusions as to what to monitor in CPU performance, you need to make sure that you know what affects CPU performance. Things that can affect CPU performance include:

- **CPU affinity**: When you pin down a virtual CPU to a physical CPU, it may happen that your resource gets imbalanced. So this is not advised, until you have a strong reason to do that.
- **CPU prioritization**: When CPU contention happens, the CPU scheduler will be forced to prioritize VMs based on entitlement and queue requests.
- **SMP VMs**: If your application is not multithreaded, then there is no benefit in adding more CPU resources in VMs. In fact, the extra idle vCPUs add overhead that prevents some more useful work from being done.
- **Idle VMs**: You may have too many idle VMs, which you think should not eat up resources. However, in reality, However, in reality, even idle VMs can affect CPU performance if the VM shares or reservations have been changed from their default values.

So, now you know what affects CPU performance. You can now look at what it takes to monitor it.

You can categorize the factors that should be monitored for CPU performance into three main sections:

- Host CPU usage
- VM CPU usage
- VM CPU ready time

To monitor these sections, you need to know the esxtop counters, and they are:

- **PCPU Used (%)**
- Per group statistics:
    - **%Used**
    - **%Sys**
    - **%RDY**
    - **%Wait**
    - **%CSTP**
    - **%MLMTD**

Getting ready

To step through this recipe, you need a running ESXi Server with SSH enabled, a couple of running CPU-hungry VMs, and an SSH client (Putty). No other prerequisites are required.

How to do it...

Let's get started:

1. Log in to the ESXi host using an SSH client (Putty).
2. Run `esxtop` and monitor the statistics. The following screenshot is an example output:

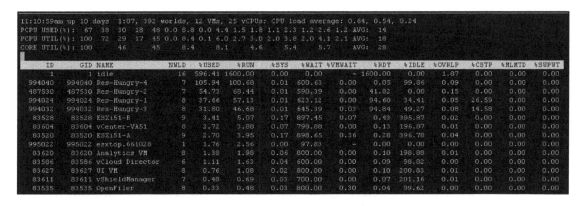

3. Now, look at the performance counters as mentioned previously. In the following example output, look at the different metrics:

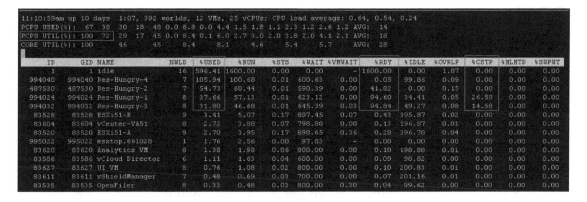

In the preceding example, you can see our **PCPU** 0 and **PCPU** 1 are being used heavily (**100** percent and **73** percent **UTIL**, respectively), and it shows the following figure:

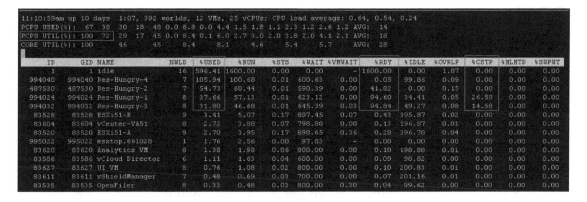

Now in the preceding example, you see that the **%Used** value of the four CPU-hungry virtual machines is pretty high.

Also, look at the **%RDY** screen and you will see high ready time, which indicates a performance problem.

The following list is a quick explanation of each of these metrics:

- **PCPU USED (%)**: This refers to the CPU utilization per physical CPU. **%USED**: This is the physical CPU usage per group.
- **%SYS**: This is the VMkernel system's activity time.
- **%RDY**: This is the ready time. It is referred to as the amount of time that the group spent ready to run but waiting for the CPU to be available. Note that this is not adjusted for the number of vCPUs. You should expand the group to see **%Ready** for each vCPU, or at least divide this by the number of vCPUs to use an average per vCPU.
- **%WAIT**: This is the percentage of time spent in the blocked or busy state. It includes idle time and also the time waiting for I/O from the disk or network.
- **%CSTP**: This is referred to as the percentage of time spent in VMkernel on behalf of the group for processing interrupts.
- **%CSTP** for a vCPU indicates how much time the vCPU has spent not running in order to allow extra vCPUs in the same VM to catch up. High values suggest that this VM has more vCPUs than it needs and the performance might be suffering.
- **%MLMTD**: This is the amount of time spent ready to run, but not scheduled because of a CPU limit.

CPU performance best practices

CPU virtualization adds varying amounts of overhead. Because of this, you may need to fine-tune the CPU performance and need to know what the standard best practices are.

The following are the standard CPU performance best practices:

- You need to avoid using SMP VMs unless it is required by the application running inside the guest OS. This means if the application is not multithreaded, then there is no benefit of using the SMP VM.
- You should prioritize VM CPU usage with a proportional share algorithm.
- Use **Distributed Resource Scheduler** (**DRS**) and vMotion to redistribute VMs and reduce contention.
- Use the latest available virtual hardware for the VMs.
- Reduce the number of VMs running on a single host. This way, you can not only reduce contention, but also reduce the fault domain configuration.
- You should leverage the application-tuning guide from the vendor to tune your VMs for best performance.

Getting ready

To step through this recipe, you need a running ESXi Server (licensed with Enterprise Plus for DRS), a couple of running VMs, and vSphere Web Client. No other prerequisites are required.

How to do it...

Let's get started:

1. For the first best practice, you need to check whether the application is single threaded or multithreaded. If it is single threaded, then avoid running an SMP VM:

    1. You need to log in to vCenter using vSphere Web Client, then go to the **Home** tab.
    2. Once there, go to the VM and look at the **VM Hardware** tile.
    3. Now you can see whether the VM has one vCPU or multiple vCPUs. You see whether it's using them by looking at **%Utilization** or a similar metric for each vCPU:

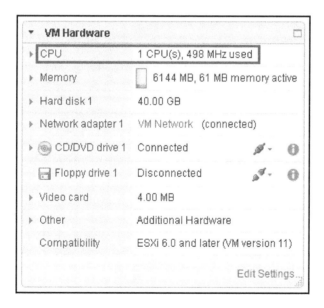

This **Summary** tab doesn't tell us whether the app is single threaded or multithreaded.

2. For the second best practice, you need to prioritize the VM CPU using shares and reservation. Depending on the customer SLA, this has to be defined:
    1. You need to log in to vCenter using vSphere Web Client, then go to the **Home** tab.
    2. Once there, go to the VM, right-click on it, and then select **Edit Resource Settings**.
    3. In the **CPU** section, you need to define the **Shares** and **Reservation** values depending on your SLA and the performance factors.

By default, ESXi is efficient and fair. It does not waste physical resources. If all the demands could be met, all is well. If all the demands are not satisfied, the deprivation is shared equitably among VMs by default.

VMs can use and then adjust the shares, reservation, or limit settings. But be sure that you know how they work first:

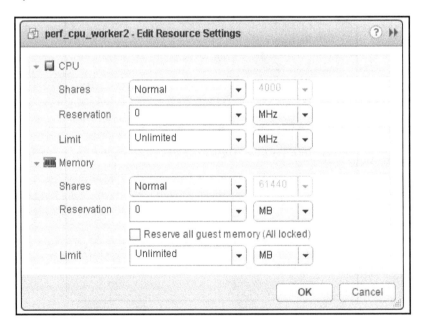

3. For the third best practice, you need to have a vSphere Cluster and have DRS enabled for this. DRS will load balance the VMs across the ESXi hosts using vMotion.

   The first screenshot shows that the DRS is enabled on this vSphere Cluster:

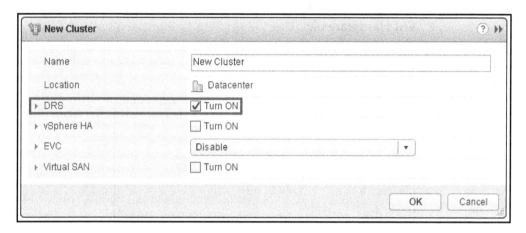

   The second screenshot shows the automation level and migration threshold:

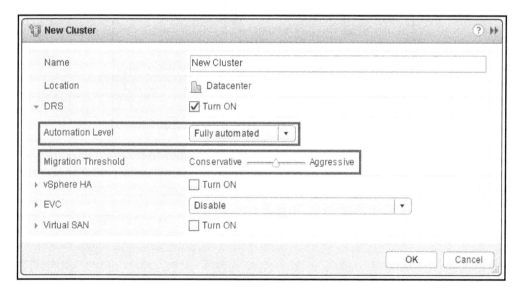

4. For the fourth best practice, you first need to see what virtual hardware the VM is running on; if it is not current, then you need to upgrade it. A virtual hardware version can limit the number of vCPUs:

   1. You need to log in to vCenter using vSphere Web Client, then go to the **Home** tab.

   2. Once there, go to **Hosts and Clusters**, then click on **VM** and look at the **VM Hardware** tile.

   In the following example, it is version 10, which is old, and we can upgrade it to version 13.

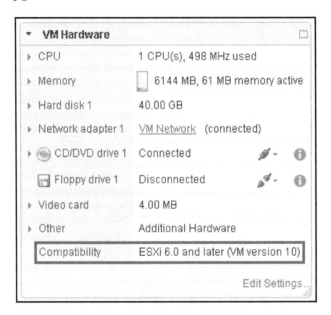

 Take a VM snapshot prior to upgrading in order to mitigate the rare occurrence of a failure to boot the guest operating system after upgrading. For further information, refer to https://kb.vmware.com/kb/1010675.

3. Now, to upgrade the virtual hardware of a VM, it has to be powered off. Then, start it again, right-click on **VM**, go to **Compatibility**, and then **Upgrade VM Compatibility**. It should give you a warning:

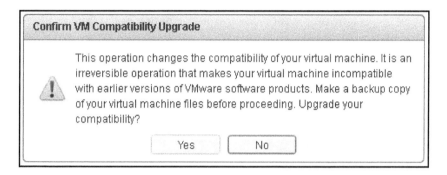

4. Once you click on Yes, the virtual hardware version will be upgraded.

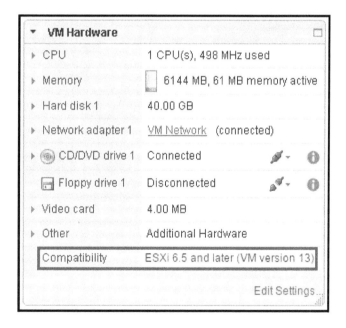

5. For the fifth recommendation, you need to limit the number of vCPUs required by the VMs that would run on the host and the number of sockets/cores available in each physical host:

    1. Try to balance the CPU load of your VMs across all of your hosts

    2. Monitor the VMs for performance and adjust as necessary.

6. For the last recommendation, you need to get the vendor-application-tuning guide and follow that to tune your virtual environment. A typical example is *Microsoft Exchange Server 2016 Best Practices Guide*.

For further information, refer to `https://blogs.vmware.com/apps` `/2016/01/now-updated-microsoft-exchange-server-vmware-vsphere-` `best-practices-guide.html.`

2
Memory Performance Design

In this chapter, we will cover the tasks related to memory performance design. You will learn the following aspects of memory performance design:

- Virtual memory reclamation techniques
- Monitoring a host-swapping activity
- Monitoring a host-ballooning activity
- Keeping memory free for VMkernel
- Key memory performance counters to monitor
- What counters not to use
- Identifying when memory is the problem
- Analyzing host and VM memory
- Memory performance best practices

Introduction

Although VMware vSphere uses various mechanisms to efficiently allocate memory, you might still encounter a situation where VMs are allocated with insufficient physical memory.

You should know how to monitor memory usage of both host machines and VMs. You should also know how to troubleshoot common memory performance problems, such as those involving a demand for memory.

Virtual memory reclamation techniques

VMs perform memory allocation in the same way an operating system handles memory allocation and deallocation. The guest operating system frees a piece of physical memory by adding memory page numbers to the guest free list.

The guest operating system's free list is not accessible to the hypervisor; thus, it is difficult for the hypervisor to know when to free the host physical memory and when the guest physical memory needs to be freed. The hypervisor is completely unaware of which pages are free or allocated to the guest operating system, and because of this, it cannot reclaim the host physical memory when the guest operating system frees guest physical memory.

So the VMware hypervisor relies on memory reclamation techniques to reclaim the host physical memory that is freed by the guest operating system. These are the memory reclamation techniques:

- **Transparent Page Sharing (TPS)**
- Memory ballooning
- Host-level (or hypervisor) swapping

Getting ready

To step through this recipe, you will need a running ESXi Server, a couple of running VMs, and vSphere Web Client. No other prerequisites are required.

How to do it...

Most likely, you don't need to do anything to enable Transparent Memory Page Sharing, as it is enabled by default on your ESXi hypervisor.

Memory ballooning is driven by the VMware Tools software, so you'll need it installed on all your VMs. It will load the `vmmemctl` driver, which is responsible for memory ballooning.

Perform the following steps if VMware Tools is not installed or is out of date:

1. Log in to VMware vSphere Web Client.
2. In the VM inventory, right-click on the VM, select **Guest OS**, then click on **Install VMware Tools** or **Upgrade VMware Tools**.
3. Go to the VM Console and follow the onscreen instructions to install or upgrade it.

Similarly, host-level or hypervisor swapping is enabled by default. You don't need to perform any additional steps to enable it.

How it works...

Let's look at how these techniques work.

TPS

When there are multiple VMs running on the same hypervisor, most of the time some of them might have identical sets of memory content (known as memory pages). This creates opportunities for sharing memory across VMs. The ESXi hypervisor can reclaim redundant copies and keep only one copy using TPS. You can think of it as **Memory Deduplication**.

Traditionally, in x86 systems, memory is split into 4 kilobytes of pages, and that happens only if you are using small pages with shadow page tables. The TPS process runs every 60 minutes. It scans all the memory pages and calculates a hash value for each one of them. These hashes are saved in a separate table and compared to each other by the kernel. Every time the ESXi kernel finds two identical hashes, it starts a bit-by-bit comparison of the corresponding memory pages. If these pages are absolutely the same, the kernel leaves only one copy of the page in memory and removes the second one. When one of your VM requests to write to this page, the kernel creates a new page because the change made by one VM must not affect the memory contents of another VM.

VMware ESXi scans the guest physical pages randomly, with a base scan rate specified by `Mem.ShareScanTime`. The maximum number of scanned pages per second in the host and the maximum number of per-VM-scanned pages (that is, `Mem.ShareScanGHz` and `Mem.ShareRateMax`, respectively) can also be specified in ESXi's advanced settings.

Memory ballooning

Memory ballooning tells the guest operating system that it does not have enough memory from the host so that the guest operating system could free some of its memory. When there is a memory crisis, the hypervisor tells the balloon driver to request some number of megabytes from the guest operating system. The hypervisor knows that pages occupied by the balloon driver will never store data, so the pages of pRAM requested by the balloon driver can then be reallocated safely to other VMs. It is the guest operating system's call to decide which pages of vRAM it should allocate to the balloon driver, and it will start with free pages. If it has plenty of free or idle guest physical memory, inflating the balloon will induce no guest-level paging and thus it will not affect guest performance. However, in the case of memory contention within the guest, the VM OS decides which guest physical pages are to be paged out to the virtual swap device in order to satisfy the balloon driver's allocation requests.

The balloon driver reclaims the guest operating system's allocated memory using **Idle Memory Tax** (**IMT**). IMT may reclaim up to 75 percent of idle memory. A guest operating system page file is necessary in order to prevent guest operating system kernel starvation. The vmmemctl driver should aggressively reclaim memory due to severe host contention (make sure that the guest operating system page file is at least 65 percent of the configured vRAM). Even here, the guest operating system can make intelligent guesses about which pages of data are least likely to be requested in future. (You'll see this in contrast with hypervisor-level swapping, which is discussed next.) Look at the following pictorial representation of memory page mapping to host memory:

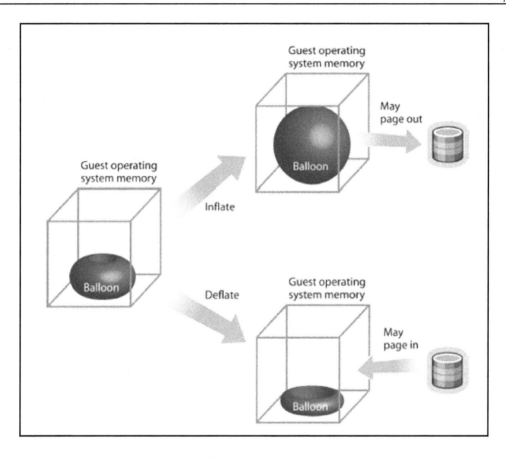

Host-level swapping in ESXi is not sufficient to reclaim memory during TPS and ballooning. To support this, when you start a VM, the hypervisor creates a separate swap file for the VM. This is primarily because if it frees pRAM for other VMs, the hypervisor can directly swap out vRAM with the swap file.

Swapping is a guaranteed technique to reclaim a specific amount of memory within a specific amount of time. However, you should be concerned about host-level swapping because it can severely penalize guest performance. This occurs when the hypervisor has no knowledge about which guest physical pages should be swapped, and the swapping might cause unintended interactions with the native memory management policies in the guest operating system. The following is a pictorial representation of host-level memory page swapping:

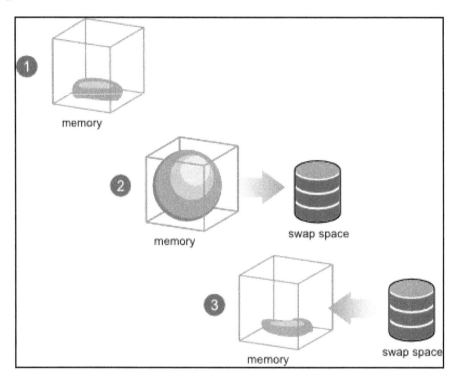

Monitoring a host-swapping activity

Excessive memory demand can cause severe performance problems for one or more VMs on an ESXi host. When ESXi is actively swapping from the memory of a VM to disk, the performance of that VM will degrade. The overhead of swapping a VM's memory to a disk can also degrade the performance of other VMs because the VM expects to be writing to RAM (speeds measured in nanoseconds), but it is unknowingly writing to disk (speeds measured in milliseconds).

The counters in vSphere Client for monitoring the swapping activity are as follows:

- **Memory Swap In Rate**: The rate at which memory is being swapped in from the disk.
- **Memory Swap Out Rate**: The rate at which memory is being swapped out to the disk.
- **Swapped**: The total amount of data that is sitting inside the `.vswp` hypervisor-level swap file. However, this doesn't tell you anything about the current state of the performance, nor about the current state of free pRAM. It just tells you that at some point in the past, there was low free pRAM. The only use of this counter is to check whether there was memory shortage in the past and whether there's a risk of Swap In (and bad performance) in future. But it's hard to estimate how likely the Swap In process will be because sometimes there's *junk data* that will be rarely requested again (for example, pages holding rarely accessed data, such as overly aggressive filesystem caching, or zeroed out pages that were actually deemed free by the guest operating system).

High values of the counter indicate insufficient memory and that performance is suffering as a result.

However, a high Swap Out rate means that the host is low on free pRAM, but essentially it does not indicate a current performance problem. A high Swap In rate indicates a current performance problem but not necessarily that the host is currently low on free pRAM.

 Swap In happens only on demand, which could be a week after the data was swapped out, and maybe a free-host-memory shortage has long since been resolved.

Getting ready

To step through this recipe, you will need a running ESXi Server, a couple of memory-hungry VMs with VMware Tools installed, a vCenter Server, and vSphere Web Client. No other prerequisites are required.

How to do it…

To monitor a host-swapping activity in vSphere Web Client, view the **Performance** screen. A few useful counters are **Swapped**, **Swap In**, and **Swap Out**. These counters represent total swapping of a virtual machine on the host.

To see the swapping activity of a single VM in action, perform the following steps:

1. Open vSphere Web Client.
2. Log in to your vCenter Server.
3. On your Home screen, select **Hosts and Clusters**.
4. Choose **memory-hungry VM**.
5. Go to the **Monitor** tab, then the **Performance** tab and click on **Advanced**.
6. Switch the view to **Memory**.
7. Click on **Chart Options**.
8. Select the three counters: **Swapped**, **Swap in Rate in KBps**, and **Swap Out Rate in KBps**.
9. Click on **OK**. Now you should see something similar to the following image if there are swapping activities on your VM:

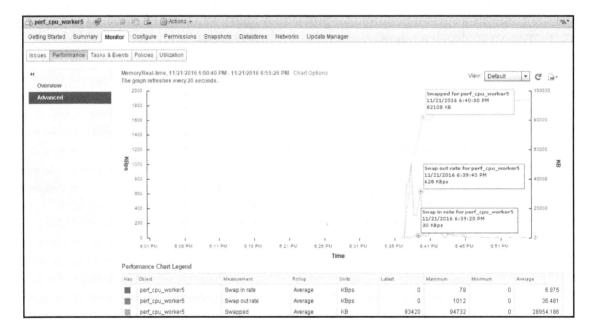

In the preceding example, you can see that this VM swapped out **82108 KB**, and its Swap Out rate was **682 KBps** and Swap In was **30 KBps**.

Now to see the overall swapped activity for all VMs on a single ESXi Server, perform the following steps:

1. Open vSphere Web Client.
2. Log in to your vCenter Server.
3. On your Home screen, select **Hosts and Clusters**.
4. Choose the poorly performing ESXi host.
5. Go to the **Monitor** tab, then the **Performance** tab, and then click on **Advanced**.
6. Change the view to **Memory**.
7. Click on **Chart Options**.
8. Select the three counters: **Active**, **Swap in Rate in KBps**, and **Swap Out Rate in KBps**.
9. Click on **OK**. Now you should see something similar to the following image if there are swapping activities on your ESXi host:

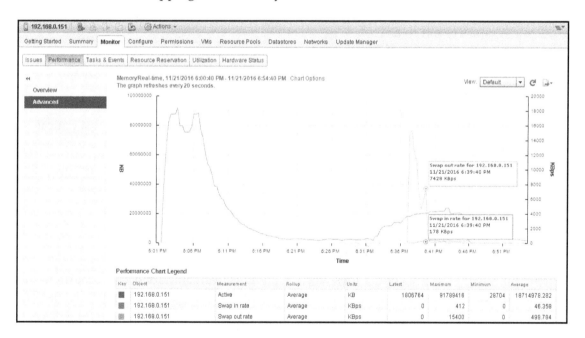

In this example, you can see that this ESXi host's Swap In rate was **178 KBps** and its Swap Out rate was **7428 KBps**.

How it works...

We talked about *How it works...* section in the previous recipe. Please refer to the *Virtual memory reclamation technique* recipe.

There's more...

The basic cause of host-level swapping is memory overcommitment from running memory-intensive VMs whose combined configured memory is greater than the amount of host physical memory available.

To resolve this problem, consider the following factors:

- Reduce the level of memory overcommitment (for example, reduce oversized VMs and add more memory where necessary, add more hosts to the cluster if necessary, and so on).
- Enable the balloon driver in all the VMs by installing VMware Tools.
- Reduce memory reservations. This will be covered in *Chapter 5, vSphere Cluster Design*.
- Use resource controls (Shares, Reservations, and Limits) with careful understanding and planning to reduce memory contention on the most critical VMs.

Note that this will not reduce the total memory contention on this host, but it will allow you to mitigate the risk to the performance of your most important VMs.

Monitoring a host-ballooning activity

Ballooning is part of normal operations when memory is overcommitted. The occurrence of ballooning is not necessarily an indication of a resource-deficient infrastructure. The use of the balloon driver enables the guest to give up physical memory pages that are not being used. In fact, ballooning can be a sign that you're getting extra value out of the memory you have in the host.

However, if ballooning causes the guest to give up memory that it actually needs, performance problems can occur due to guest operating system paging.

 Note, however, that this is fairly uncommon because the guest operating system will always assign memory that is already free to the balloon driver whenever possible, thereby avoiding any guest operating system swapping.

In vSphere Web Client, use the Memory Balloon counter to monitor a host's ballooning activity. This counter represents the total amount of memory claimed by the balloon drivers of the VMs on the host. The memory claimed by the balloon drivers can be used by other VMs. Again, this is not a performance problem, but it represents that the host takes memory from the less needful VMs for those with large amounts of Active Memory. If the host balloons, check the swap rate counters (Memory Swap In Rate and Memory Swap Out Rate), which might indicate performance problems, but it does not mean that you have a performance problem presently. It means that the unallocated pRAM on the host has dropped below a predefined threshold.

In a world where a vast majority of VMs have oversized vRAM, much of the vRAM -> pRAM mapping just holds zeroed out free pages, and these will be freed up by ballooning without displacing real data and risking poor performance in future.

Getting ready

To step through this recipe, you will need a running ESXi Server, a couple of running VMs with VMware Tools installed, a vCenter Server, and vSphere Web Client. No other prerequisites are required.

How to do it...

Balloon activity can also be monitored in **Performance Chart** through vSphere Web Client. The counter that you should follow in this case is **Balloon Average** in kilobytes.

You should select the same counter when you monitor the ballooning activity for ESXi as well.

To monitor the ballooning activity using the vSphere client for individual VM, follow these steps:

1. Open vSphere Web Client.
2. Log in to your vCenter Server.
3. On your **Home** screen, select **Hosts and Clusters**.
4. Choose the memory-hungry VM.
5. Click on the **Monitor** tab, then the **Performance** tab, and then click on **Advanced**.
6. Change the view to **Memory**.
7. Click on **Chart Options**.
8. Select the **Active**, **Ballooned Memory**, and **Consumed** counters.
9. Click on **OK**. Now you should see something similar to the following image if there is ballooning activity on your VM:

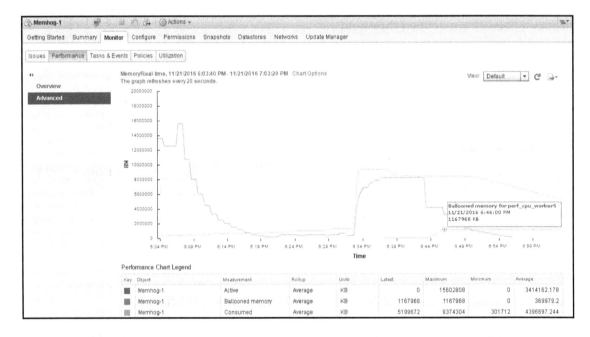

In this example, you can see that this VM (Memhog-1) is releasing its inactive Memory pages to the host memory. Here it is **1167968 KB**.

To monitor the ballooning activity for your ESXi using the vSphere client, follow these steps:

1. Open vSphere Web Client.
2. Log in to your vCenter Server.
3. On your **Home** screen, select **Hosts and Clusters**.
4. Choose the poorly performing ESXi host.
5. Go to the **Monitor** tab, then the **Performance** tab, and finally click on **Advanced**.
6. Switch the view to **Memory**.
7. Select **Chart Options**.
8. Select the **Active**, **Ballooned Memory**, and **Consumed** counters.
9. Click on **OK**. Now you should see something similar to this if there is ballooning activity on your ESXi host:

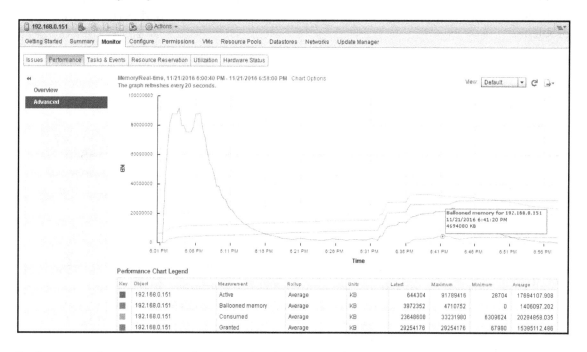

In this example, you can see that this ESXi host is involved in ballooning and its VMs are actively releasing inActive Memory pages.

How it works...

In our previous recipe, we talked about how it works. Refer to How it works... section of *Virtual memory reclamation technique* recipe.

There's more...

Memory ballooning is caused by the overcommitment of memory-intensive VMs. However, this is just indicative, which means that the presence of ballooning does not always say it's a performance problem. Ballooning is an effective way to use pRAM more efficiently, usually with no negative performance impact.

In order to maximize the ability of ESXi to recover idle memory from VMs, the balloon driver should be enabled on all VMs. The balloon driver should never be deliberately disabled on a VM. Disabling the balloon driver might cause unintended performance problems.

Keeping memory free for VMkernel

The amount of memory VMkernel will try to keep free can be set through the `Mem.MemMinFreePct` parameter. `MemMinFreePct` determines the amount of memory that VMkernel should keep free. vSphere 4.1 introduced a dynamic threshold for the Soft, Hard, and Low states to set appropriate thresholds and prevent VM performance issues while protecting VMkernel. The different states, based on `%pRAM`, which is still free, determines what type of memory reclamation techniques would be used.

For `MemMinFreePct`, using a default value of 6 percent can be inefficient when 256 gigabytes, 512 gigabytes, or even 1 TB hosts are becoming more mainstream. Having a 6 percent threshold on 512 gigabytes results in 30 gigabytes idling most of the time. However, not all customers use large systems; some prefer to scale out rather than scale up. If you choose to scale out and have more servers with less RAM in each system, a 6 percent `MemMinFreePct` threshold might be suitable. To have the best of both the worlds, vSphere 5 and above uses a sliding scale to determine the `Mem.MemMinFreePct` threshold, based on the amount of RAM installed in the hosts.

Getting ready

To step through this recipe, you will need a running ESXi Server and vSphere Web Client. No other prerequisites are required.

How to do it...

VMkernel uses a sliding scale to determine the `Mem.MinFreePct` threshold, based on the amount of RAM installed on the host, and it is automatic. However, if you need to change this behavior and set something on your own, follow these steps:

1. Open vSphere Web Client.
2. Log in to your vCenter Server.
3. On your **Home** screen, select **Hosts and Clusters**.
4. Choose the ESXi host where you want to perform this activity.
5. Go to the **Configure** tab and click on **Advanced System Settings**.
6. Scroll down to **Mem.MemMinFreePct** or search for it.
7. Choose a value between 0 and 50, where 0 indicates automatic.

Here you can set the percentage of host memory to reserve for accelerating memory allocations when free memory is low, which means this percentage determines when you could start using memory reclamation techniques (besides TPS).

The following is a sample screenshot when you configure this parameter:

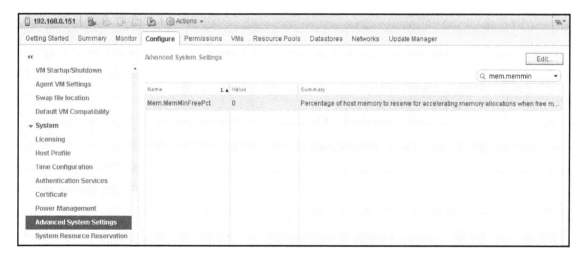

How it works...

When the `Mem.MemMinFreePct` value is set to 0, ESXi will calculate the `MemMinFreePct` threshold using the following formula and adding the results:

Threshold	Memory range	Result (host with 256GB)	Result (host with 512GB)
6%	0-4GB	245.76MB	245.76MB
4%	4-12GB	327.68MB	327.68MB
2%	12-28GB	327.68MB	327.68MB
1%	Remaining memory	2334.72MB	4956.16MB
Total High Threshold	3235.84MB (3.16GB)	5857.28MB (5.72GB)	

Total High Threshold is then used to activate the memory reclamation method for the Soft, Hard, and Low thresholds:

Free memory state	Threshold	Reclamation method	Threshold (host with 256GB)	Threshold (host with 512GB)
Soft	64%	Balloon	2070.93MB (2.02GB)	3748.65MB (3.66GB)
Hard	32%	Balloon, compress	1035.46MB (1.01GB)	1874.32MB (1.83GB)
Low	16%	Balloon, compress, swap	517.73MB (0.50GB)	937.16MB (0.91GB)

In a nutshell, the `MemMinFreePct` parameter defines the minimal amount of free memory desired in the system. Falling below this level will cause the system to reclaim memory through ballooning or swapping.

So, the amount of memory VMkernel keeps free is controlled by the value of `MemMinFreePct`, which is now determined using a sliding scale. This means that when free memory is greater than or equal to the derived value, the host is not under memory pressure.

Even if a host is under memory pressure, it just means that less free pRAM is available than is preferred. It does not mean that a performance problem is currently present. Because VMs often have extra vRAM and because the hypervisor doesn't know how much vRAM is considered free by the guest operating system, pRAM is often allocated to back vRAM, which holds junk data and could be freed for use elsewhere without any negative performance impact.

Key memory performance counters to monitor

To troubleshoot memory performance in a VMware vSphere environment, you should monitor the memory performance very carefully. In this aspect, you should monitor the following counters:

- **Average memory active**: The memory estimated to be used, based on recently touched memory pages.
- **Average memory swapped in or out**: Virtual memory swapped to or from disk.
- **Average memory swapped**: Total amount of memory swapped out. This indicates a possibility (with an unknown likelihood) of poor performance in future.

Getting ready

To step through this recipe, you will need a running ESXi Server, a couple of running VMs with VMware Tools installed, and vSphere Web Client. No other prerequisites are required.

How to do it...

To spot the average Active Memory, you should check both the VM level and host level. To monitor at the VM level, perform the following steps:

1. Open up vSphere Web Client.
2. Log in to your vCenter Server.
3. On the **Home** screen, select **VMs and Templates**.
4. Choose the VM where you want to monitor Active Memory.

5. Go to the **Monitor** tab, then the **Performance** tab, and then click on **Advanced**.

6. Change the view to **Memory**, then click on **Chart Options**.

7. Select the **Active**, **Balloon memory**, **Consumed**, and **Granted** counters from the list and click on **OK** to continue. Active is the counter that usually estimates how much the VM would actually need.

One of the biggest myths is that when a host is low on memory, performance problems are likely or that the VM needs more memory than it has installed because you're looking at a **Granted** or **Consumed** type of counter instead of the **Active-type** counter.

The following is a sample screenshot that you see once you select the **Active** counter to monitor memory performance:

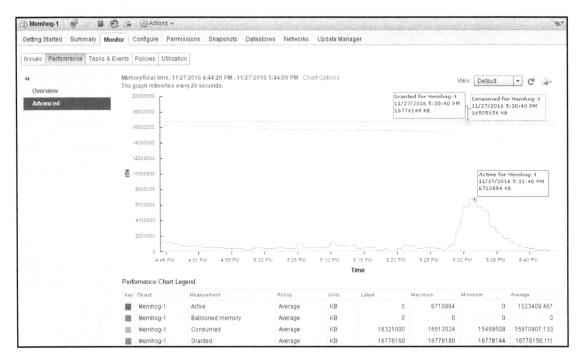

In the preceding example, you can see that **Memhog-1** is using close to 6.4 gigabytes of memory, which means the Active Memory is 6.4 gigabytes, whereas the granted memory for this VM is 16 gigabytes.

If you want to monitor this counter at the ESXi host level, perform the following steps:

1. Open up vSphere Web Client.
2. Log in to your vCenter Server.
3. On the **Home** screen, select **Hosts and Clusters**.
4. Choose the ESXi host where you want to monitor the Active Memory.
5. Go to the **Monitor** tab, then the **Performance** tab, and then click on **Advanced**.
6. Change the view to **Memory**, then click on **Chart Options**.
7. Select the **Active**, **Balloon memory**, **Consumed**, and **Granted** counters from the list and click on **OK** to continue.

The following is a sample screenshot that you see once you select the **Active** counter to monitor memory performance:

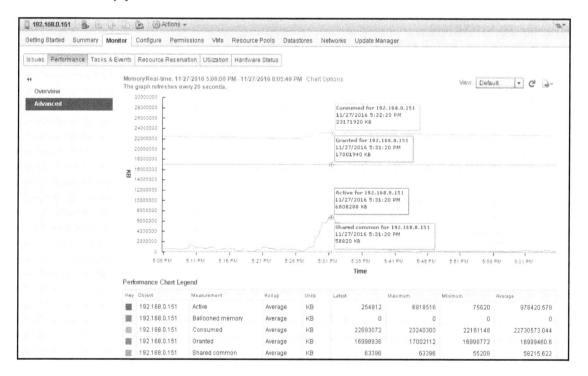

In this example, you can see that the ESXi host is using **6811516** kilobytes (6.49GB) of Active Memory.

 You may notice the **Shared common** counter here. This is a measure of savings due to TPS. Having TPS run does not have any downside and does not provide any reason to monitor it either. You could get into the most shared pages being zeroed pages, and the VDI is more likely to share the memory if all the guest operating systems are the same. TPS doesn't work with large pages, which are standard now until you hit a threshold, where large pages are broken down. Then, TPS is started.

Now, to monitor **Swapped**, **Swap in**, and **Swap out**, follow the *Monitoring host swapping activity* recipe.

How it works...

To understand how swapping happens, check the *Monitoring host swapping activity* recipe.

Average Active Memory refers to the average amount of memory that is actively used in kilobytes.

What counters not to use

A lot of the time, we assume that some very popular counters would be better to monitor memory performance. However, many times, it leads to something else. This means that these are not an indication of a memory performance issue. If this counter is combined with something else, then it may indicate performance degradation.

In this aspect, don't use two of the most popular counters just to understand whether the memory is under pressure or not:

- Mem.consumed (Consumed Memory)
- Mem.vmmemctl (ballooned memory)

Let me show you what they essentially indicate.

The `Mem.consumed` counter is the amount of memory consumed by one or all VMs. This is calculated as memory granted minus memory saved by sharing. Now the question is why we should not use this. The reason is that memory allocation will vary dynamically based on the VM's entitlement. It is important that a VM should get whatever it actually demands.

Similarly, `Mem.vmmemctl` is the amount of ballooned memory. This does not indicate a performance problem as well. However, when it gets combined with host swapping, then it indicates a performance problem.

Getting ready

To step through this recipe, you will need a running ESXi Server, a couple of running VMs with VMware Tools installed, and vSphere Web Client. No other prerequisites are required.

How to do it...

To spot the Consumed Memory counter value within the vSphere infrastructure, this is what you should do:

1. Open up vSphere Web Client.
2. Log in to your vCenter Server.
3. In the **Home** screen, select **VMs and Templates**.
4. Choose the VM where you want to monitor the Consumed Memory.
5. Go to the **Monitor** tab, then the **Performance** tab, and then click on **Advanced**.
6. Select the **Memory** view.
7. Click on **Chart Options**.
8. Select the **Consumed** counter and then click **OK** to continue.

Now you should see something similar to the following screenshot:

In this example, you can see that the consumed value of the **Memhog-1** VM is **16505156** kilobytes.

To understand the Mem.vmmemctl counter, you should follow the *Monitoring a host-ballooning activity* recipe.

Identifying when memory is the problem

Both your host memory and VM memory can indicate that they are under pressure. But the main challenge to a VMware admin is how to determine that there is a memory performance issue.

There are a few things that a VMware admin should understand to confirm whether there is a memory performance issue, and they are:

- Your host memory consumption is approaching your total host memory
- Active Memory in your host is approaching your total memory
- Ballooning is occurring
- Host swapping is occurring

Now if you wonder what is the Active Memory here in relation to Consumed Memory, let me tell you that Active Memory is the amount of memory that is actively used, as estimated by VMkernel, based on recently touched memory pages. For a VM, this is referred to the amount of guest physical memory that is actively used.

The ESXi host calculates Active Memory using the sum of all the active counters for all the powered-on VMs plus vSphere services on the host.

There could be another side to it, which can depict that VM is under memory pressure, to determine that you could combine the factors described previously. You should check whether VM memory has a high amount of Active Memory.

Getting ready

To step through this recipe, you will need a running ESXi Server, a couple of running VMs with VMware Tools installed, and vSphere Web Client. No other prerequisites are required.

How to do it...

To check memory utilization of a VM, follow the ensuing steps:

1. Open up vSphere Web Client.
2. Log in to your vCenter Server.
3. On the **Home** screen, select **VMs and Templates**.
4. Choose the VM where you want to monitor the utilization of memory.
5. Go to the **Monitor** tab, then the **Performance** tab, and then click on **Advanced**.
6. Select **Memory** from the drop-down list.
7. Click on **Chart Options**.

8. Select the **Active**, **Ballooned**, **Consumed**, and **Host consumed %** counters and click on **OK** to continue.

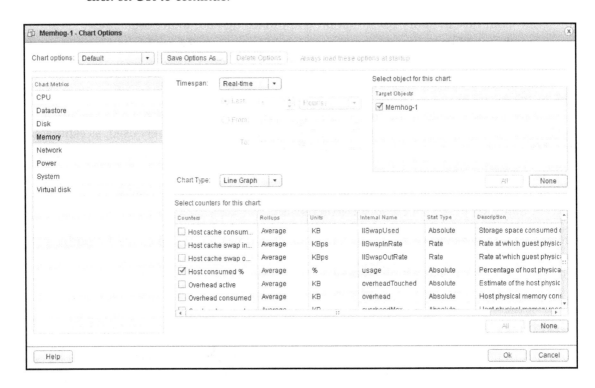

The following is an example where you can see the utilization of this VM is almost 96 percent:

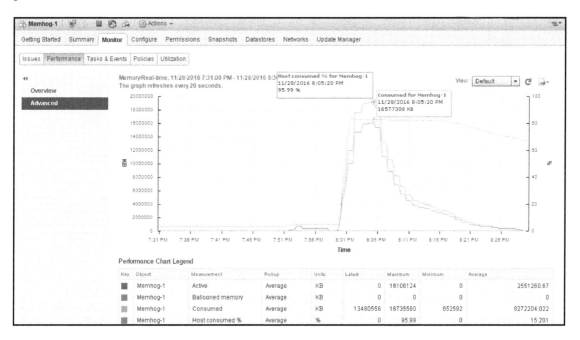

Now to check the overall host memory consumption and active host memory consumption, you need to perform the following steps:

1. Open up vSphere Web Client.
2. Log in to the vCenter Server.
3. On the **Home** screen, select **Hosts and Clusters**.
4. Choose the ESXi host where you want to monitor the memory consumption.
5. Go to the **Monitor** tab, then the **Performance** tab.
6. Select **Memory** from the drop-down list.
7. Click on **Chart Options**.
8. Select the **Active, Ballooned, Consumed**, and **Host consumed** % counters and click on **OK** to continue.

Now let us look at a sample screenshot and see what it looks like:

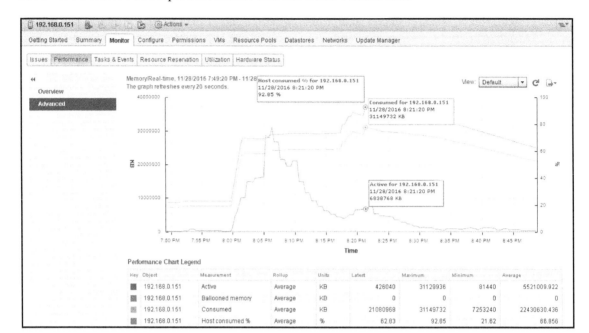

You can see in this example that we have an ESXi host that has 32 gigabytes of physical memory and we are consuming almost every bit of it.

However, if you look at the Active Memory here, we are using a little under 7 gigabytes. This means that although we have more than 30 gigabytes of Consumed Memory, we only have 7 gigabytes of Active Memory. It should not create many issues. This could indicate overprovisioning of resources; if applicable, VMs should be right-sized by removing the allocated RAM that is not required.

Analyzing host and VM memory

Often, you need to monitor VM and host memory usage; the good part about this is that VMware vSphere Client exposes two memory statistics in the **Summary** tab of a VM. These are **Consumed Host Memory** and **Active Guest Memory**.

Consumed Host Memory is the amount of host physical memory that is allocated to the VM. Please note that this value includes virtualization overhead as well.

 Note that many VMs have oversized vRAM, and the guest operating system is likely to opportunistically fill up its vRAM with unnecessary things (for example, caching everything read from the disk, no matter how unlikely it will be requested again). Consumed Memory only means that the VM used this memory at some point, not that it's likely to use it again.

Active Guest Memory is defined as the amount of guest physical memory that is currently being used by the guest operating system and its applications.

These two statistics are quite useful for analyzing the memory status of the VM and providing hints to address potential performance issues.

For host memory usage, you may want to look at the **Resources** section of the **Summary** tab for an ESXi host. To understand how much is the actual VM usage, you need to check the **Memory** section of the **Configuration** page.

Getting ready

To step through this recipe, you will need a running ESXi Server, a couple of running VMs with VMware Tools installed, and vSphere Web Client. No other prerequisites are required.

How to do it...

1. Open up vSphere Web Client.
2. Log in to your vCenter Server.
3. On the **Home** screen, select **VMs and Templates**.
4. Click on the VM where you want to monitor **Utilization of Memory**.

5. Go to the **Summary** tab and locate **Memory Usage** in the summary at the top and **Memory Active** in the **VM Hardware** tile:

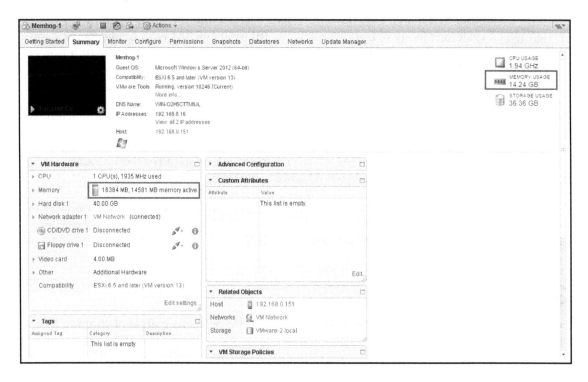

You can see in the preceding example that the Consumed Host Memory of the VM is **16384 MB** and its Active Guest Memory is **14581 MB**.

You can also check this through the performance graph of the VM. Here is what you need to do to get to this:

1. Open up vSphere Web Client.
2. Log in to your vCenter Server.
3. On the **Home** screen, select **VMs and Templates**.
4. Choose the VM where you want to monitor **Utilization of Memory**.
5. Go to the **Monitor** tab, then the **Performance** tab.
6. Select **Memory** from the drop-down list.
7. Click on **Chart Options**.

8. Make sure that the **Active** and **Consumed** counters are selected and click on **OK** to see the result:

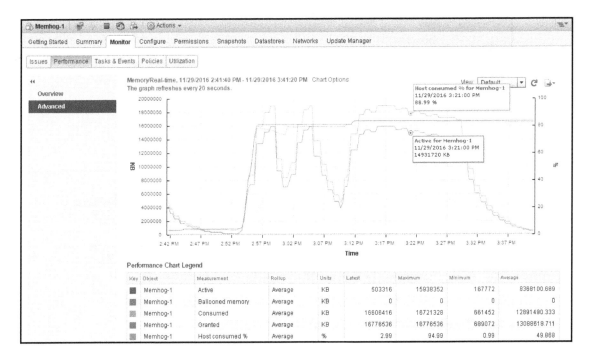

You can see in this example that the memory usage of this VM is 89 percent. Guest Active Memory and Consumed Host Memory are also quite high.

Now to check the host memory, follow these steps:

1. Open up vSphere Web Client.
2. Log in to your vCenter Server.
3. On the **Home** screen, select **Hosts and Clusters**.
4. Choose the ESXi host where you want to monitor **Utilization of Memory**.
5. Go to the **Summary** tab.

6. On the top-right corner, you will see **Host Memory Usage**:

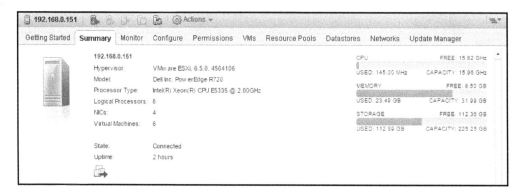

7. Now go to the **Configure** tab, then on the left scroll down to the **Hardware** section, and then click on **Memory** to see VM memory usage:

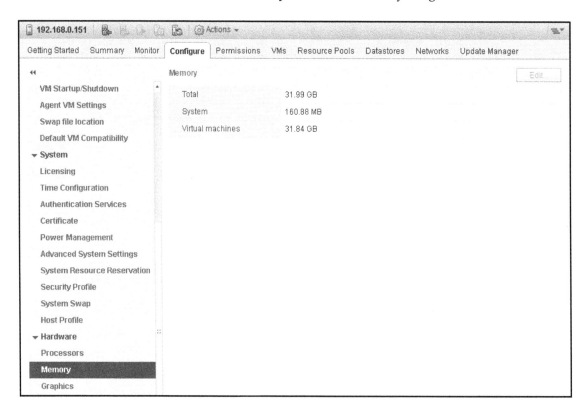

How it works...

Sometimes, you may see that Consumed Host Memory is greater than Active Guest Memory. The reason for this is that for physical hosts that are not overcommitted on memory, Consumed Host Memory represents the highest amount of memory usage by a VM. It is possible that in the past, this VM was actively using a very large amount of memory.

Because the host physical memory is not overcommitted, there is no reason for the hypervisor to invoke ballooning or host-level swapping to reclaim memory. Therefore, you can find the VM in a situation where its active guest memory use is low, but the amount of host physical memory assigned to it is high. This is a perfectly normal situation, so there is nothing to be concerned about.

 Please note that the Consumed Memory on the host being close to 100 percent does not reliably indicate that a performance problem is likely to happen.

If the Consumed Host Memory is less than or equal to active guest memory, this might be because the active guest memory of a virtual machine might not completely reside in the host physical memory. This might occur if a guest's Active Memory has been reclaimed by the balloon driver, or if the VM has been swapped out by the hypervisor. In both cases, this is probably due to high memory overcommitment.

Memory performance best practices

Virtualization causes an increase in the amount of physical memory required due to the extra memory needed by ESXi for its own code and data structures, and you need to know what are the best practice standards you have.

There are four basic principles that you should keep in mind:

- Allocate enough memory to hold the working set of applications that you will run on the VM, thus minimizing swapping. You can estimate the working set by monitoring the Active Memory counter.
- Do not disable the balloon driver.
- Keep TPS enabled. It's free!
- Avoid overcommitting memory to the point that it results in heavy memory reclamation, especially complicated Swap In rates (KBps).

How to do it...

So you may ask how can we determine the total required data center memory?

Well, there are several methods to determine the total memory capacity requirement:

- Use the information gathered during the current state analysis to determine the current memory capacity requirements
- Use application vendor documentation to estimate memory capacity requirements
- Actual data center usage analysis is typically more accurate

Do not plan on fully utilizing host memory resources. You will want to have enough memory so you can remove one host from any cluster and still run all the VMs. This will allow you to perform maintenance on a host or have a host fail without the need to power off VMs. Also, leave some headroom for such things as:

- Increase in short-term utilization as part of the normal business cycle
- Failover from other data centers during disaster recovery
- VMkernel overhead
- VM overhead
- Future growth

3
Networking Performance Design

In this chapter, we will cover the tasks related to networking performance design. You will learn the following aspects of networking performance design:

- Designing a vSphere Standard Switch for load balancing and failover
- Designing a vSphere Distributed Switch for load balancing and failover
- What to know when offloading checksum
- Selecting the correct virtual network adapter
- Improving performance through VMDirectPath I/O
- Improving performance through NetQueue
- Improving network performance using the SplitRx mode for multicast traffic
- Designing a multi-NIC vMotion
- Improving network performance using network I/O control
- Monitoring network capacity and performance matrix

Introduction

Device and I/O virtualization involves managing the routing of I/O requests between virtual devices and the shared physical hardware. Software-based I/O virtualization and management, in contrast to a direct pass through to the hardware, enables a rich set of features and simplified management. With networking, virtual NICs and virtual switches create virtual networks between VMs that are running on the same host, without the network traffic consuming bandwidth on the physical network.

NIC Teaming consists of multiple physical NICs and provides failover and load balancing for VMs. VMs can be seamlessly relocated to different systems using VMware vMotion while keeping their existing MAC addresses and the running state. The key to effective I/O virtualization is to preserve these virtualization benefits while keeping the added CPU overhead to a minimum.

A hypervisor virtualizes the physical hardware and presents each VM with a standardized set of virtual devices. These virtual devices effectively emulate well-known hardware and translate VM requests to the system hardware. This standardization on consistent device drivers also helps with VM standardization and portability across platforms because all VMs are configured to run on the same virtual hardware, regardless of the physical hardware in the system. In this chapter, we will discuss the following:

- Various network performance problems
- Causes of network performance problems
- Solutions to correct network performance problems

Designing a vSphere Standard Switch for load balancing and failover

The load balancing and failover policies that are chosen for the infrastructure can have an impact on the overall design. Using NIC Teaming, we can group several physical network adapters attached to a vSwitch. This grouping enables load balancing between the different physical NICs and provides fault tolerance if a network card or link failure occurs.

Network adapter teaming offers a number of available load balancing and load distribution options. Load balancing is load distribution based on the number of connections, not network traffic. In most cases, load is managed only for the outgoing traffic, and balancing is based on four different policies:

- Route based on IP hash
- Route based on source MAC hash
- Route based on the originating virtual port (default)
- Using the explicit failover order

Also, we have two network failure detection options and these are:

- Link status only (default)
- Beacon probing

Getting ready

To step through this recipe, you will need one or more running ESXi hosts, a vCenter Server, and vSphere Web Client. No other prerequisites are required.

How to do it...

To change the load balancing policy and select the right one for your environment, and to also select the appropriate failover policy, follow these steps:

1. Open up VMware vSphere Web Client.
2. Log in to your vCenter Server.
3. On the left-hand side, choose any ESXi Server and choose **Configuration** from the right-hand pane.
4. Click on the **Networking** section and select the vSwitch for which you want to change the load balancing and failover settings.

 You may wish to override this per port group as well.

5. Click on **Properties**.
6. Select the vSwitch and click on **Edit**.
7. Go to the **Teaming and failover** tab.
8. Select one of the available policies from the **Load balancing** drop-down menu.
9. Select one of the available policies from the **Network failure detection** drop-down menu.

10. Click on **OK** to make it effective.

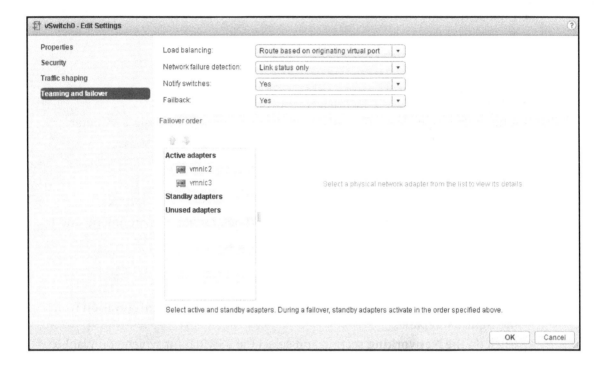

How it works...

Here we will explain each of the four balancing policies and how they work.

Route based on the originating virtual port (default policy)

In this configuration, load balancing is based on the number of physical network cards and the number of virtual ports used. With this configuration policy, a virtual network card connected to a vSwitch port will always use the same physical network card. If a physical network card fails, the virtual network card is redirected to another physical network card.

 You typically do not see individual ports on a vSwitch. However, each vNIC that gets connected to a vSwitch implicitly uses a particular port on the vSwitch. (It's just that there's no reason to ever configure which port because that is always done automatically.)

It does a reasonable job of balancing your egress uplinks for the traffic leaving an ESXi host as long as all the VMs using these uplinks have similar usage patterns.

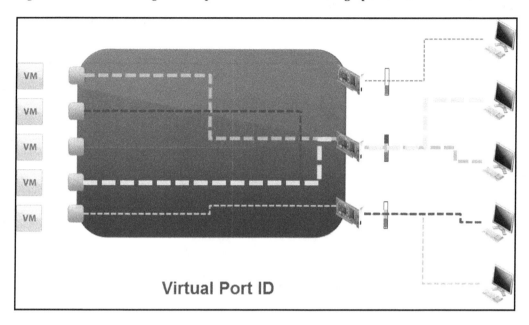

Virtual Port ID

It is important to note that port allocation occurs only when a VM is started or when a failover occurs. Balancing is done based on a port's occupation rate at the time the VM starts up. This means that which pNIC is selected for use by this VM is determined at the time the VM powers on, based on which ports in the vSwitch are occupied at the time. For example, if you start 20 VMs in a row on a vSwitch with two pNICs, the odd-numbered VMs would use the first pNIC and the even-numbered VMs would use the second pNIC, and this would persist even if you shut down all the even-numbered VMs; the first pNIC would have all the VMs and the second pNIC would have none. It might happen that two heavily loaded VMs are connected to the same pNIC; if this happens, load would not be balanced.

This policy is the easiest one, and we always call for the simplest one to map it to a best operational simplification.

Now when speaking of this policy, it is important to understand that if, for example, teaming is created with two 1 GB cards and if one VM consumes more than one card's capacity, a performance problem will arise because traffic greater than 1 Gbps will not go through the other card and there will be an impact on the VMs sharing the same port as the VM consuming all the resources. Likewise, if two VMs each wish to use 600 Mbps and they happen to go to the first pNIC, the first pNIC will not be able to meet the 1.2 Gbps demand, no matter how idle the second pNIC is.

Route based on source MAC hash

This principle is the same as the default policy but is based on the number of MAC addresses. This policy may put those VM vNICs on the same physical uplink depending on how the MAC hash is resolved.

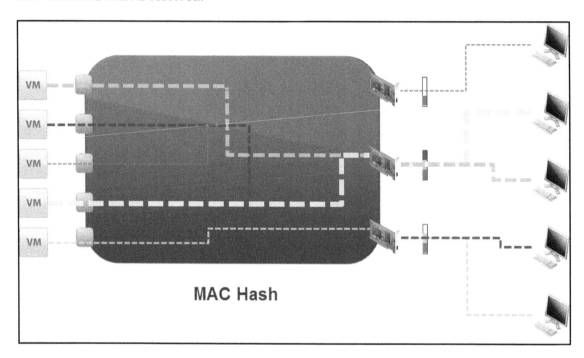

MAC Hash

For MAC hash, VMware has a different way of assigning ports. It's not based on the dynamically changing port (after a power off and power on, the VM usually gets a different vSwitch port assigned) but is based on fixed MAC address instead. As a result, one VM is always assigned to the same physical NIC unless the configuration is not changed. With the port ID, the VM could get different pNICs after a reboot or VMotion.

If you have two ESXi Servers with the same configuration, the VM will stay on the same pNIC number even after a vMotion. But again, one pNIC may be congested while others are bored. So there is no real load balancing.

Route based on IP hash

The limitation of the two previously discussed policies is that a given virtual NIC will always use the same physical network card for all its traffic. IP hash-based load balancing uses the source and destination of the IP address to determine which physical network card to use. Using this algorithm, a VM can communicate through several different physical network cards, based on its destination. This option requires the configuration of the physical switch's ports to EtherChannel. Because the physical switch is configured similarly, this option is the only one that also provides inbound load distribution, where the distribution is not necessarily balanced.

There are some limitations and reasons why this policy is not commonly used. These reasons are described as follows:

- The route based on the IP hash load balancing option involves added complexity and configuration support from upstream switches. **Link Aggregation Control Protocol** (**LACP**) or EtherChannel is required for this algorithm to be used. However, this does not apply to a vSphere Standard Switch.
- For IP hash to be an effective algorithm for load balancing, there must be many IP sources and destinations. This is not a common practice for IP storage networks, where a single VMkernel port is used to access a single IP address on a storage device.

 The same NIC will always send all its traffic to the same destination (for example, google.com) through the same pNIC, though another destination (for example, bing.com) might go through another pNIC.

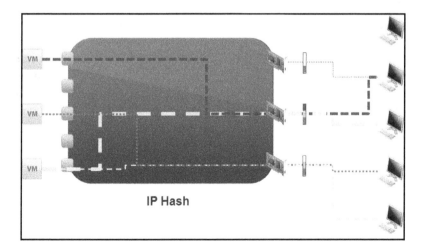

IP Hash

So, in a nutshell, due to the added complexity, the upstream dependency on the advanced switch configuration, and the management overhead, this configuration is rarely used in production environments. The main reason is that if you use IP hash, pSwitch must be configured with LACP or EtherChannel. Also, if you use LACP or EtherChannel, the load balancing algorithm must be IP hash. This is because, with LACP, inbound traffic to the VM could come through either of the pNICs, and the vSwitch must be ready to deliver that to the VM and only IP hash will do that (other policies will drop the inbound traffic to this VM that comes in on a pNIC that the VM doesn't use).

Using the explicit failover order

In this failover mode, the system will use the highest order uplink for all of the traffic, as defined in the **Active Adapter** section of the vSwitch settings. If this uplink fails, the system will move all of the traffic to the next highest order uplink.

The two network failure detection options (as mentioned earlier) are discussed next.

Link status only (default)

The link status option enables the detection of failures related to the physical network's cables and switch. However, be aware that configuration issues are not detected. Also, this option cannot detect the link state problems with upstream switches; it works only with the first hop switch from the host.

Beacon probing

The beacon probing option allows the detection of failures unseen by the link status option by sending the Ethernet broadcast frames through all the network cards. These network frames authorize the vSwitch to detect faulty configurations or upstream switch failures and force the failover if the ports are blocked. When using an inverted U physical network topology in conjunction with a dual NIC server, it is recommended that you enable link-state tracking or a similar network feature in order to avoid traffic black holes.

According to VMware's best practices, it is recommended that you have at least three cards before activating this functionality. However, if IP hash is going to be used, beacon probing should not be used as a form of network failure detection in order to avoid an ambiguous state due to the limitation that a packet cannot hairpin on the port it is received. Beacon probing works by sending out and listening to beacon probes from the NICs in a team. If there are two NICs, then each NIC will send out a probe and the other NICs will receive that probe. Because EtherChannel is considered one link, this will not function properly as the NIC uplinks are not logically separate uplinks. If beacon probing is used, this can result in MAC address flapping errors, and the network connectivity may be interrupted.

Designing a vSphere Distributed Switch for load balancing and failover

The load balancing and failover policies are chosen so the infrastructure can have an impact on the overall design. Using NIC Teaming, we can group several physical network switches attached to a vSwitch. This grouping enables load balancing between different physical NICs and provides fault tolerance if a card or physical switch failure occurs.

A vSphere Distributed Switch offers a load balancing option that actually takes the network workload into account when choosing the physical uplink. This is route-based on a physical NIC load. This is also called **Load Based Teaming** (**LBT**). We recommend this load balancing option over others when using a distributed vSwitch. The benefits of using this load balancing policy are as follows:

- It is the only load balancing option that actually considers NIC load when choosing uplinks
- It does not require upstream switch configuration dependencies, like the route based on the IP hash algorithm does
- When the route based on physical NIC load is combined with network I/O control, a truly dynamic traffic distribution is achieved

Getting ready

To step through this recipe, you will need one or more running ESXi Servers (licensed with Enterprise Plus for vDS), a configured vSphere Distributed Switch, a vCenter Server, and vSphere Web Client. No other prerequisites are required.

How to do it...

To change the load balancing policy and the appropriate failover policy, follow these steps:

1. Open up VMware vSphere Web Client.
2. Log in to your vCenter Server.
3. Navigate to **Networking** on the home screen.
4. Navigate to **Distributed Port group** and right-click on it and select **Edit Settings**.
5. Click on the **Teaming and failover** section.
6. From the **Load balancing** drop-down menu, select **Route based on physical NIC load** as the load balancing policy.
7. Choose the appropriate network failover detection policy from the drop-down menu.
8. Click on **OK** and your settings will be effective.

How it works...

Load-based teaming, also known as **Route based on physical NIC load**, maps vNICs to pNICs and remaps the vNIC to pNIC affiliation if the load exceeds specific thresholds on a pNIC. LBT uses the originating port ID's load balancing algorithm for the initial port assignment, which results in the first vNIC being affiliated to the first pNIC, the second vNIC to the second pNIC, and so on. Once the initial placement is over after the VM is powered on, LBT will examine both the inbound and outbound traffic on each of the pNICs and then distribute the load across if there is congestion.

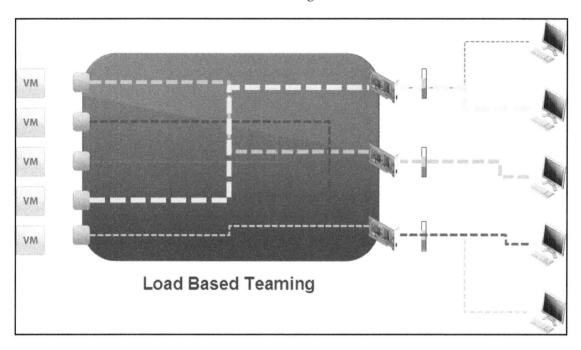

Load Based Teaming

LBT will send a congestion alert when the average utilization of a pNIC is 75 percent over a period of 30 seconds. The 30-second interval is used to avoid MAC flapping issues. However, you should enable PortFast on the upstream switches if you plan to use STP. VMware recommends LBT over IP hash when you use, vSphere Distributed Switch, as it does not require any special or additional settings in the upstream switch layer. In this way, you can reduce unnecessary operational complexity. LBT maps vNIC to pNIC and then distributes the load across all the available uplinks, unlike IP hash which just maps the vNIC to pNIC but does not do load distribution. LBT reduces the chance of pNIC imbalance compared to IP hash.

What to know when offloading checksum

VMware takes advantage of many of the performance features from modern network adapters.

In this section, we are going to talk about two of them and they are:

- TCP checksum offload
- TCP segmentation offload

Getting ready

To step through this recipe, you will need a running ESXi Server with SSH enabled and an SSH client (Putty). No other prerequisites are required.

How to do it...

The list of network adapter features that are enabled on your NIC can be found in the `/etc/vmware/esx.conf` file on your ESXi Server. Look for the lines that start with `/net/vswitch`.

However, do not change the default NIC's driver settings unless you have a valid reason to do so. A good practice is to follow any configuration recommendations that are specified by the hardware vendor. Carry out the following steps in order to check the settings:

1. Log in to the ESXi host using an SSH client (Putty).
2. Open the `etc/vmware/esx.conf`. file.
3. Look for the line that starts with `/net/vswitch`.

4. Your output should look like the following screenshot:

```
/net/vswitch/child[0000]/uplinks/child[0000]/pnic = "vmnic2"
/net/vswitch/child[0000]/name = "vSwitch0"
/net/vswitch/child[0000]/teamPolicy/maxActive = "1"
/net/vswitch/child[0000]/teamPolicy/uplinks[0000]/pnic = "vmnic2"
/net/vswitch/child[0000]/teamPolicy/linkCriteria/beacon = "ignore"
/net/vswitch/child[0000]/teamPolicy/team = "lb_srcid"
/net/vswitch/child[0000]/teamPolicy/notifySwitch = "true"
/net/vswitch/child[0000]/teamPolicy/rollingRestoration = "false"
/net/vswitch/child[0000]/teamPolicy/hasUplinkOrder = "true"
/net/vswitch/child[0000]/shapingPolicy/enabled = "false"
/net/vswitch/child[0000]/cdp/status = "listen"
/net/vswitch/child[0000]/capabilities/HighDMA = "true"
/net/vswitch/child[0000]/capabilities/ChecksumOffloadIPv6ExtHdrs = "true"
/net/vswitch/child[0000]/capabilities/ChecksumOffload = "true"
/net/vswitch/child[0000]/capabilities/VlanUntag = "true"
/net/vswitch/child[0000]/capabilities/VlanTag = "true"
/net/vswitch/child[0000]/capabilities/Offload8Offset = "true"
/net/vswitch/child[0000]/capabilities/TcpSegmentationOffloadIPv6ExtHdrs = "true"
/net/vswitch/child[0000]/capabilities/UplinkReadOnlyInetHeaders = "true"
/net/vswitch/child[0000]/capabilities/ScatterGatherTx = "true"
/net/vswitch/child[0000]/capabilities/TcpSegmentationOffload256k = "true"
/net/vswitch/child[0000]/capabilities/TcpSegmentationOffload = "true"
/net/vswitch/child[0000]/capabilities/TcpSegmentationOffloadIPv6 = "true"
/net/vswitch/child[0000]/capabilities/ScatterGatherSpanPagesTx = "true"
/net/vswitch/child[0000]/capabilities/Offload16Offset = "true"
/net/vswitch/child[0000]/capabilities/ChecksumOffloadIPv6 = "true"
/net/vswitch/child[0000]/securityPolicy/macChange = "true"
/net/vswitch/child[0000]/securityPolicy/promiscuous = "false"
/net/vswitch/child[0000]/securityPolicy/forgedTx = "true"
/net/vswitch/child[0000]/portgroup/child[0000]/vlanId = "0"
/net/vswitch/child[0000]/portgroup/child[0000]/name = "VM Network"
```

How it works...

A TCP message must be broken down into Ethernet frames. The size of each frame is determined by the **maximum transmission unit** (**MTU**). The default maximum transmission unit is either 1,500 bytes or 9,000 bytes for jumbo frames. The process of breaking messages into frames is called segmentation.

Modern NIC adapters have the ability to perform checksum calculations natively. TCP checksums are used to determine the validity of transmitted or received network packets based on the error-correcting code. These calculations are traditionally performed by the host's CPU. By offloading these calculations to the network adapters, the CPU is freed up to perform other tasks. As a result, the system as a whole runs better. **TCP segmentation offload** (**TSO**) allows a TCP/IP stack from the guest OS inside the VM to emit large frames (up to 64 KB) even though the MTU of the interface is smaller.

Earlier operating systems used the CPU to perform segmentation. Modern NICs try to optimize this TCP segmentation using a larger segment size as well as offloading the work from the CPU to the NIC hardware. ESXi utilizes this concept to provide a virtual NIC with TSO support, without requiring specialized network hardware.

- With TSO, instead of processing many small MTU frames during the transmission, the system can send fewer, larger virtual MTU frames.
- TSO improves the performance of the TCP network traffic coming from a VM and the network traffic sent out of the server.
- TSO is supported at the VM level and in the VMkernel TCP/IP stack.
- TSO is enabled on the VMkernel interface by default. If TSO becomes disabled for a particular VMkernel interface, the only way to enable it is to delete the VMkernel interfaces and recreate them with TSO enabled.
- TSO is used in the guest when the VMXNET 2 (or later) network adapter is installed. To enable TSO at the VM level, you must replace the existing VMXNET or flexible virtual network adapter with a VMXNET 2 (or later) adapter. This replacement might result in a change in the MAC address of the virtual network adapter.

Selecting the correct virtual network adapter

When you configure a VM, you can add NICs and specify the adapter type. The types of network adapters that are available depend on the following factors:

- The version of the VM, which depends on which host created it or most recently updated it
- Whether or not the VM has been updated to the latest version for the current host
- The guest operating system

The following virtual NIC types are supported:

- Vlance
- VMXNET
- Flexible
- E1000
- E1000e
- Enhanced VMXNET (VMXNET 2)
- VMXNET 3

If you want to know more about these network adapter types, refer to the KB article at `http ://kb.vmware.com/kb/1001805`.

Getting ready

To step through this recipe, you will need one or more running ESXi Servers, a vCenter Server, and vSphere Web Client. No other prerequisites are required.

How to do it...

You cannot change the network adapter type on an existing network adapter. The only time you can choose the network adapter type is when creating a new VM or when adding a new network adapter to an existing VM.

The steps to choose a network adapter while creating a new VM are as follows:

1. Open vSphere Web Client.
2. Log in to your vCenter Server.
3. Click on your cluster and select **New Virtual Machine** | **New Virtual Machine**.

4. Go through the steps and hold on to the **Customize hardware** step. Here you need to choose how many network adapters you need, which port group you want them to connect to, and the adapter type.

To choose an adapter type while adding a new network interface to an existing VM, follow these steps:

1. Open vSphere Web Client.
2. Log in to your vCenter Server.
3. Navigate to **VMs and Templates** on your home screen.
4. Select an existing VM where you want to add a new network adapter, then right-click on it and select **Edit Settings**.
5. Select **Network** from the **New device** drop-down menu at the bottom, then click on the **Add** button.
6. Expand the **New Network** section at the bottom.
7. Select the port group and **Adapter Type**.

8. Click on **OK** to finish.

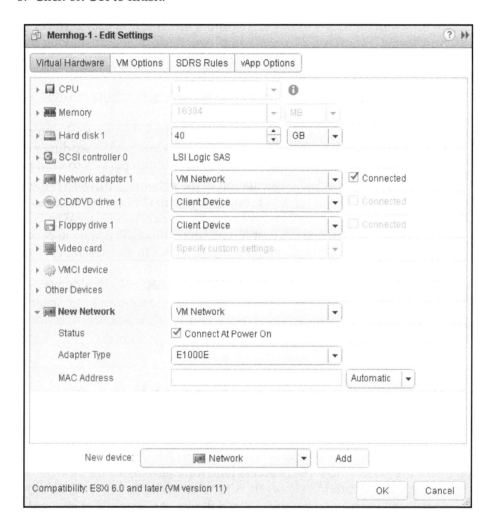

How it works...

Among the entire supported virtual network adapter types, VMXNET is the paravirtualized device driver for virtual networking. The VMXNET driver implements an idealized network interface that passes through the network traffic from the VM to the physical cards with minimal overhead. The three versions of VMXNET are VMXNET, VMXNET 2 (enhanced VMXNET), and VMXNET 3.

The VMXNET driver improves performance through a number of optimizations, as follows:

- It shares a ring buffer between the VM and VMkernel and uses zero-copy, which in turn saves CPU cycles. Zero-copy improves performance by having the VMs and VMkernel share a buffer, reducing the internal copy operations between buffers to free up CPU cycles.
- It takes advantage of transmission packet coalescing to reduce address space switching.
- It batches packets and issues a single interrupt rather than multiple interrupts. This improves efficiency, but in some cases, with slow packet-sending rates, it could hurt the throughput while waiting to get enough packets to send them.
- It offloads the TCP checksum calculation to the network hardware rather than use the CPU resources of the VM monitor. Use vmxnet3 or the most recent model if you can. Use VMware Tools where possible. For certain unusual types of network traffic, sometimes the best model isn't optimal; if you have poor network performance, experiment with other types of vNICs to see which performs best.

 We recommend that you use the VMXNET3 adapter in deployments where performance is the top concern.

Improving performance through VMDirectPath I/O

VMware vSphere DirectPath I/O leverages Intel VT-d and AMD-Vi hardware support to allow guest operating systems to directly access hardware devices. In the case of networking, vSphere DirectPath I/O allows the VM to access a physical NIC directly rather than using an emulated device or a paravirtualized device. An example of an emulated device is the E1000 virtual NIC, and examples of paravirtualized devices are the VMXNET and VMXNET 3 virtual network adapters. vSphere DirectPath I/O provides limited increases in throughput, but it reduces the CPU cost of networking-intensive workloads.

vSphere DirectPath I/O is not compatible with certain core virtualization features. However, when you run ESXi on certain vendor configurations, vSphere DirectPath I/O for networking is compatible with the following:

- VMware vMotion
- Hot adding and removing of virtual devices, suspend, and resume
- VMware vSphere high availability
- VMware vSphere **Distributed Resource Scheduler** (DRS)
- Snapshots

Typical VMs and their workloads do not require the use of vSphere DirectPath I/O. However, for workloads that are networking-intensive and do not need the core virtualization features just mentioned, vSphere DirectPath I/O might be useful to reduce CPU usage and/or latency. Another potential use case of this technology is passing through a network card to a guest when the network card is not supported by the hypervisor:

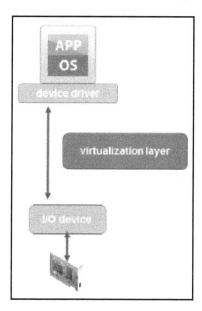

Getting ready

To step through this recipe, you will need one or more running ESXi Server; the ESXi Server hardware should have Intel VT-d or AMD-Vi, a vCenter Server, and vSphere Web Client. No other prerequisites are required.

How to do it...

To configure direct PCI device connections for VMs, using VMDirectPath I/O, follow these steps:

1. Open vSphere Web Client.
2. Log in to your vCenter Server.
3. On your home screen, select **Hosts and Clusters**.
4. Select an ESX host from the inventory of VMware vSphere Client.
5. In the **Configure** tab, click on **Advanced** under **Networking**. Make sure that **DirectPath I/O** shows **Supported**:

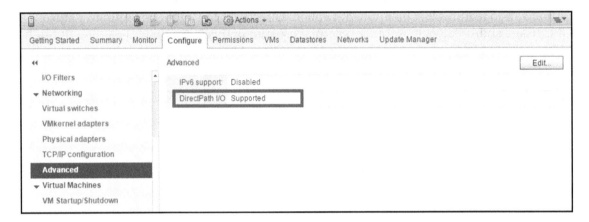

6. In the **Configure** tab, click on **PCI Devices** under **Hardware**.
7. Click on the pencil icon to edit. You will see a list of devices.
8. Check the devices you want to use for DirectPath I/O.
9. When the devices are selected, they are marked **Available (pending)**. Reboot the system for the changes to take effect:

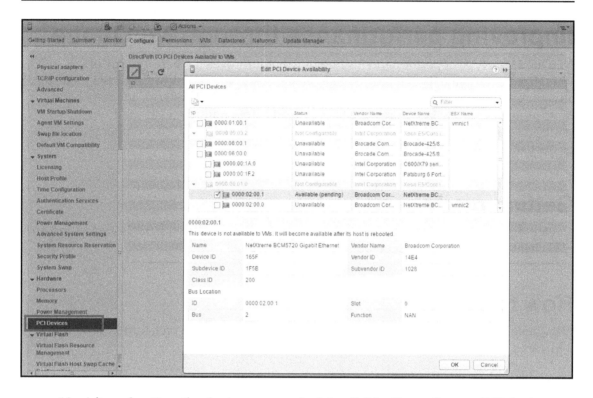

10. After rebooting, the devices are marked **Available**. To configure a PCI device on a VM, perform these steps:

    1. From the inventory in vSphere Client, right-click on the VM and choose **Edit Settings**. Please note that the VM must be powered off to complete this operation.
    2. Click on the **Virtual Hardware** tab.
    3. Click on **Add**.
    4. Choose **PCI Device** as **New device** and click on **Add**.
    5. Click on **OK**.

 When the device is assigned, the VM must have memory reservation for the fully configured memory size.

Improving performance through NetQueue

NetQueue is a type of performance technology that improves the performance of virtualized environments that use 10 GigE adapters supported by VMware. NetQueue takes advantage of the multiple queue capability that newer physical network adapters have. Multiple queues allow I/O processing to be spread across multiple CPUs in a multiprocessor system. So while one packet is queued up on one CPU, another packet can be queued up on another CPU at the same time.

Getting ready

To step through this recipe, you will need a running ESXi Server with SSH enabled and an SSH client (Putty). No other prerequisites are required.

How to do it...

NetQueue is enabled by default. Disabling or enabling NetQueue on a host is done using VMware's **vSphere Command-Line Interface (vCLI)**.

To enable and disable this feature, perform the following activity:

1. Log in to the ESXi host using an SSH client (Putty).
2. Now run the `esxcli system settings kernel` with the following command:

```
~ # esxcli system settings kernel set --setting="
netNetqueueEnabled" --value="TRUE"
```

3. Run the following command to find the network driver:

```
~ # esxcfg-nics -l
```

4. Use the VMware vSphere CLI to configure the NIC driver to use NetQueue. The following command assumes that you are using the `s2io` driver:

```
~ # esxcli system module parameters set -m s2io -p "intr_type=2
rx_ring_num=8"
```

5. Once you set the parameter, use the following command to list the parameters and options:

```
~ # esxcli system module parameters list -m s2io | more
```

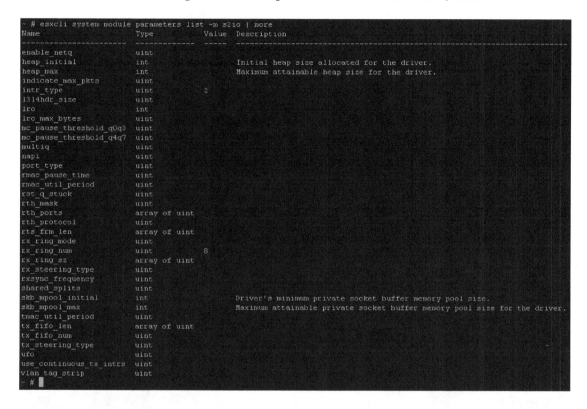

6. Reboot the host.

If you want to disable the NetQueue feature for any reason, follow these steps:

1. Log in to the ESXi host using an SSH client (Putty).

2. Now run the esxcli system settings kernel with the following command:

```
~ # esxcli system settings kernel set --setting="
netNetqueueEnabled" --value="FALSE"
```

3. Run the following command to find the network driver:

```
~ # esxcfg-nics -l
```

4. Now disable the NIC driver to use NetQueue, using the following command:

```
~ # esxcli system module parameters set -m s2io -p "intr_type=
rx_ring_num="
```

5. Now list the parameters as follows to check whether it has been taken off or not:

```
~ # esxcli system module parameters list -m s2io | more
```

```
~ # esxcli system module parameters list -m s2io | more
Name                      Type           Value  Description
-----                     ----           -----  -----------
enable_netq               uint
heap_initial              int                   Initial heap size allocated for the driver.
heap_max                  int                   Maximum attainable heap size for the driver.
indicate_max_pkts         uint
intr_type                 uint
l314hdr_size              uint
lro                       int
lro_max_bytes             uint
mc_pause_threshold_q0q3   uint
mc_pause_threshold_q4q7   uint
multiq                    uint
napi                      uint
port_type                 uint
rmac_pause_time           uint
rmac_util_period          uint
rst_q_stuck               uint
rth_mask                  uint
rth_ports                 array of uint
rth_protocol              uint
rts_frm_len               array of uint
rx_ring_mode              uint
rx_ring_num               uint
rx_ring_sz                array of uint
rx_steering_type          uint
rxsync_frequency          uint
shared_splits             uint
skb_mpool_initial         int                   Driver's minimum private socket buffer memory pool size.
skb_mpool_max             int                   Maximum attainable private socket buffer memory pool size for the driver.
tmac_util_period          uint
tx_fifo_len               array of uint
tx_fifo_num               uint
tx_steering_type          uint
ufo                       uint
use_continuous_tx_intrs   uint
vlan_tag_strip            uint
~ #
```

6. Reboot the host.

How it works...

NetQueue can use multiple transmit queues to parallelize access that is normally serialized by the device driver. Multiple transmit queues can also be used to get some sort of guarantee. A separate, prioritized queue can be used for different types of network traffic.

NetQueue monitors the load of the VMs as they receive packets and assigns queues to critical VMs. All other VMs use the default queue.

Improving network performance using the SplitRx mode for multicast traffic

Multicast is an efficient way of disseminating information and communicating over the network. Instead of sending a separate packet to every receiver, the sender sends one packet that is then distributed to every receiver that has subscribed to this multicast. Multiple receivers can be enabled on a single ESXi host only when you use multicast traffic. Because multiple receivers reside on the same host, packet replication is carried out in the hypervisor instead.

SplitRx mode uses multiple physical CPUs in an ESXi host to process network packets received in a single network queue. As it does not transfer the same copy of the network packet, it provides a scalable and efficient platform for multicast receivers. SplitRx mode improves the throughput and CPU efficiency for multicast traffic workloads.

Only the VMXNET 3 network adapter supports SplitRx mode. This feature is disabled on vSphere 5.0 by default; however, it is enabled in 5.1 and later versions by default.

SplitRx mode is individually configured for each virtual NIC.

Getting ready

To step through this recipe, you will need one or more running ESXi Servers, a couple of running VMs, a vCenter Server, and vSphere Web Client. No other prerequisites are required.

How to do it...

The behavior of SplitRx can be enabled or disabled entirely on an ESXi Server using the following steps:

1. Open vSphere Web Client.
2. Log in to your vCenter Server.
3. Select **Hosts and Clusters** on the home screen.
4. Select the ESXi host you wish to change.

5. Navigate to the **Configure** tab.

6. Under the **System** section on the left-hand side, click on **Advanced System Settings**.

7. Search for NetSplit.

8. Click on the value to be changed and configure it as you wish.

The possible values of NetSplitRxMode are `NetSplitRxMode = "0"`, which disables SplitRx mode for the ESXi host and, the default, `NetSplitRxMode = "1"`, which enables SplitRx mode for the ESXi host. The change will take effect immediately and does not require the ESXi host to be restarted.

The SplitRx mode feature can also be configured individually for each virtual NIC using the `ethernetX.emuRxMode` variable in each VM's `.vmx` file (where X is replaced with the network adapter's ID).

The possible values of this variable are `ethernetX.emuRxMode = "0"`, which disables SplitRx mode for ethernetX, and `ethernetX.emuRxMode = "1"`, which enables SplitRx mode for ethernetX.

So if you want to change this value on individual VMs through vSphere Client, follow these steps with the VM powered off:

1. Select the VM that you wish to change and click on **Edit Settings**.

2. Go to the **VM Options** tab.

3. Click on the down arrow next to **Advanced**, then click on **Edit Configuration**.

4. Look for `ethernetX.emuRxMode` (where *X* is the number of the desired NIC). If the variable isn't present, enter the name and value at the bottom, then click on **Add** to enter it as a new variable.

5. Click on **OK** to save the parameter.

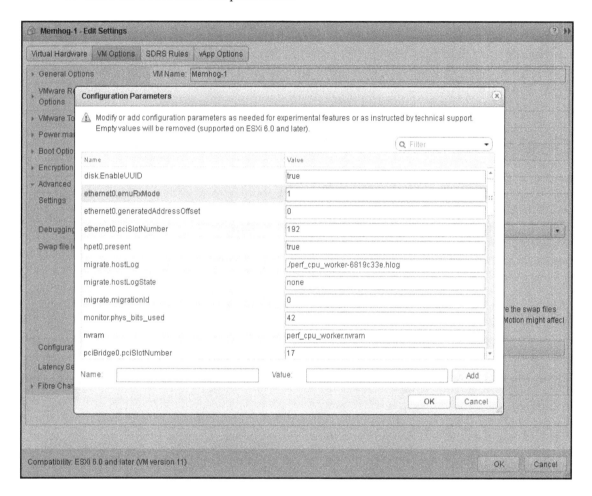

How it works...

SplitRx mode uses multiple physical CPUs to process network packets received in a single network queue. This feature can significantly improve the network performance of certain workloads.

These workloads include:

- Multiple VMs on one ESXi host, all receiving multicast traffic from the same source.
- Traffic via the DVFilter API between two VMs on the same ESXi host.

vSphere 5.1 and later versions automatically enable this feature for a VMXNET 3 virtual network adapter (the only adapter type on which it is supported). They do so when they detect that a single network queue on a physical NIC is both heavily utilized and servicing more than eight clients (that is, VMs or vmknic) that have evenly distributed loads.

Designing a multi-NIC vMotion

Before the release of VMware vSphere 5, designing a vMotion network was relatively easy as it was straightforward. vMotion in VMware vSphere 5.0 and above is able to leverage multiple NICs. By default, a single vMotion will use only one NIC regardless of how many NICs are set up for vMotion. Running multiple vMotions at the same time will utilize multiple NICs. Implementing a multi-NIC vMotion will allow a single vMotion operation to use multiple NICs at once and reduce the duration of that operation.

Getting ready

To step through this recipe, you will need one or more running ESXi Servers (licensed with Enterprise Plus for vDS), each with two available NICs, a vCenter Server, and vSphere Web Client. No other prerequisites are required.

How to do it...

These steps will walk you through the process of creating a new vSphere-Distributed Switch that will be capable of multi-NIC vMotion. This assumes that you have two network adapters available for this new vSwitch:

1. Open up vSphere Web Client.
2. Log in to your vCenter Server.
3. Navigate to the **Networking** section.
4. Right-click on the cluster and select **Distributed Switch**, then **New Distributed Switch**.

5. Call the `MultiNICvMotion` switch and confirm it's at the correct location. Click on **Next**.

6. Select the switch version appropriate to your environment, then click on **Next**.

7. Change the number of uplinks to 2. Leave the check next to **Create a default port group**, then change the port group name to `vMotion-01`. Click on **Next**. Click on **Finish**.

8. Expand **MultiNICvMotion**, then right-click on **vMotion-01** and select **Edit Settings**.

9. In the **VLAN** section, change the VLAN type to **VLAN** and assign a VLAN.

10. In the **Teaming and failover** section, move **Uplink 2** down to **Standby uplinks**. Click on **OK**.

11. Right-click on **MultiNICvMotion** and select **Distributed Port Group**, then **New Distributed Port Group**.

12. Call the port group `vMotion-02` and click on **Next**.

13. Change the VLAN type to **VLAN** and change the VLAN ID to the same ID as step 9. Click on **Next**. Click on **Finish**.

14. Right-click on **vMotion-02** and select **Edit Settings**.

15. In the **Teaming and failover** section, move **Uplink 1** down to **Standby uplinks**. Click on **OK**.

Now we need to add hosts to the vSphere-Distributed Switch. Edit the switch at the host level and assign IP addresses to the port groups, then follow these steps:

1. From the **Networking** view, right-click on **MultiNICvMotion** and select **Add and Manage Hosts**.
2. Select the **Add Hosts** task. Click on **Next**.
3. Click on the **New Hosts** button and add your hosts to the list. Click on **Next**.
4. Check the **Manage physical adapters** and **Manage VMkernel adapters** tasks, then click on **Next**.
5. From the NICs listed, select the two you want to assign to MultiNICvMotion and click on the **Assign uplink** button. Assign the first NIC to **Uplink 1** and the second to **Uplink 2**. Repeat this for each host. Click on **Next**.
6. On the **Manage VMKernel network adapters** page, select the first server and then click on **New adapter**.
7. Choose **Select an existing network** and then browse to select **vMotion-01**. Click on **Next**.
8. Enable the **vMotion** service, then click on **Next**.
9. Set the IP address and subnet mask and click on **Next**. Click on **Finish**.
10. Repeat steps 6-9 for **vMotion-02**.
11. Repeat steps 6-10 for any other servers.
12. Click on **Next**, then **Next**, then **Finish**.
13. You can view the settings of **MultiNICvMotion** at the host level by going back to **Hosts and Clusters**. Click on the host, then go to **Configure** | **Networking** | **Virtual switches**:

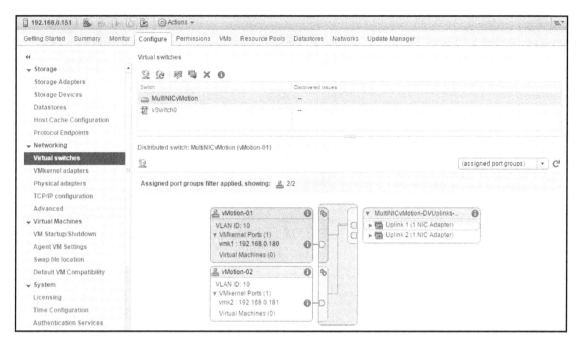

Now you have a multi-NIC vMotion Network.

Improving network performance using network I/O control

The 1 GigE era is coming to an end and is rapidly being replaced by 10 GigE. This means less physical network connections and that network traffic with different patterns and needs will merge together on the same network.

This may directly impact performance and predictability due to lack of isolation, scheduling, and arbitration. Network I/O control can be used to prioritize different network traffic on the same pipe.

You cannot have guaranteed bandwidth as long as you don't limit other traffic, so there'll always be enough available bandwidth.

As some traffic (that is, vMotion) might not be used all the time, we'll have temporarily unused bandwidth with static limits. As long as there is no congestion, this doesn't really matter, but if there is, then you're limiting the bandwidth for traffic even when there is bandwidth available, which is not a good way to deal with congestion.

For some VMkernel traffic, VMware recommends dedicated 1 GB NICs to guarantee bandwidth for them. So it's very likely that there will be no dedicated NIC anymore for VM traffic. Without some **QoS** or guaranteed bandwidth, you're wasting the bandwidth with the previous static traffic shaping. So there needs to be a more dynamic solution for it.

So the solution is **network I/O control** (**NIOC**) for vDS.

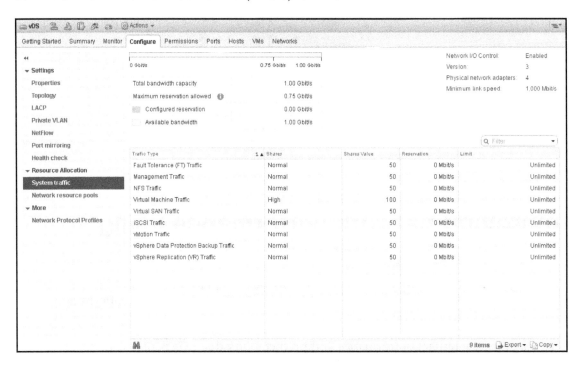

VMware has predefined resource groups, as shown in the previous screenshot.

These traffic groups are based on vDS ports. So with the connection to a specified port, the traffic on this port belongs to one of these predefined groups. This means that if we mount an NFS share inside a VM, it's treated as VM traffic instead of NFS traffic. Again, assignment to a group is based on the switch port, not on traffic characteristics.

Two values that you can edit for the predefined **Network resource pool** are **Physical adapter shares** and **Host limit**.

Shares work like the shares on VMs (CPU and memory). NIOC will sum up all the shares and set the shares in relation to the sum. So a value of 50 does not necessarily mean the group is entitled to 50 percent of bandwidth (although, it could be possible if the shares of the other groups sum up to 50).

The share does not reflect the number of ports in this group. So it doesn't matter if we have 10 or 100 VMs running. The percentage of all will be the same. Therefore, inside a resource group, there is no sublevel possible.

The defined share values are:

- Normal = 50
- Low = 25
- High = 100
- Custom = any values between 1 and 100

The default share value of VM traffic is 100 and all other traffic is 50, which is normal:

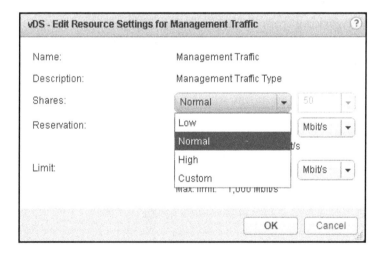

In case some resource groups aren't used at all--that is, no FT (short for fault tolerance), no NFS, and no vSphere Replication)--the shares still apply but as there will be no traffic claiming bandwidth, the bandwidth will be given to other groups based on the share values.

So if all of the traffic together doesn't need the full bandwidth of pNIC, there might still be unused bandwidth. But it will be dynamically given to a resource group requesting more bandwidth later. Previously, this bandwidth was not used at all as the limits were configured with peak rates and bursts.

Limits are useful if you don't want to have other traffic affected too much, that is, by vMotion. Let's assume that the VM and iSCSI traffic usually uses nearly all of the available bandwidth. Now, if vMotion starts consuming 14 percent of bandwidth by default, then this will affect the traffic of the VMs and iSCSI, so you might want to limit it to 1 Gbit/s.

Getting ready

To step through this recipe, you will need one or more running ESXi Servers (licensed with Enterprise Plus), a vCenter Server, and vSphere Web Client. No other prerequisites are required.

How to do it...

To check the NIOC resource pool and enable it, follow these steps:

1. Log in to your vCenter Server.
2. Select **Networking** from the home screen.
3. Right-click on the appropriate vDS and go to **Settings**, then **Edit Settings**.
4. On the **General** screen, click on the **Network I/O Control** drop-down menu and select **Enabled**:

vSphere 5 and above has the ability to create user-defined network resource pools and modify system network resource pools. When editing or creating a new network resource pool, two settings are configurable, which are as follows:

- **Physical adapter shares**: These prioritize access to the physical NICs when contention arises. One of these four settings can be configured: **Low**, **Normal** (default), **High**, and **Custom** (a value of 1 to 100 may be specified).
- **Host limit**: Host limit places a limit on the amount of network bandwidth (Mbps) that a particular resource pool has access to. The default setting of **Unlimited** puts the onus on the card to control limits.

Perform the following steps to edit an existing network resource pool:

1. Navigate to the **Networking** section and click on your vSphere Distributed Switch.
2. Click on the **Configure** tab, then click on **System traffic** under **Resource Allocation**.
3. Click on the desired resource pool, for example, the **Fault Tolerance (FT)** traffic, and click on the pencil icon to edit.
4. On the **Edit Resource Settings** screen, adjust the settings for **Physical adapter shares** and **Host limit** as needed.
5. Click on **OK** to apply the changes.

Optionally, an administrator may also create a user-defined network resource pool, as follows:

1. Navigate to the **Networking** section and click on your vSphere Distributed Switch.
2. Click on the **Configure** tab, then click on **Network resource pools** under **Resource Allocation**.
3. Click on the plus sign to create a network resource pool.
4. On the **Network Resource Pool Settings** screen, supply the resource pool name.
5. Adjust the settings for **Physical adapter shares** and **Host limit** as needed.

6. Click on **OK** to apply the changes.

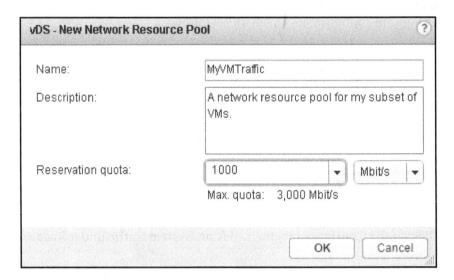

Once a user-defined resource pool has been selected, perform the following steps to associate a port group with it:

1. From the **Networking** view, select the appropriate vDS.
2. Right-click on the appropriate port group and navigate to **Edit Settings**.
3. On the port group's **General** tab, click on the **Network resource pool** drop-down menu and select **MyVMTraffic**.
4. Click on **OK**.
5. Click on the vDS and go to the **Configure** tab, then **Network resource pools** under **Resource Allocation**. Click on the resource pool to see the associated port group.

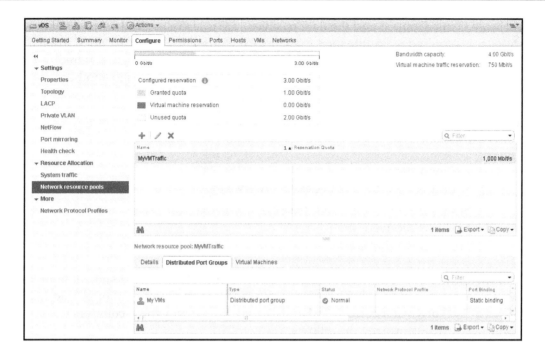

Monitoring network capacity and performance matrix

Network performance is dependent on application workload and network configuration. Dropped network packets indicate a bottleneck in the network. To determine whether packets are being dropped, use resxtop/esxtop or the VMware vSphere Client advanced performance charts to examine the droppedTx and droppedRx network counter values.

If packets are being dropped, adjust the VM CPU shares. This just intensifies the problem for other VMs. The root solution is to reduce the overall CPU load on the host. If you just adjust CPU shares up for this VM, you'd expect other VMs to start dropping packets or having higher CPU latency (%RDY). If packets are not being dropped, check the size of the network packets and the data received and transmitted rates. In general, the larger the network packets, the faster the network speed. When the packet size is large, fewer packets are transferred, which reduces the amount of CPU required to process the data. When network packets are small, more packets are transferred, but the network speed is slower because more CPU is required to process the data. In some instances, large packets can result in high latency. To rule out this issue, check the network latency.

If packets are being dropped and the data received rate is also slow, the host may lack the CPU resources required to handle the load. Check the number of VMs assigned to each physical NIC. If necessary, perform load balancing by moving the VMs to different virtual switches or adding more NICs to the host. You can also move the VMs to another host or increase the CPU resources of the host or VMs.

Check out the following key metrics. These are the significant network statistics in a vSphere environment:

- Network usage
- Host droppedRx (received packets dropped)
- Host droppedTx (transmitted packets dropped)
- Net packets received
- Net packets transmitted

You can use the vSphere Client performance charts to track the network statistics per host, VM, or NIC (virtual or physical). However, a single chart can display either physical objects (host and vmnic#) or virtual objects (VM and virtual NIC). Track these counters to determine network performance as follows:

- **Network packets transmitted**: Number of packets transmitted in the sampling interval
- **Network packets received**: Number of packets received in the sampling interval
- **Network data transmit rate**: Amount of data transmitted in Kbps
- **Network data receive rate**: Amount of data received in Kbps
- **droppedTx**: Number of outbound packets dropped in the sampling interval
- **droppedRx**: Number of inbound packets dropped in the sampling interval

Getting ready

To step through this recipe, you will need one or more running ESXi Servers, a vCenter Server, and vSphere Web Client. No other prerequisites are required.

How to do it...

Now to check the network statistics of the ESXi Server or VM, you should follow the proceeding steps:

1. Open up vSphere Web Client.

2. Log in to your vCenter Server.
3. Navigate to **Hosts and Clusters** on the home screen.
4. Choose the ESXi Server where you want to monitor the utilization and performance of the network.
5. Go to the **Monitor** tab, then the **Performance** tab.
6. Click on the **Advanced** tab, then select **Network** from the drop-down menu.
7. Click on **Chart Options**.
8. Now select the metrics and click on **OK** to continue.
9. The counters that you need to select are:

- **Usage**
- **Data receive rate**
- **Data transmit rate**
- **Packets transmitted**
- **Packets received**
- **Transmit packets dropped**
- **Receive packets dropped**

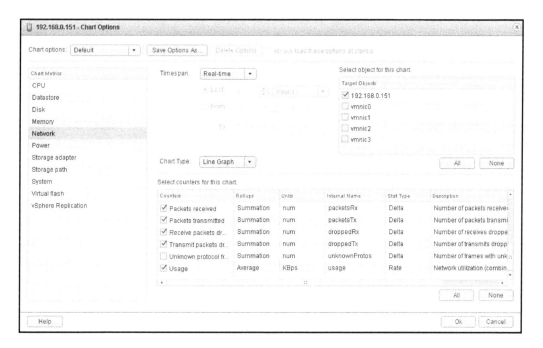

The following is an example screenshot where you can see the utilization of the ESXi network:

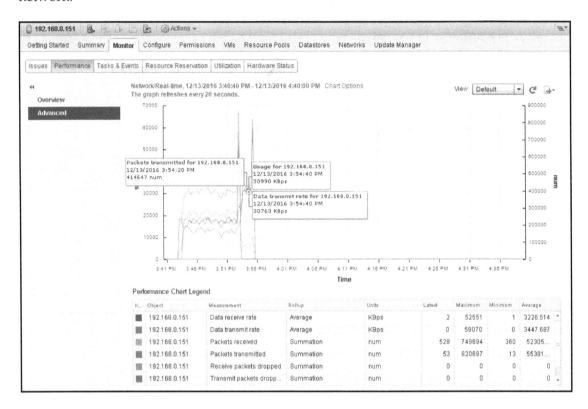

It's worth noting that in practice, dropped packets should be exactly zero. Also, in practice, network usage for typical VMs is a simple load on the host compared to storage I/O, CPU, and memory demand. The network is the least likely physical bottleneck, as long as it's configured reasonably.

4

DRS, SDRS, and Resource Control Design

In this chapter, we will cover the tasks related to , and Resource Control Design. You will learn the following aspects of DRS and SDRS design:

- Using DRS algorithm guidelines
- Using resource pool guidelines
- Avoiding the use of a resource pool as a folder structure
- Choosing the best SIOC latency threshold
- Using storage capability and policy-driven storage
- Anti-affinity rules in the SDRS cluster
- Avoiding the use of the SDRS I/O metric and array-based automatic tiering together
- Using VMware SIOC and array-based automatic tiering together

Introduction

ESXi provides several mechanisms to configure and adjust the allocation of CPU, memory, and network and storage resources to the VMs running on it. If you create additional storage capability, configurations can have a significant impact on VM performance.

In this chapter, we will discuss the guidelines for resource allocation settings, such as shares, reservation, and limits. We will also discuss guidelines for the DRS algorithm and resource pools. Some of the advanced storage concepts will also be unveiled.

Using DRS algorithm guidelines

DRS aligns resource usage with workload priority by automatically load balancing across hosts. It continuously monitors utilization across vSphere ESXi Servers and intelligently allocates available resources among VMs according to workload needs.

DRS aggregates vSphere ESXi host resources into clusters and automatically distributes these resources to VMs by monitoring the utilization and continuously optimizing VM distribution across vSphere ESXi hosts. DRS operates on a continuous 60-minute cycle in a default configuration.

It also continuously balances computing capacity in resource pools to deliver a level of performance, scalability, and availability that is not possible with a physical infrastructure.

DRS assigns priorities to its recommendations in the range of 1-5. The DRS migration threshold can be set from conservative (1) to aggressive (5). Depending on the migration threshold, DRS will apply recommendations at the corresponding priority and the ones below it. For example, if the migration threshold is set at 3, DRS will apply 1, 2, and 3 priority items and ignore 4 and 5 items. So, when you choose the DRS migration threshold, remember these two things:

- Moderate threshold, which is also the default setting, works well for most of the cases, for example, the majority of business applications that exhibit stable workload characteristics.
- However, you may wish to change the migration threshold of the following type of workloads in order to provide a more balanced workload distribution:
    - Clusters that are homogenous
    - Where resource demand for VMs is relatively constant
    - Have few affinity and anti-affinity rules

Use affinity and anti-affinity rules only when absolutely necessary. The more rules that are used, the less flexibility DRS has when determining on which hosts to place VMs.

Also, always make sure that DRS is in automatic mode, cluster-wide. If you need more control over your critical VMs, override the cluster-wide setting by setting manual or partially automated mode on selected VMs. To change these options at the VM level, click on your DRS-enabled cluster, then go to the **Configure** tab and select **VM Overrides** under **Configuration**. Here you can add VMs and change their DRS configuration:

With the automatic mode cluster-wide setting, DRS can make migration recommendations only for the VMs that can be migrated with vMotion.

The following are some things to consider before you allow DRS to use vMotion:

- Ensure that the hosts in the DRS cluster have compatible CPUs. Within the same hardware platform (Intel or AMD), there might be differences in the CPU family, which means different CPU feature sets. As a result, VMs will not be able to migrate across hosts. However, **Enhanced vMotion Compatibility** (**EVC**) automatically configures server CPUs with Intel FlexMigration or AMD-V Extended Migration technologies so they could be compatible with older servers. EVC works by masking newer CPU features. Enabling EVC may require VM downtime if those newer features are in use. This prevents migrations with vMotion from failing due to incompatible CPUs.

- Leave some unused CPU capacity in your cluster for vMotion operations. When a vMotion operation is in progress, ESXi opportunistically reserves CPU resources on both the source and destination hosts. CPU resources are reserved to ensure the ability of vMotion operations to fully utilize the network bandwidth. The amount of CPU reservation thus depends on the number of vMotion NICs and their speeds: 10 percent of a processor core for each Gigabit Ethernet network interface is reserved. 100 percent of a processor core for each 10 Gigabit Ethernet network interface is reserved.

- The network configuration should be consistent across all the hosts in your DRS cluster. In addition, the VM network and the datastores on which the VMs reside should be available on all the hosts in your cluster.
- Disconnect VM devices that map to localhost devices, such as the local CD-ROM drive, the local floppy drive, local serial ports, and local USB ports.
- For example, an MS cluster with raw device mapped could also prevent a VM from being migrated.

Getting ready

To step through this recipe, you will need a couple of running ESXi Servers (licensed with Enterprise Plus for DRS), an instance of vCenter Server, and vSphere Web Client. No other prerequisites are required.

How to do it...

To create a DRS cluster, carry out the following steps:

1. Open up vSphere Web Client and log in to the vCenter Server.
2. Select **Hosts and Clusters** on the home screen.
3. If you don't have a datacenter object, right-click on the vCenter name and select **New Datacenter**.
4. Select the **Datacenter** object where you want to create the cluster.
5. Right-click on the object and select **New Cluster**.
6. Give a name to the new cluster and check the **Turn ON** DRS checkbox.
7. Now select **Automation level** and **Migration Threshold**.
8. Turn on vSphere HA if you wish and set its parameters.
9. You can now select the **EVC** settings. If you are using homogenous hosts, then select leave EVC **Disabled**; otherwise, select the EVC mode that is compatible with your oldest processor.

10. Click on **OK** to create the cluster.

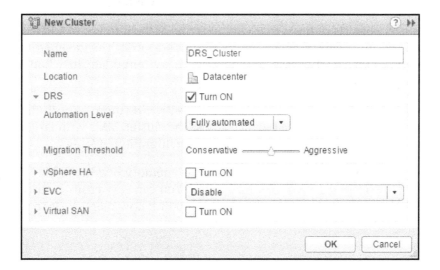

Once the cluster has been created, you can further modify the properties of the cluster by clicking on the cluster and going to the **Configure** tab.

A good EVC CPU matrix for Intel CPUs can be found at `http://www.virten.net/2013/04/intel-cpu-evc-matrix/`.

A good EVC CPU matrix for AMD CPUs can be found at `http://www.virten.net/2014/01/amd-cpu-evc-matrix-vmware-enhanced-vmotion-compatibility/`.

How it works...

For a better DRS placement algorithm, you need to always remember the points we will discuss now.

Always choose homogenous hosts that include the same CPU and memory architecture. However, differences can exist in the memory cache architecture of hosts in your DRS cluster. For example, some of your hosts in the DRS cluster might have the NUMA architecture and others might not. This difference can result in differences in performance numbers across your hosts. DRS does not consider the memory cache architecture because accounting for these differences results in minimal benefits at the DRS granularity of scheduling.

If you have more hosts in your cluster, then DRS will get more opportunities to place your VMs. The maximum number of hosts in a cluster is 32 in vSphere 5.x and 64 in 6.x.

If your DRS cluster consists of hosts that vary in terms of the number of CPUs and memory sizes, then DRS tries to place your VMs on the largest host first. The idea here is that DRS wants the VM to run on a host with excess capacity to accommodate any changes in resource demands of the VM.

VMs with smaller memory sizes and/or fewer vCPUs provide more opportunities for DRS to migrate them in order to improve balance across the cluster. VMs with larger memory sizes and/or more vCPUs add more constraints to the migration of VMs.

Every VM that is powered on incurs some amount of memory overhead. This overhead is not factored in as a part of the VMs' memory usage. You can very easily overlook the overhead when sizing your resource pools and estimating how many VMs to place on each host.

Using resource pool guidelines

ESXi provides several mechanisms to configure and adjust the allocation of CPU and memory resources to VMs. Thus, resource management configurations have a significant impact on VM performance.

If you expect flexibility in the total available resources, then use shares, not reservations. It will allocate resources fairly across the VMs. Even if you upgrade your hardware, each VM will stay at the same relative priority, using shares. The relative priority remains the same even though each share represents a larger amount of memory or CPU.

Remember that shares will only be effective in the case of resource contention. So, if you think you can have an immediate effect on the resources of a VM by increasing the number of shares, you are mistaken. Share values are used in order to determine the dynamic entitlement of a VM. Dynamic entitlement is used in order to determine fairness and also opportunistically distribute unused resources. Therefore, while shares are enforced during contention, their configured priority is also leveraged in non-contentious situations as well.

You may want to use reservations to specify the minimum amount of guaranteed CPU or memory. After all the resource reservations have been met, VMkernel allocates the remaining resources based on the number of shares and limits configured on the VM. If you choose to have a reservation for your VM, then just remember that you may limit the ability of the DRS cluster in regard to the placement of other VMs.

So carefully specify the memory limit and memory reservation. If these two parameters are misconfigured, users might observe ballooning or swapping, even when the host has plenty of free memory. For example, a VM's memory might be reclaimed when the specified limit is too small or when other VMs reserve too much host memory. If a performance-critical VM needs guaranteed memory allocation, the reservation must be specified carefully because it might affect other VMs.

Getting ready

To step through this recipe, you will need a couple of running ESXi Servers (licensed with Enterprise Plus), an instance of vCenter Server, and vSphere Web Client. No other prerequisites are required.

How to do it...

Let's get started with the implementation of the guidelines:

1. Log in to the vCenter Server using vSphere Web Client.
2. Select **Hosts and Clusters** on the home screen.
3. Select the cluster where you want to create the resource pool.

4. Right-click on the resource pool and select **New Resource Pool**:

In order to create a resource pool, you need to have the following information in hand:

- **Name**: This refers to the name of the resource pool.
- **Shares**: This indicates the total number of shares to be allocated to the VMs in the resource pool.
- **Reservation**: This indicates the minimum resources guaranteed to the VMs.

- **Reservation Type**: If **Expandable** is checked and a VM is powered on that pushes the resource pool beyond its reservation, the resource pool can use resources from its parent or ancestors. If **Expandable** is not checked and a VM is powered on that pushes the resource pool beyond its reservation, the VM will not be allowed to power on.
- **Limit**: This refers to the maximum number of resources any VM under this resource pool will get.

Similar options are available for memory configuration. Once this step is completed, you might see a yellow warning triangle, which suggests that something is incorrect.

How it works...

Resource pools hierarchically partition the available CPU and memory resources. When you configure separate resource pools, you have more options when you need to choose between resource availability and load balancing.

You may want to use resource pools to isolate performance. Isolation can prevent one VM's performance from affecting the performance of other VMs. This way, your defined limits provide more predictable service levels and less resource contention. If you define limits on your resource pool, then it also protects the resource pool from a VM going into a runaway condition. You may also want to set a firm limit on a resource pool, which reduces the negative effect that the VM might have in the resource pool.

VMware recommends that resource pools and VMs should not be made siblings in a hierarchy. Instead, each hierarchy level should contain only resource pools or VMs. By default, resource pools are assigned share values that might not compare appropriately with those assigned to VMs, potentially resulting in unexpected performance.

Avoiding the use of a resource pool as a folder structure

It is common to use resource pools to create a folder structure in the host, have a cluster view of vCenter, and categorize your VMs. Administrators may place these VMs into these resource pools for sorting, but this is not the true sense of using resource pools. Resource pools should be used to prioritize VM workloads and guarantee and/or limit the number of resources available to a group of VMs. The issue is that even though a particular resource pool may have a higher level of shares, by the time the pool is subdivided, the VM ends up with fewer shares than a VM that resides in a resource pool with a lower number of shares.

If you create a resource pool with the default settings, then by default, this resource pool will be assigned 4,000 shares. Also, a VM has a default of 1,000 shares. In this way, if you place three VMs on a resource pool, even with default settings, the resources will be divided by three. This means that each VM will get one-third of the resources assigned to that resource pool by default.

Now if you take one VM out of that resource pool, it will have a performance impact.

How to do it...

Let's get started with the configuration of the folders rather than the resource pool:

1. Open up vSphere Client and log in to the vCenter Web Server.
2. Select **VMs and Templates** on the home screen.
3. Select the datacenter where you want to categorize the VMs.
4. Right-click on the datacenter and select **New Folder** and then **VM and Template Folder**.
5. Give a name to this folder and click on **OK**.
6. Now move the existing VMs to this folder based on the categorization.

How it works...

Let's say you create a resource pool with all the default settings. Now add eight VMs to this pool called Prod. If you have another resource pool and some other VMs at the root resource pool (cluster), then your resource pool will get 4,000 shares by default, and those VMs that are in the root resource pool will get 1,000 shares.

In this case, the percentage of shares of the resource pool will be same for all the pools. But if you keep on placing VMs inside the pool, then it will be divided amongst all of them. The following is an example of what could happen in this situation.

You have a Prod resource pool with 1,000 shares of CPU and four VMs within it and a Dev resource pool with 4,000 shares of CPU and 50 VMs.

The Prod resource pool with 1,000 shares and four VMs is greater than or equal to 250 units per VM (small pie, a few big slices):

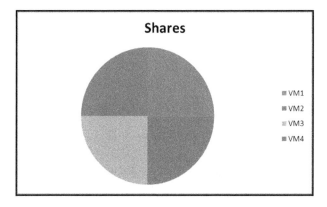

The Dev resource pool with 4,000 shares and 50 VMs is greater than or equal to 80 units per VM (bigger pie, many small slices):

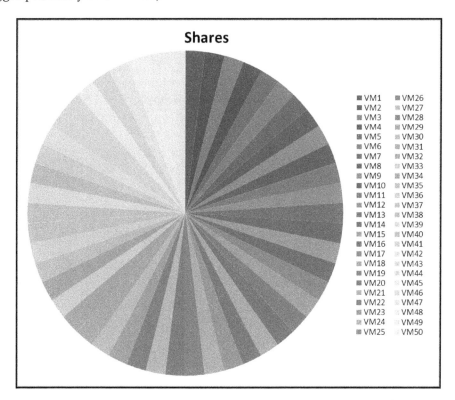

Also, note that shares will only come into play when there is contention. However, if the shares for the VMs aren't allocated properly, this can be an issue. It may happen that your non-production VMs may get higher priority than the more critical VMs.

Folders provide a simple structure and nothing else. You can have as many folders as you want.

Choosing the best SIOC latency threshold

Storage I/O Control (SIOC) extends the constructs of shares and limits to handle storage I/O resources. SIOC is a proportional share scheduler that, under contention, throttles IOPS. You can control the amount of storage I/O that is allocated to VMs during periods of I/O congestion. Controlling storage I/O ensures that more important VMs get preference over less important VMs for I/O resource allocation.

There are two thresholds: one for standalone SIOC and one for Storage DRS. For Storage DRS, latency statistics are gathered by SIOC for an ESXi host and sent to the vCenter Server and stored in the vCenter Server database. With these statistics, Storage DRS can make the decision on whether a VM should be migrated to another datastore.

The default latency threshold of SIOC is 30 milliseconds. The default setting might be acceptable for some storage devices, but other devices might reach their latency threshold well before or after the default setting is reached. For example, **Solid State Disks** (**SSD**) typically reach their contention point sooner than the default setting protects against. Not all devices are created equally.

Getting ready

To step through this recipe, you will need a couple of running ESXi Servers (licensed with Enterprise Plus), an instance of vCenter Server, a couple of datastores attached to ESXi, and vSphere Web Client. No other prerequisites are required.

How to do it...

To enable SIOC on a datastore:

1. Log in to the vCenter Server using vSphere Web Client.
2. In the **Datastores and Datastore Clusters** inventory view, select a datastore and click on the **Configure** tab.
3. In the **General** section, click on **Edit** under **Datastore Capabilities**.
4. Click on **Enable Storage I/O Control**.
5. Click on the **OK** button.

To set the storage I/O shares and limits, carry out the following steps:

1. Right-click on the VM in the inventory and select **Edit Settings**.
2. In the **Virtual Hardware** tab, expand the drive where you want to set the shares or limits.

By default, all the VM shares are set to normal (1000) with unlimited IOPS.

How it works...

SIOC provides quality of service capabilities for storage I/O in the form of I/O shares and limits that are enforced across all the VMs accessing a datastore, regardless of which host they are running on. Using SIOC, vSphere administrators can ensure that the most important VMs get adequate I/O resources, even in times of congestion.

In vSphere 5.1, SIOC can automatically determine the optimal latency threshold using injector-based models to determine the latency setting. In vSphere 5.1 and above, this injector determines and sets the latency threshold when 90 percent of the throughput is reached.

When SDRS is enabled, SIOC is set to stats only mode by default. Stats only mode collects and stores statistics but does not perform throttling on the storage device. Storage DRS can use the stored statistics immediately after the initial configuration or when new data stores are added.

When you enable SIOC on a datastore, ESXi begins to monitor the device latency that hosts observe when communicating with that data store. When device latency exceeds a threshold, the data store is considered to be congested, and each VM that accesses this data store is allocated I/O resources in proportion to their shares.

When you allocate storage I/O resources, you can limit the IOPS that are allowed for a VM. By default, the number of IOPS allowed for a VM is unlimited. If the limit that you want to set for a VM is in terms of megabytes per second instead of IOPS, you can convert megabytes per second into IOPS based on the typical I/O size of that VM. For example, a backup application has a typical I/O size of 64 KB. To restrict a backup application to 10 MB per second, set a limit of 160 IOPS (10 MB per second per 64 KB I/O size, which is equal to 160 I/OS per second). However, this setting needs an eye on it as an application with a 4 KB I/O size would be very slow if limited to 160 IOPS. An IOPS limit is applied to the sum of the limits of all the virtual disks attached to a VM.

Using storage capability and policy-driven storage

It is always a cumbersome task to manage datastores and match the SLA requirements of VMs with the appropriate datastore. vSphere 5.0 introduced profile-driven storage, which allows you to have rapid and intelligent placement of VMs based on SLA, availability, performance, or other requirements, and provided storage capabilities. It was later reintroduced in vSphere 6.x and beyond as VM Storage Policies.

You can request various storage characteristics, typically defined as a tier, in a VM storage policy using policy-driven storage. These policies are used during provisioning, cloning, and storage vMotion to ensure that only those datastores or datastore clusters that are compliant with the VM storage .

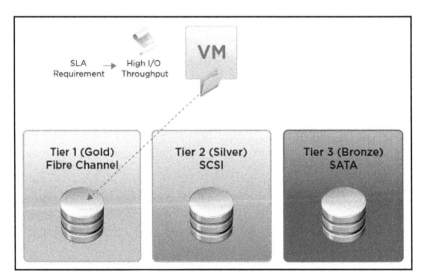

Policy-driven storage is achieved by using two key components: storage capabilities and VM storage policies.

Storage capability outlines the quality of service that a storage system can deliver. It is a guarantee that the storage system can provide a specific set of characteristics. The two types of storage capabilities are system-defined and user-defined.

A system-defined storage capability is one that comes from a storage system that uses the **VASA** (short for **vStorage API for Storage Awareness**) vendor provider. The vendor provider informs the vCenter Server that it can guarantee a specific set of storage features by presenting them as a storage capability. The vCenter Server recognizes this capability and adds it to the list of storage capabilities for that storage vendor. It also assigns the system-defined storage capability to each datastore that you create from that storage system.

A user-defined storage capability is one that you can define and associate with datastores. Examples of user-defined capabilities are as follows:

- Storage array type
- Replication status
- Storage tiers, such as gold, silver, and bronze datastores
- VM encryption policies
- Virtual SAN and VVol characteristics' policies

A user-defined capability can be associated with multiple datastores. It is possible to associate it with a datastore that already has a system-defined capability.

Storage capabilities are used to define a VM storage policy. A VM storage policy lists the storage capabilities that VM home files and virtual disks require to run the applications on the VM. It is created by an administrator who can create different storage policies to define different levels of storage requirements. The VM home files (.vmx, .vmsd, .nvram, .log, and so on) and virtual disks (.vmdk) can have separate VM storage policies.

With a VM storage policy, a VM can be checked for storage compliance. If the VM is placed on storage that has the same capabilities as those defined in the VM storage policy, the VM is storage-compliant.

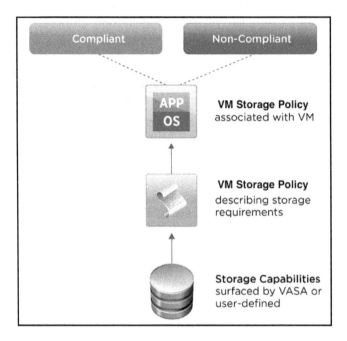

Getting ready

To step through this recipe, you will need a couple of running ESXi Servers (licensed with Enterprise Plus), an instance of vCenter Server, a couple of datastores attached to ESXi, and vSphere Web Client. No other prerequisites are required.

How to do it...

Let's get started:

1. Create a VM storage policy. While in vSphere Web Client, click on the Home icon and select **Policies and Profiles**. This will take you to the **Policies and Profiles** view. Then, select **VM Storage Policies** from the left sidebar. This will take you to the **VM Storage Profiles** view:

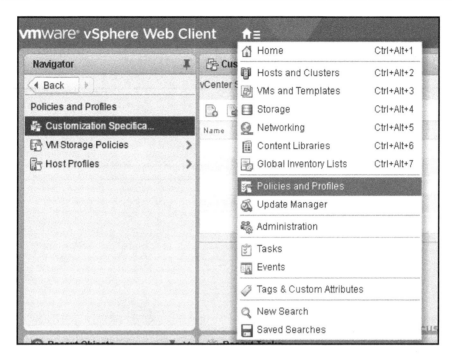

Now we can see the default VM storage policies as shown in the image below:

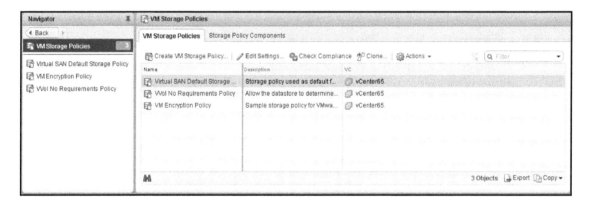

2. The next step is to start adding a new VM storage policy. To do this, select **Create VM Storage Policy**. If we stick to the gold/silver/bronze example, here is how you would create a `Gold` user-defined storage policy:

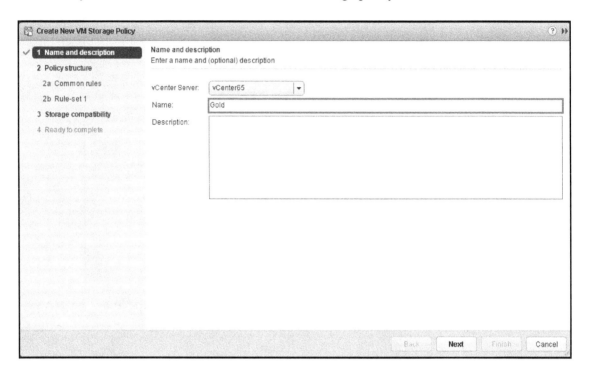

3. If you create additional storage capabilities, you can use them to classify different types of storage.

4. The next page of the VM storage policy is **Policy Structure**, which provides a breakdown of how the levels of service are applied to the VMs:

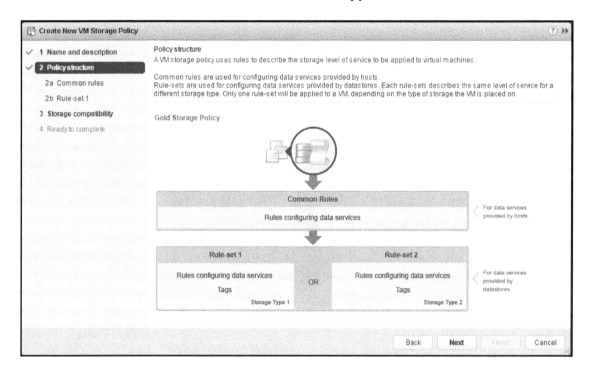

5. Through the **Common Rules** option, you can provide additional rules applicable to encryption, I/O control, and caching. These are user-configurable storage policy components you can establish:

6. **Rule-set 1** is where we define the rule sets applicable to the VM storage policy; in this example, we use tag-based placement:

7. The tag used for placement will be based on the datastore speed:

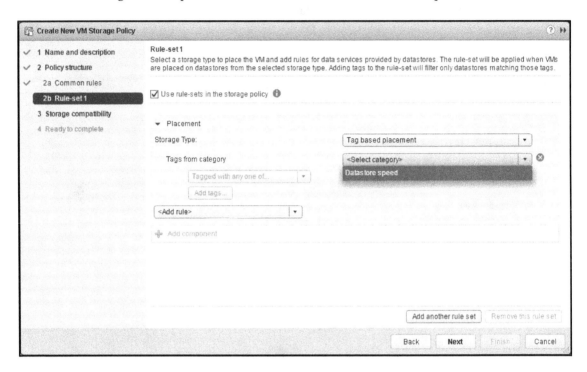

8. In our example, this category will tag storage based on it being present under **All flash datastore**:

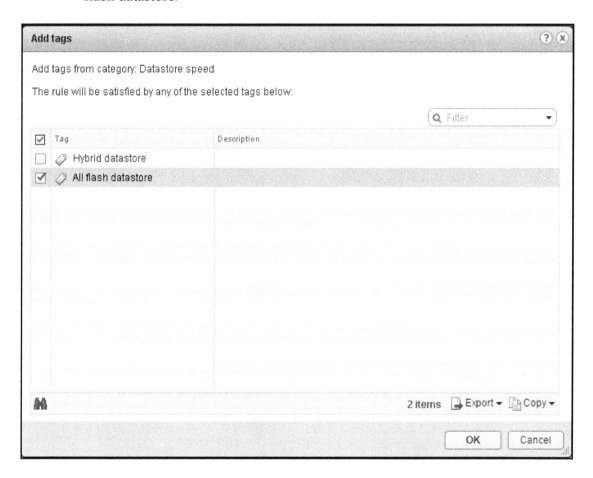

9. After selecting **Rule-set 1**, our Gold VM storage policy is configured to be usable, based on the VMs tagged with the **All flash datastore** tag for datastore speed:

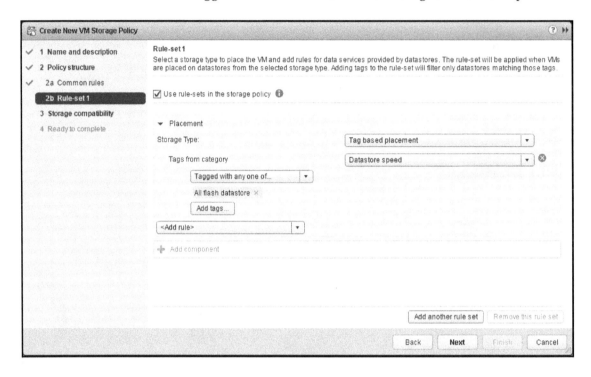

10. As we proceed, the **Storage compatibility** screen shows which storage is compatible with this policy:

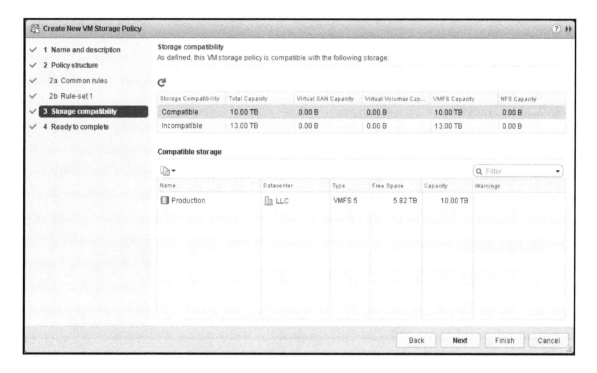

11. Then, we proceed to the final screen to finish and create the Gold policy:

12. Upon completion, we have a new VM storage policy named Gold, which we can assign to our VMs:

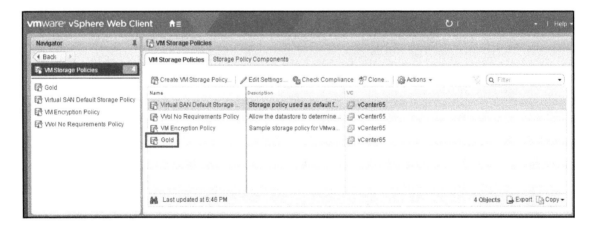

13. Using the VM storage policy, at this point, the profile is created and the user-defined capabilities are added to the datastore. Now we can use the profile to select the correct storage for the VM. The profile is automatically attached to the VM during the deployment phase. Later, we can check whether the datastore on which the VM is placed has the same capabilities as the profile. If it does, then the VM is said to be compliant. If it does not, then the VM is said to be non-compliant.

VM Storage Policies can be used during deployment or migrations or can be attached on the fly.

How it works...

Profile-driven storage enables the creation of datastores that provide varying levels of service. With profile-driven storage, you can use storage capabilities and VM storage profiles to ensure that VMs use storage that provides a certain level of capacity, performance, availability, redundancy, and so on.

Profile-driven storage minimizes the amount of storage planning that the administrator must do for each VM. For example, the administrator can use profile-driven storage to create basic storage tiers. Datastores with similar capabilities are tagged to form gold, silver, and bronze tiers. Redundant, high-performance storage might be tagged as the gold tier, and non-redundant, medium performance storage might be tagged as the bronze tier.

It can be used during the provisioning of a VM to ensure that its disks are placed on the storage that is best for its situation. For example, profile-driven storage can help you ensure that the VM running a critical I/O-intensive database is placed in the gold tier. Ideally, an administrator will always want to create the best match of predefined VM storage requirements with the available physical storage properties.

Anti-affinity rules in the SDRS cluster

Storage DRS makes sure that a VM's data is assigned to the optimal storage location initially, then it uses ongoing load balancing between datastores to avoid bottlenecks. Storage DRS provides smart VM placement and load balancing mechanisms, based on I/O and space utilization.

Similar to the vSphere DRS, aggregates the resources of several datastores into a single datastore cluster to simplify storage management at scale with vSphere SDRS. To create a datastore cluster, navigate to the storage view and click on the **Create a new datastore cluster** icon. Follow the wizard to create the datastore cluster:

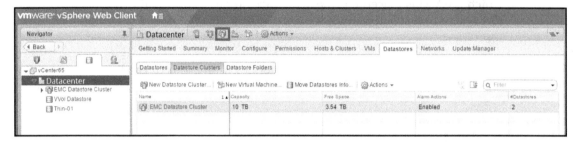

During VM provisioning, Storage DRS provides intelligent VM placement, based on the I/O load and the available storage capacity of the datastores. Storage DRS performs ongoing load balancing between data stores to ensure space and/or I/O bottlenecks are avoided as per predefined rules that reflect business needs and changing priorities.

Similar to the vSphere DRS, SDRS also has a mechanism for placing VMs' data. It is called affinity and anti-affinity rule. But affinity and anti-affinity rules work on **virtual machine disk (VMDK)** and datastores.

By default, all the disks of a virtual machine can be on the same datastore. However, an end user might want the virtual disks on different datastores. For example, a user can place a system disk on one datastore and place the data disks on another. In this case, the user can set up a VMDK anti-affinity rule, which keeps a VM's virtual disks on separate datastores.

If you change the default setting of keeping VMDKs together, then Storage DRS will have far more options for moving virtual disks around, as it can make decisions per disk instead of per VM. By changing the default, Storage DRS will find the optimal placement per disk.

The VM anti-affinity rules keeps VMs on separate datastores. This rule is useful when redundant VMs are available.

The following is a table that specifies how it behaves in different cases:

Intra-VM VMDK Affinity	Intra-VM VMDK Anti-Affinity	VM Anti-Affinity
Keep a VM's VMDKs together on the same datastore	Keep a VM's VMDKs on different datastores	Keep VMs on different datastores
Maximize VM availability when all the disks are needed in order to run	Rules can be applied to all, or a subset of, a VM's disks	Rule is similar to the DRS anti-affinity rule
Rule is on by default for all VMs	Maximize the availability of a set of redundant	

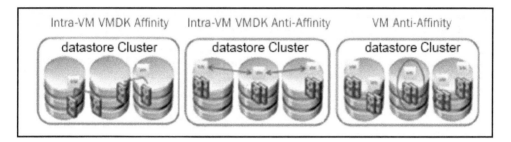

Getting ready

To step through this recipe, you will need a couple of running ESXi Servers, an instance of vCenter Server, a couple of datastores attached to ESXi, a couple of VMs on those datastores, and vSphere Web Client. No other prerequisites are required.

How to do it...

To change the default setting of the SDRS affinity rule, carry out the following steps:

1. Log in to the vCenter Server using vSphere Web Client.
2. Go to the **Storage** tab.
3. Select **Datastore Cluster**, where you want to change the setting.
4. Go to the **Configure** tab, then **Rules** under the **Configuration** section. Click on **Add**.

5. Give the rule a name, select the type, then add the VMs to the rule:

Avoiding the use of the SDRS I/O metric and array-based automatic tiering together

While we can employ array-based automatic LUN tiering and VMware Storage DRS, we need to disable the I/O-metric-based calculation in SDRS. This way, we would not employ both of them for the same job. Now let's see what it does in the backend.

SDRS triggers action in either capacity and/or latency. Capacity stats are constantly gathered by vCenter, where the default threshold is 80 percent. I/O load trend is evaluated (by default) every 8 hours, based on the past day's history; the default threshold is 15 ms. This means that the Storage DRS algorithm will be invoked when these thresholds are exceeded. Now, in the case of utilized space, this happens when vCenter collects datastore statistics and notices that the threshold has been exceeded in the case of I/O load balancing.

Every 8 hours, Storage DRS evaluates the I/O imbalance and makes recommendations if and when the thresholds are exceeded. Note that these recommendations will only be made when the difference between the source and destination is at least 5 percent and the cost/risk/benefit analysis has a positive result.

I/O latency is the datastore's response time, measured in milliseconds. The default value is 15 ms, which means that the datastore will not consider relocations until the datastore restore time exceeds 15 ms and the imbalance rules are also satisfied.

In some cases, it might be best to avoid latency assessment because of variability in the application workload or storage configuration. For example, auto-tiered storage can provide varied I/O response times, depending on the class of storage used by the tiered device. Additionally, storage array technologies, such as EMC's **Fully Automated Storage Tiering for Virtual Pools** (**FAST VP**), is designed to migrate blocks at a sub-LUN level. Since both SDRS and FAST VP address the same problem, although at a slightly different level, use only one of them to perform the migrations to avoid duplicate relocation operations. Do not allow both SDRS and FAST VP to perform automated relocations.

When using EMC FAST VP, use SDRS but disable the I/O metric. This combination gives you the simplicity benefits of SDRS for automated placement and capacity balancing.

So, the thumb rule is, *do not* enable I/O metric for SDRS recommendations. Let that be done by the array-based automatic LUN tiering at the storage layer.

Getting ready

To step through this recipe, you will need a couple of running ESXi Servers, an instance of vCenter Server, a couple of datastores attached to ESXi, a couple of VMs on these datastores, and vSphere Web Client. No other prerequisites are required.

However, we presume that FAST is enabled on the storage side. Showing how to enable FAST on the storage side is not in the scope of this recipe.

How to do it...

To do this, carry out the following steps:

1. Open up vSphere Web Client and log in to the vCenter Server.
2. Select **Storage** on the home screen.
3. Click on the cluster, then go to the **Datastores** tab.
4. Click on the **Datastore Clusters** section and then **New Datastore Cluster**.
5. Give a name to this datastore cluster; leave a check mark next to **Turn On Storage DRS** and click **Next**.
6. Select your automation level and click **Next**.

 Manual mode indicates that Storage DRS will only make recommendations and the user will need to apply these. Fully automated means that Storage DRS will make recommendations and apply these directly by migrating VMs or virtual disks to the proposed destination datastore.

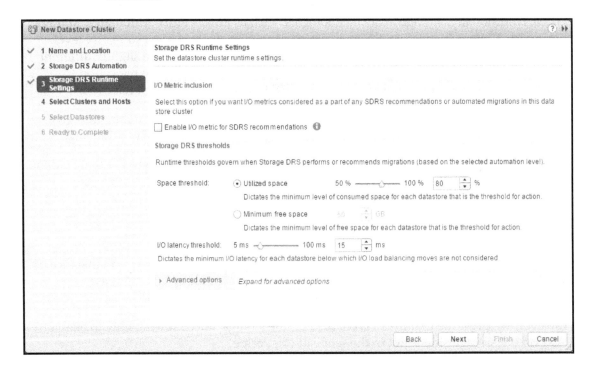

7. Here, do not select **Enable I/O metric for SDRS recommendations**.
8. Accept all the default settings and click **Next**.
9. Select the cluster to which you want to add this **Datastore Cluster**. Click on **Next**.
10. Select the datastores that should be part of this **Datastore Cluster**. Click on **Next**.
11. Review your selections, ensure that all the hosts are connected to the datastores in the datastore cluster, and click **Finish**.
12. A datastore cluster will now be created and a new object should appear on the **Datastores** and **Datastore Clusters** view. This object should contain the selected datastores.

Using VMware SIOC and array-based automatic tiering together

SIOC and array-based automatic tiering always complement each other, and we should use them together wherever possible.

Fully automated storage tiering for virtual pools, or FAST VP, intelligently manages data placement at the sub-LUN level, thus increasing overall performance. When implemented on a storage system, FAST VP measures, analyzes, and implements a storage-tiering policy much faster and more efficiently than any user could.

A FAST VP-enabled storage pool contains disks of varying performance levels and costs. It may contain a tier of SSD disks, a tier of 10k SAS disks, and a tier of 7.2k NLSAS disks. Flash or SSD drives perform the fastest, followed by SAS and NL-SAS, respectively. LUNs are created from the capacity from this pool as needed. FAST VP collects the statistics of the LUNs based on the I/O activity in 256 MB slices. These statistics are then analyzed and the most active slices are moved to the highest tier available. A single LUN may have its slices stored on SSD, 10k and 7.2k disks. This is only specific to newer EMC arrays, such as VNX/Unity or VMAX and so on.

At the user's discretion, relocation of the data can be initiated either manually or by an automated scheduler.

All of the data goes through a life cycle and experiences varying levels of activity during that lifetime. For example, when data is first created, it is typically used heavily, and as it ages, data is accessed less often. FAST dynamically matches these data characteristics to the tier of disk drives best suited to the data access patterns. Data will initially sit on the fastest tier available and move to the lower tiers as it ages.

Getting ready

To step through this recipe, you will need a couple of running ESXi Servers, an instance of vCenter Server, a couple of datastores attached to ESXi, and vSphere Web Client. No other prerequisites are required.

However, we presume that FAST is enabled on the storage side. Configuring FAST VP on EMC storage is not in the scope of this recipe.

How to do it...

Let's get started:

1. Open up vSphere Web Client and log in to the vCenter Server.
2. In the **Storage** section, select **Datastores**.
3. Choose the datastore from the list of datastores in the left panel where you want to prioritize the I/O:

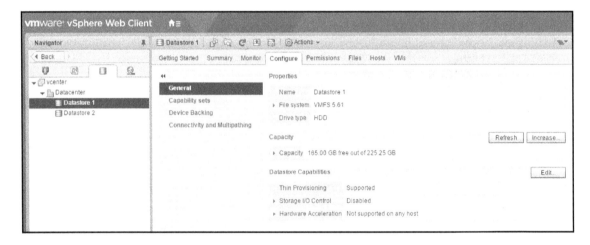

4. Click on the **Configure** tab, then click on the **Edit** button in the **General** section.

5. At this stage, you can enable SIOC by simply selecting the checkbox labeled **Enable Storage I/O Control**. Click on the **OK** button when you're done:

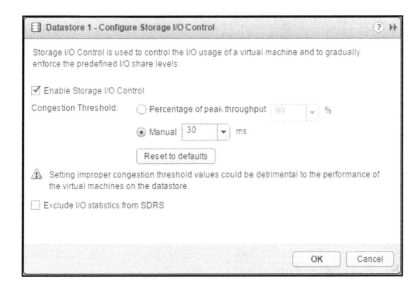

6. You'll know you were successful if, in the vSphere Web Client window, you now see **Enabled** under the **Storage I/O Control** item of the **Datastore Details** section:

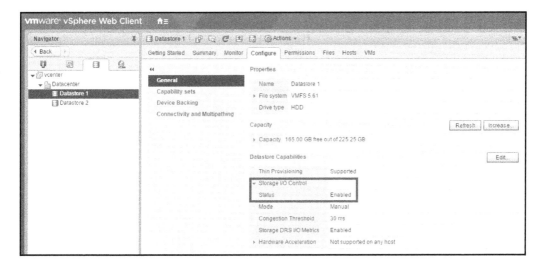

7. Do the same thing on your other shared storage datastores.

How it works...

FAST supports SIOC. SIOC is a technology that allows users to configure I/O shares at a datastore level so that the critical VM receives the I/O throughput and response time when needed, without worrying that another VM on that same datastore would hinder the performance of a critical VM. One works at the VM level and the other works at the drive level—both complement each other.

For example, let's say you have two VMs, each running SQL, and one VM is critical and the other is not.

FAST will service the I/O from both the SQL databases equally. However, you can design these VMs as HIGH and LOW in SOIC and ensure the correct performance is given to your VMs.

This is a situation where we need to assign a response time value based on the weakest link (NL-SAS).

 Use these guidelines for drive type and response times: EFD (flash drives)-15 ms, SAS drives-30 ms, and NLSAS drives-30 to 50 ms.

In this case, FAST VP Pool with NL-SAS would need to be set to 50.

Of course, it does not help if all of the data resides on EFD and the LUN experience's contention.

5
vSphere Cluster Design

In this chapter, we will cover the tasks related to vSphere Cluster Design for best performance. You will learn the following aspects of vSphere Cluster Design:

- Trade-off factors while designing scale-up and scale-out clusters
- Using VM Monitoring
- vSphere Fault Tolerance design and its impact
- DPM and its impact
- Choosing the reserved cluster failover capacity
- Choosing the correct vSphere HA cluster size

Introduction

Downtime always brings significant costs to any environment, so implementing a high availability solution is always necessary. Traditionally, however, it brings complexity in terms of manageability and cost.

VMware **vSphere High Availability (vSphere HA)** makes it simpler, easier, and cheaper to provide high availability for your applications. You can configure it with a couple of simple steps through VMware vCenter Server. You can create a vSphere HA cluster with multiple ESXi Servers, which will enable you to protect VMs and the services running on them. In the event of a failure of one of the hosts in the cluster, impacted VMs would be automatically restarted on other ESXi hosts within that same VMware vSphere Cluster.

There are many details to consider when configuring your HA cluster:

- Determining the size of your vSphere HA cluster
- Determining the number of resources to keep in reserve
- Determining when to use vSphere **Fault Tolerance** (**FT**)
- Determining when to use **Distributed Power Management** (DPM)

In this chapter, you will learn what you need to know about these to make sure you are running a balanced environment and thus achieving good performance in your vSphere Cluster.

Trade-off factors while designing scale-up and scale-out clusters

One of the initial decisions you need to make when designing a vSphere Cluster is if you will build a small cluster with larger hosts (scale-up cluster) or a large cluster with smaller hosts (scale-out cluster). There are many factors that work as a catalyst when you choose a scale-up or scale-out cluster. Some of them are as follows:

- Which hardware is ideal for lowering cost, a few larger hosts or a large number of smaller hosts? The answer to this varies in different situations.
- What is the operational cost and complexity over the period of time in maintaining either of these two models?
- What about the other infrastructure components, such as power, cooling, and floor space?
- What is the purpose of this cluster? Is it a desktop virtualization cluster or a server virtualization cluster?

The design decision that you choose depends on the answers to the preceding questions. If you choose to virtualize servers, then this typically requires a large number of hosts with fair capacity. This cluster typically hosts fewer VMs per host. However, the picture is totally different when you virtualize desktops, where you choose fewer hosts with a large capacity to host more VMs per host. You should also consider the maximum capacity of a host in an HA cluster.

Getting ready

To step through this recipe, you need to have two different sets of ESXi Servers: some of them should be rich and thick (four-socket servers with more memory) in terms of capacity and other should be thin (two-socket servers with less memory) in terms of capacity. You also need a vCenter Server and vSphere Web Client. No other prerequisites are required.

How to do it...

Perform the following steps to create a scale-out cluster:

1. Using vSphere Web Client, log in to the vCenter Server.
2. Select the **Hosts and Clusters** view on the **Home** screen.
3. Right-click on **Datacenter** in the Inventory tree and click on **New Cluster**.
4. Name this cluster `scale-out` in **Cluster Creation Wizard**.
5. Click on the checkbox to enable vSphere DRS.
6. Click on the checkbox to enable vSphere HA. Click on **OK**.
7. Once your cluster is created, right-click on it and select **Add Host**.
8. Specify the hostname or IP Address of the ESXi hosts that you will select for the scale-up cluster (thick hosts) and click **Next**.
9. Enter the username and password that vSphere will use to connect to the host, then click **Next**.
10. Take the default settings in the next four pages, then click on **Finish**.
11. Repeat this step for adding the rest of the scale-out hosts.

Now you are ready to create a scale-up cluster that has fewer hosts with rich configurations/capacity for your server workload.

To create a scale-up cluster, repeat the previous steps except:

1. In step 4, name the cluster `scale-up`.
2. Choose the scale-up hosts in step 10 and add subsequent hosts there.

How it works...

Scale-up and scale-out clusters have their advantages and disadvantages.

The primary advantage of a scale-up cluster is that it takes less effort to manage and monitor; thus, it is less expensive (in terms of operational cost). When it comes to the other infrastructure components, such as power, cooling, and space, this cluster is also beneficial as it might consume less than a scale-out cluster. If you choose to virtualize user desktops, then a scale-up cluster is preferable.

However, a scale-up cluster has disadvantages as well. Consider a failure domain of a scale-up cluster. A single host failure in a scale-up cluster can affect many VMs at the same time. vSphere HA will need to restart those failed VMs. Also, the reservation of failover capacity is also huge, as reserving a single host also impacts cluster resource reservation.

DRS migration options are very limited in a scale-up cluster. This may result in workloads that are not balanced perfectly between all the hosts.

You may need to consider the HA maximum VM limit as well. In a scale-up cluster, you may end up reaching that limit very fast (8,000 VMs per cluster in vSphere 6.5); then HA will not be able to restart those VMs after a failure.

Similarly, a scale-out cluster also has several advantages and disadvantages. As opposed to the scale-up cluster, only fewer VMs are affected in a scale-out cluster due to a single host failure, and the failover takes effect quickly as well. Also, fewer resources will be reserved for the failover.

With DRS enabled, a scale-out cluster has the option to provide more choices to VMs, in terms of migration and load balancing. Also, it is hard to reach the per-host VM limits in a scale-out cluster.

However, it can consume more power, cooling, and floor space. For example, four-socket servers take 2U-4U of space in the rack, whereas two-socket servers take 1U-2U of space in the rack. Additional cost could be related to the network port. Operational complexity and costs are also high in the case of a scale-out cluster.

Using VM Monitoring

The VM Monitoring service, which is serviced by VMware Tools, evaluates whether each VM in the cluster is running or not. Regular heartbeats and I/O activity from the VMware Tools process will be checked by the VM Monitoring service to determine the running guest.

Sometimes, VM heartbeats or I/O activity is not received by the VM Monitoring service because the guest operating system fails or VMware Tools is not being allocated time to complete its tasks. If the VM Monitoring service does not hear those heartbeats, then it declares that the VM has failed and the VM is rebooted to restore service.

The VM Monitoring service also monitors a VM's I/O activity just to avoid unnecessary resets. If there are no heartbeats received within the failure interval, the I/O stats interval (a cluster-level attribute) is checked. The I/O stats interval (by default, 120 seconds) determines whether any disk or network activity has occurred for the VM during the previous 2 minutes. If not, then the VM is reset.

 This default value (120 seconds) can be changed using the advanced attribute, namely `das.iostatsinterval`.

You should enable VM Monitoring to restart a failed VM. To be effective, the application or service running on the VM must be capable of restarting successfully after a reboot.

The default monitoring and restart settings are acceptable. VM monitoring does not adversely affect VMs that are protected by FT and **Microsoft Clustering Services** (**MSCS**). FT and MSCS monitor VM failure, but they detect and react to a VM failure well before vSphere HA VM Monitoring.

You can also configure the level of monitoring. If you select the sensitivity as high, then a quick conclusion will be reached regarding the failure occurrence. However, it may result in negative impact on the monitoring service and might not get a heartbeat because of resource constraints and may trigger a false alarm. Low sensitivity monitoring results in longer interruptions in service between actual failures and VMs being reset. You should select an option that is an effective compromise for your needs.

VM Monitoring settings are as follows:

Setting	Failure Interval	Minimum Uptime	Reset Period
High	30 seconds	120 seconds	1 hour
Medium	60 seconds	240 seconds	24 hours
Low	120 seconds	480 seconds	168 hours (7 days)

Getting ready

To step through this recipe, you should have an existing vSphere Infrastructure and a vCenter Server. No other prerequisites are required.

How to do it…

To configure VM Monitoring while creating a vSphere HA cluster, carry out the following steps:

1. Using vSphere Web Client, log in to the vCenter Server.
2. Select the **Hosts and Clusters** view on the **Home** Screen.
3. Right-click on **Datacenter** in the Inventory tree and click on **New Cluster**.
4. Give a name to this cluster.
5. Check **Turn On vSphere DRS** and **vSphere HA** and **Turn ON** boxes.
6. Leave the default settings for the DRS Automation level.

7. In the **VM Monitoring** section, select **VM Monitoring Status** as **VM Monitoring Only** (by default, it will be disabled) from the drop-down menu and select **Monitoring Sensitivity**:

8. Choose the default **Monitoring Sensitivity** as Low, Medium, or High.
9. Review the cluster configuration and click **OK**.

To configure VM Monitoring on an existing cluster, do the following:

1. Using vSphere Web Client, log in to the vCenter Server.
2. Select the **Hosts and Clusters** view on the **Home** Screen.
3. Go to the **Configure** tab, then click on **vSphere Availability** under the **Services** section.
4. Click on **Edit** at the top-right corner of the screen.
5. Go to the **Failures and Responses** section.
6. Click on **VM Monitoring** to enable this feature and either set the sensitivity as **Preset** or customize the sensitivity:

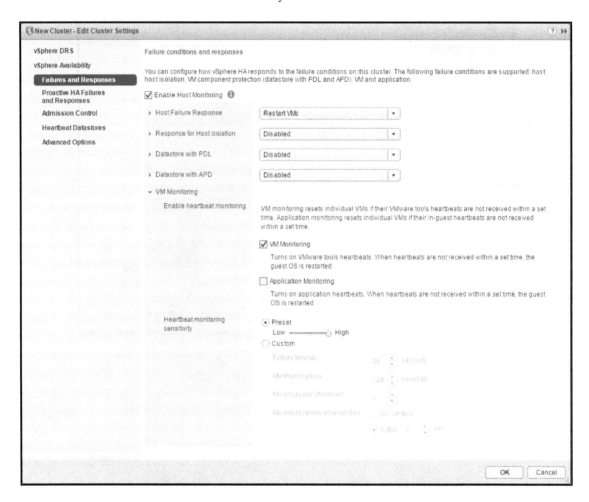

vSphere Fault Tolerance design and its impact

Deciding whether or not to configure FT depends on the workloads of the protected VMs. One of the major reasons to choose FT is if you require zero or near zero downtime for a critical workload. If you perform a current state analysis of an existing infrastructure and find some critical workloads already protected in the physical infrastructure, it is most likely that these workloads require protection in a VMware virtual infrastructure as well. FT is simple to configure and can offer a wide range of workloads to be protected. However, it works for uniprocessor VMs, which is a deal killer for most VMs that would otherwise get FT.

However, there are a number of limitations associated with the configuration of FT. Many fundamental virtualization benefits are lost, including the use of VM snapshots and VMware vSphere Storage vMotion.

There are a number of prerequisites and configurations on the infrastructure side, which should be in place before you configure FT. They are as follows:

- FT can only be configured in a vSphere HA cluster. You should have at least three hosts in the cluster because if one host fails, there will be two hosts servicing two FT VMs (one vCPU limitation per VM).
- To avoid performance problems, every host that you have in the HA cluster should have a similar CPU configuration. Say you have slower CPUs on some hosts and faster CPUs on some other hosts. In this case, when the secondary VM runs on the slower CPU host, the primary machine has to stop continuously to allow the secondary server to catch up.
- ESXi hosts must have access to the same datastore and networks.

There is a varied number of infrastructure impacts on the FT. One of them, which is crucial, is contention on the FT logging network. VMware requires at least one physical 1 GB Ethernet network for the logging network. You should have another 1 GB Ethernet for vMotion. Also, vMotion and FT should be on a separate subnet.

VMware also recommends that you configure no more than four FT-protected VMs per host, with 1 GB logging network. The number of VMs that are protected by FT that you can safely run on each host is based on the sizes and workloads of the ESXi host and the VMs.

To reduce the contention over the FT network, you should configure a 10 Gbps logging network, which increases the available bandwidth. Also, you should distribute the primary hosts across multiple physical hosts because logging traffic is asymmetric. Distributing primaries across different hosts allow the logging network to benefit from the Ethernet's bidirectional capability.

Getting ready

To step through this recipe, you should have an existing vSphere Infrastructure, an existing vCenter Server, a couple of ESXi Servers (licensed with Enterprise Plus) connected to vCenter Server, and the HA cluster. Shared storage is required. A dedicated gig Ethernet is required. The same version of ESXi is required for all three hosts. The VM to protect needs to be one per CPU. No other prerequisites are required.

How to do it...

Before you start configuring FT in your vSphere Infrastructure, you should have the prerequisites configured.

Infrastructure prerequisites:

- Your ESXi host should support vLockstep technology to support FT.
- All CPUs must be vMotion-compatible or the cluster must have EVC enabled.
- Intel CPUs must be Sandy Bridge or later. AMD CPUs must be Bulldozer or later.
- All your ESXi hosts should run on the same build and have a license to run FT VMs.
- Shared storage should be between the ESXi hosts.
- You should have an HA cluster enabled for FT to work
- You should have a dedicated NIC for the FT logging network and a separate vMotion network.
- Host certificate checking must be enabled in the vCenter Server.

VM prerequisites:

- VMs must be configured with four or fewer CPUs.
- The VM's disk must be 2 TB or smaller.
- There are no non-replayable devices on the VM.
- Snapshots must be removed before FT can be enabled on the VM.

- vMotion is supported on FT-enabled VMs, but you cannot vMotion both the primary and secondary VMs at the same time.
- Storage vMotion is not supported on FT-enabled VMs.

Once the requirements have been met, you can work on the actual FT configuration. First, we will configure a VMkernel port for FT logging:

1. Using vSphere Web Client, log in to the vCenter Server.
2. Select **Hosts and Clusters** on the **Home** Screen.
3. Select an ESXi host, then go to the **Configure** tab.
4. Click on **VMkernel adapters** under the **Networking** section.
5. Click on **Add Host Networking** to add a VMkernel port.
6. Select **VMkernel Network adapter** as the connection type. Click on **Next**.
7. Select an existing switch or create a new switch. Click on **Next**.
8. Give the VMkernel port a label and specify a VLAN number (optional).
9. Select the checkbox for **Fault Tolerance logging** and click on **Next**:

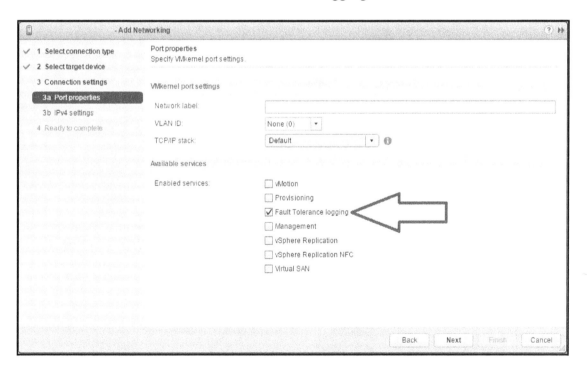

10. Specify DHCP or enter the **IP address** and **Subnet Mask** on the **IP Settings** page. A static IP is preferred over DHCP. Click on **Next**.

11. Review the configuration and click **Finish**.

Now as you have configured VMkernel for FT logging, you should be able to enable your VM for FT protection, as follows:

1. Choose the VM, right-click on it, and navigate to **Fault Tolerance** | **Turn on Fault Tolerance**.

2. Select the datastore for the secondary VM. Click on **Next**.

3. Select the host for the secondary VM. Click on **Next**.

4. Review the selections and click on **Finish**.

5. Once the setup is complete, you will be able to see the FT status, **Secondary VM location**, and **Log Bandwidth** information for the **Fault Tolerance** tile on the VM's summary tab:

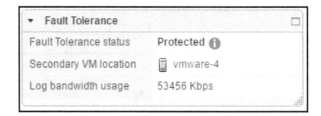

6. To test the FT feature, right-click on the VM, select **Fault Tolerance**, and click on **Test Failover**.

How it works...

FT creates a secondary VM on another ESX host that shares the same virtual disk file as the primary VM. Then it transfers the CPU and virtual device input from the primary VM (record) to the secondary VM (replay) via an FT logging NIC so that it is in sync with the primary and ready to take over in case there's a failure.

Data from the primary VM is copied to the secondary VM using a special FT logging network that is configured on each ESXi Server.

 VMware has a formula that you can use to determine the FT logging bandwidth requirements: *VMware FT logging bandwidth = (Avg disk reads (MB/s) × 8 + Avg network input (Mbps)) × 1.2 [20% headroom].*

DPM and its impact

VMware **vSphere Distributed Power Management** (also known as **vSphere DPM**) continuously monitors resource requirements and power consumption across a VMware vSphere DRS cluster. When your vSphere HA cluster needs fewer resources, it consolidates workloads and powers off unused ESXi hosts so that it can reduce power consumption. However, VMs are not affected because DRS moves the running VMs around as needed without downtime before the hosts power off. ESXi hosts are kept powered off during periods of low resource use. But when there is a need for more resources, then DPM powers on these ESXi hosts for the VMs to use. vSphere DPM uses three techniques to bring the host out of standby mode, and these techniques are as follows:

- **Intelligent Platform Management Interface (IPMI)**
- Hewlett-Packard **Integrated Lights-Out (iLO)**
- **Wake on LAN (WOL)**

If a host supports all of them, then the order of the technique chosen for use by DPM is as shown in the preceding list. However, for each of these protocols, you need to perform specific configuration on each host before you enable vSphere DPM for the cluster.

Note that the vCenter Server marks those hosts standby that has been powered off by DPM, but standby mode indicates that the host is available for being powered on in case it is required.

Getting ready

To step through this recipe, you will need a couple of ESXi Servers that support either IPMI, iLO, or WOL; a vCenter Server; and vSphere Web Client. No other prerequisites are required.

How to do it...

To enable DPM on a vSphere Cluster, perform the following steps:

1. Using vSphere Web Client, log in to the vCenter Server.
2. Select **Hosts and Clusters** on the **Home** screen.
3. Click on **vSphere Cluster** and go to **Configure** | **Services** | **vSphere DRS**.
4. Click on **Edit** in the top-right corner.

5. In the **Power Management** section, select **Manual** or **Automatic** as **Automation Level**:

6. Once you are done, click **OK**.

 Note that once you are done with the Cluster configuration, you need to configure IPMI/iLO for each host as well.

7. On the home screen of the vCenter Server, select **Hosts and Clusters**.
8. Select the Host for which you want to enable IPMI/iLO (you should configure IPMI/iLO on all the hosts in your cluster).
9. Click on the **Configure** tab and select **Power Management** under **System**.
10. Click on **Properties**.

11. Enter the **Username**, **Password**, **BMC IP Address**, and **BMC MAC Address** (use colons) fields. Click on **OK**. You will get immediate feedback if this were unsuccessful:

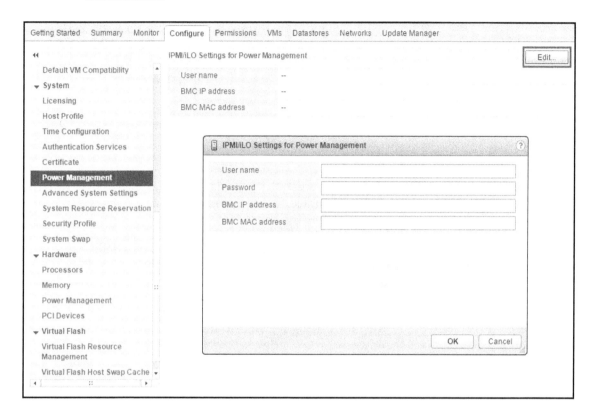

If you want to test the DPM configuration, carry out the following steps:

1. Right-click on a powered host within the cluster, select **Power**, then select **Enter Standby mode**.
2. Once complete, the host will have a moon icon next to the name.
3. Right-click on the host, select **Power**, then select **Power On**.
4. Click on the cluster containing the DPM-enabled cluster and go to the **Configure** tab.
5. Select **Host Options** under **Configuration**.
6. Verify that the host's **Last Time Exited Standby** option is updated with the most recent attempt and that it was successful.

How it works...

vSphere DPM wakes up an ESXi host from a powered off state through WOL packets. WOL packets are broadcast traffic and require that the vCenter and ESXi hosts be in the same layer 2 networks. The vMotion VMkernel interface is used to send these WOL packets to other hosts, so vSphere DPM keeps at least one host powered on at all times. VMware recommends that you need to test the *exit standby* procedure for the host where DPM is going to be enabled. You need to make sure it can be successfully powered on through WOL.

The vSphere DPM algorithm does not frequently power servers on and off in response to transient load variations. Rather, it powers off a server only when it is very likely that it will stay powered off for some time. The history of the cluster workload is used to account this.

To minimize the power cycling frequency across all the hosts in the cluster, vSphere DPM cycles through all the comparable hosts enabled for vSphere DPM hosts when trying to find a power off candidate.

In conjunction with vSphere HA, if HA Admission Control is disabled, then failover constraints are not passed on to the DPM; thus, those constraints are not enforced. vSphere DPM does not care about failover requirements and puts the hosts in standby mode.

With cluster configuration settings, users can define the reserve capacity to always be available. Users can also define the time during which load history can be monitored before the power off decision is made. Power on is also triggered when not enough resources are available to power on a virtual machine, or when more spare capacity is required for vSphere HA.

You should enable DPM only after you are done with the testing of standby mode and wake on protocol configuration.

Priority ratings are based on the amount of overutilization or underutilization found in the DRS cluster, and the improvement that is expected from the intended host power state changes.

When you disable vSphere DPM, hosts are taken out of standby mode. Taking hosts out of standby mode ensures that when vSphere DPM is disabled, all the hosts are powered on and are ready to accommodate load increases.

Also, when you enable vSphere DPM, hosts in the DRS cluster inherit the power management automation level of the cluster by default.

VMware strongly recommends that you disable any host with a **Last Time Exited Standby status of Never** until you ensure that WOL is configured properly. You do not want vSphere DPM to power off a host for which wake has not been successfully tested.

Choosing the reserved cluster failover capacity

By now, we all know that VMware has introduced a percentage-based cluster resource reservation model. Using this setting, you need to specify how many resources you want to reserve to accommodate a host failure. It also allows us to select different percentages for CPU and memory.

You might wonder how you would calculate how many resources you want to reserve for your HA cluster. While it was a straightforward approach when we used to select a number of hosts reserved for servicing a host failure, we have seen disadvantages as well. If you use the number of ESXi hosts failure in your HA cluster, you will reserve those completely; thus, it will not be efficient to tune into your HA cluster or put it to best use. Also, it avoids the commonly experienced slot size issue, where values are skewed due to a large reservation.

Percentage-based reservation is also much more effective as it considers the actual reservation per VM to calculate the available failover resources, which means that clusters dynamically adjust when resources are added.

What you get is an option to specify a percentage of failover resources for both CPU and memory:

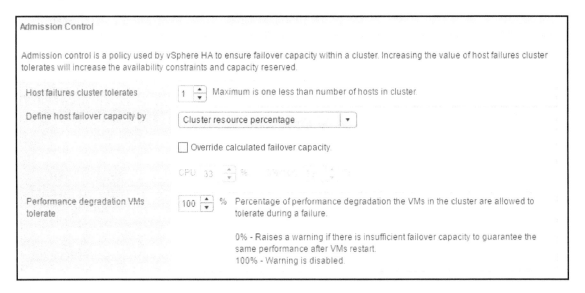

The default host failover capacity percentage is dynamic, based on the number of hosts in the cluster and the host failures to tolerate. A cluster with three hosts and one host failure to tolerate would result in a failover capacity of 33 percent. A cluster with four hosts and one host failure to tolerate would result in a failover capacity of 25 percent. You can override this default and enter your own percentage if you wish.

You can use the following formula to calculate the percentage of resources you should keep there: *(Total amount of available resources – total reserved VM resources) / total amount of available resources) < = (percentage HA should reserve as spare capacity)*. For those VMs that do not have a reservation, a default of 32 MHz will be used for the CPU and a default of 0 MB plus memory overhead will be used for memory. The total reserved VM resources include the default reservation of 32 MHz plus the memory overhead of the VM.

Getting ready

To step through this recipe, you should have an existing vSphere Infrastructure, an existing vCenter Server, a couple of ESXi Servers connected to the vCenter Server, and an HA cluster. No other prerequisites are required.

How to do it...

To set a percentage-based admission control, follow these steps:

1. Log in to vCenter Server Web Client.
2. Click on **Hosts and Clusters** on the **Home** Screen.
3. Click on the cluster and go to the **Configure** tab.
4. Click on **vSphere Availability** under the **Services** section.
5. Click on the **Edit** button in the top-left corner.
6. Click on the **Admission Control** section.
7. Set the drop-down box to **Cluster resource percentage** and click on **Override calculated capacity percentage**, then set the **CPU** and **Memory** percentages:

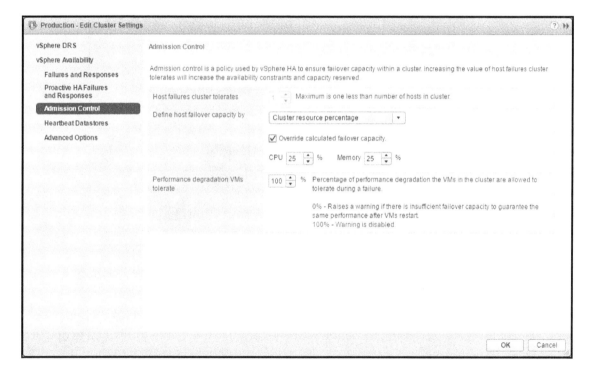

8. Click on **OK** to apply the settings.

How it works…

Let me show you how it works by way of an example scenario and a diagram:

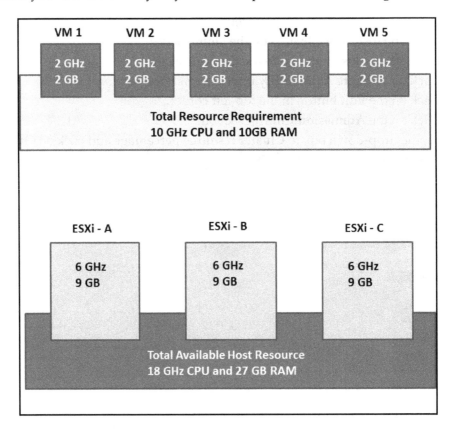

In this example, we have three ESXi hosts in a vSphere HA cluster. All the hosts are identical and have 6 GHz of CPU and 9 GB of memory.

There are five powered-on VMs that are also identical (in reality, getting identical VM requirements are rare; this is for academic purposes only). Each VM requires 2 GHz of CPU and 2 GB of memory, and a reservation is also set for the entire allocated CPU and memory.

So you have now gathered how many resources you have and how much you need.

Based on this, the current CPU failover capacity is ((18 GHz-10 GHz)/18GHz = 44%, and the current memory failover capacity is ((27 GB-10 GB)/27 GB) = 62%.

Now, because your cluster was configured with 25 percent failover capacity, 19 percent of CPU resources are still available to power on additional VMs. Also, you still have 37 of percent memory resources for additional VMs.

See also

For more information on the percentage of resources to keep, refer the VMware vSphere 6.5 vSphere Availability Guide at `http://pubs.vmware.com/vsphere-65/topic/com.vmware.ICbase/PDF/vsphere-esxi-vcenter-server-65-availability-guide.pdf`.

Choosing the correct vSphere HA cluster size

When vSphere 5 was introduced, we saw a significant change in the HA model, and that does relax the constraints on the size of your vSphere HA cluster. But, you may ask, what about storage bottlenecks while accessing the same storage via a larger cluster? We have VAAI to handle that now, and that being in the picture, it does not constrain you from choosing a larger cluster.

Also, a crucial factor is that a larger cluster creates more scheduling opportunities for DRS, and a bigger cluster does not impose a heavy lift on the cost. Does that mean, we suggest *only a* bigger cluster and not many smaller clusters? Well, not really. It all boils down to what you are going to use on that cluster and what is your requirement. If you are implementing View Manager and are going to use Linked Clone, then you are limiting yourself with eight hosts, as with Linked Clone only eight hosts can access one single file. This restriction is not there in vSphere 5.1 and above.

There are a few other factors that you need to look at before you decide your HA cluster size, and one of them is operational complexity. Maintaining a large cluster in a production environment is not an easy task. You need to have all the hosts in the cluster updated and in the same change window. This may conflict with your change management process. Also, the time required to update a cluster depends on the cluster size, the amount of time required to evacuate a host, the number of resources available to perform concurrent host updates, and so on.

Getting ready

To step through this recipe, you will need to have ESXi Servers, a vCenter Server, and the vSphere Web Client. No other prerequisites are required.

How to do it...

Perform the following steps to create your desired cluster with a determined size:

1. Using vSphere Web Client, log in to the vCenter Server.
2. Select the **Hosts and Clusters** view on the **Home** Screen.
3. Right-click on **Datacenter** in the **Inventory** tree and click on **New Cluster**.
4. Name this cluster in **Cluster Creation Wizard**.
5. Turn on **vSphere HA** and **DRS**.
6. Select all the default settings and click **OK**.
7. Once your cluster is created, right-click on it and select **Add Host**.
8. Specify the Hostname or IP Address of the ESXi hosts that you selected for your cluster and click **Next**.
9. Choose the default configuration for the rest of the steps and click on **Finish**.
10. Repeat steps 7 to 10 for the rest of the host's addition.

So, in a nutshell, if you limit the number of hosts in a vSphere HA cluster, then this reduces the number of load balancing opportunities. However, if you exceed the number of ESXi hosts beyond what you actually need, then this will cause CPU strain on your vCenter Server because DRS performs load balancing calculations every 5 minutes for each cluster. So this needs to be balanced according to your requirements.

6

Storage Performance Design

In this chapter, we will cover the tasks related to storage performance design. You will learn the following aspects of storage performance design:

- Designing the host for a highly available and high-performance storage
- Designing a highly available and high-performance iSCSI SAN
- Designing a highly available and high-performance FC storage
- Performance impact of queuing on the storage array and host
- Factors that affect storage performance
- Using VAAI or VASA to boost storage performance
- Selecting the right VM disk type
- Monitoring command queuing
- Identifying a severely overloaded storage
- Setting up VVols
- Introduction to vSAN
- Health check for vSAN

Introduction

Storage can limit the performance of enterprise workloads. It is one of the most common bottlenecks in performance. You should know how to design a storage system, monitor a host's storage throughput, and troubleshoot problems that result in overloaded storage and slow storage performance.

There are many catalysts that affect storage performance. These are:

- Improper configuration of a storage device
- Storage protocols
- Queuing and LUN queue depth
- Load balancing across available storage
- VMFS configuration:
    - Characteristics of VMFS and RDMs
    - SCSI reservations
- Virtual disk types
- Placing more I/O demand than the storage is architected to deliver

Designing the host for a highly available and high-performance storage

VMware ESXi enables multiple hosts to share the same physical storage through its optimized storage stack and VMware VMFS-distributed filesystem. Centralized storage of VMs can be accomplished using VMFS and/or NFS. Centralized storage enables virtualization capabilities, such as VMware vMotion, VMware **Distributed Resource Scheduler** (**DRS**), and VMware High Availability.

Several factors have an effect on storage performance:

- Storage protocols
- Proper configuration of your host device and storage devices
- Load balancing across available storage processors
- Storage queues

Getting ready

To step through this recipe, you will need one or more running ESXi Servers, an HBA card, an NIC card, and a **Fibre Channel** (**FC**) or an iSCSI storage. No other prerequisites are required.

How to do it...

High availability requires at least two HBA connections to provide redundant paths to the SAN or storage system.

Follow these steps to design high-performing storage:

- Having redundant HBAs mitigate the single point of failure and also increase performance. If you use more than one single-port HBA, then it helps to isolate port and path failures and may provide performance benefits. However, multiport HBA provides component cost savings and efficient port management, which results in operational simplicity. If you have only a few available I/O bus slots in your host, then multiport HBAs are useful, but you also have to consider a single point of failure. A single port HBA failure would affect only one port.
- You should put HBAs on separate host buses for performance and availability. This may not be possible on hosts that have a single bus or a limited number of bus slots. However, the likelihood of a bus failure is arguably so small that it is negligible.
- You should always use an HBA that equals or exceeds the bandwidth of the storage network. This means you should not use 8 Gb/s or slower HBAs for connections to 16 Gb/s SANs. This is mainly because FC SANs reduce the speed of the network path to the HBA's speed or to the storage system's frontend port if directly connected. It may create a performance bottleneck when you focus on optimizing bandwidth.
- Always use the most current HBA firmware and driver from the manufacturer.
- You can use NICs and/or iSCSI HBA for iSCSI environments. The differences include cost, host CPU utilization, and features such as security.
- Use the correct cables--Cat 6a or better for 10 Gb/s Ethernet and OM2 or better for 8 Gb/s and 16 Gb/s Fibre Channel.
- Ethernet networks will autonegotiate down to the lowest common device speed; thus, a slower NIC may bottleneck the storage network's bandwidth. If you use TOE, then it offloads TCP packet segmentation, checksum calculations, and optionally, IPSec from the host CPU to themselves. So, if you use TOE, then your CPU cycles will be used exclusively for application processing.
- To avoid a single point of failure, you should use redundant NICs, iSCSI HBAs, and TOEs wherever possible. You can use either single or multiport NICs. Typically, each NIC or NIC port is configured to be on a separate subnet, and this applies to IP storage and not ESXi networking in general. If you have more than one NIC, then you should place them on separate host buses.

Note this may not be possible on smaller hosts that have a single bus or a limited number of bus slots, or when the onboard host NIC is used.

Designing a highly available and high-performance iSCSI SAN

The main reason why people use iSCSI SANs is that they handle longer transmission distances and are less expensive than Fiber Channel SANs.

iSCSI SAN's performance mainly gets affected by network congestion. Most of the time, network congestion is usually the result of an inappropriate network configuration or improper network settings.

For example, a common problem that we see is a switch in the data path into the storage system that is fragmenting frames. It happens most of the time for jumbo frames, and network oversubscription also plays a crucial role there. A slow switch somewhere in the path can reduce the overall speed of the network connection because of this slowest link.

Getting ready

To step through this recipe, you will need one or more running ESXi Servers, an iSCSI SAN, and a couple of VLANs provisioned on the network switch side. No other prerequisites are required.

How to do it...

Let's discuss how jumbo frames, pause frames, and TCP-delayed Ack can improve the iSCSI network bandwidth.

Jumbo frames

A standard Ethernet network uses a frame size of 1,500 bytes. Jumbo frames allow packets configurable up to 9,000 bytes in length.

To use jumbo frames, all the switches and routers in the network path of the iSCSI storage system must be configured for jumbo frames. The performance will degrade if every hop in the path cannot pass the jumbo frames without breaking them down (fragmenting them).

Pause frames

Pause frames should be disabled on the iSCSI network used for storage, considering the characteristic flow of the iSCSI traffic. They may cause a delay in traffic unrelated to a specific host port to the storage system links. This means if Host A could send a pause frame, it would cause the array to stop sending data to Host B and other hosts too, even though Host B has no trouble handling the desired data rate.

TCP-delayed Ack

TCP-delayed Ack delays an acknowledgment for a received packet for the ESXi host.

So certainly, TCP-delayed Ack should be disabled on the iSCSI network used for storage.

If you have this feature enabled, then an acknowledgment for a packet is delayed up to 0.5 seconds or until two packets are received. Sending an acknowledgment after 0.5 seconds is a sign that the network is congested. Because there was no communication between the host computer and the storage system during those 0.5 seconds, the host computer issues inquiry commands to the storage system for all LUNs based on the delayed Ack. When there is congestion in the network and recovery of dropped packets, delayed Ack can slow down the recovery considerably, resulting in further performance degradation.

To implement this workaround in ESXi 6.5, use vSphere Web Client to disable the delayed ACK, as follows:

1. Log in to vSphere Web Client and select the host.
2. Navigate to the **Configure** tab.
3. Select **Storage Adapters**.
4. Select the **iSCSI vmhba** option to be modified.

5. Modify the delayed Ack setting, using the option that best matches your site's needs, as follows:
    - Modify the delayed Ack setting on a discovery address (recommended) as follows:
        1. Click on **Dynamic Discovery** on the **Targets** tab.
        2. Click on the iSCSI server, then click on **Advanced**.
        3. Find the **DelayedAck** option.
        4. Uncheck **Enabled in the Inherited column**, then uncheck **Enabled in the Value column**.
        5. Click on **OK**.
    - Modify the delayed Ack setting on a specific target, as follows:
        1. Click on **Static Discovery** on the **Targets** tab.
        2. Click on the iSCSI server, then click on **Advanced**.
        3. Find the **DelayedAck** option.
        4. Uncheck **Enabled in the Inherited column**, then uncheck **Enabled in the Value column**.
        5. Click on **OK**.
    - Modify the delayed Ack setting globally, as follows:
        1. Click on the **Advanced Options** tab.
        2. Click on **Edit**.
        3. Find the **DelayedAck** option.
        4. Uncheck **Enabled in the Value column**.
        5. Click on **OK**.

6. Reboot the host.

How it works...

For better performance and security, you should use separate Ethernet networks to ensure redundant communications between hosts and storage systems. In addition, paths should be handled by separate switching if direct connections are not used.

You should use a dedicated storage network; otherwise, put the iSCSI traffic in either separated network LAN segments or a **virtual LAN (VLAN)**. VLAN allows more than one logical layer 2 networks to share the same physical network while maintaining separation of data and reducing the broadcast domain and collisions.

Ethernet connections to the storage management and the iSCSI ports should use separate subnets. Also, each iSCSI port on a **storage processor** (**SP**) should be on a different subnet. Place each port from SP-A on a different subnet. Place the corresponding ports from SP-B on the same set of subnets. The following IP address ranges are available for private networking:

- 192.168.0.0 through 192.168.255.255
- 10.0.0.0 through 10.255.255.255
- 172.16.0.0 through 172.31.255.255

For example, a typical configuration for the iSCSI ports on a storage system with two iSCSI ports per SP would be:

- **A0**: 172.18.48.10 (Subnet mask 255.255.255.0; Gateway 172.18.48.1)
- **A1**: 172.18.49.10 (Subnet mask 255.255.255.0; Gateway 172.18.49.1)
- **B0**: 172.18.48.11 (Subnet mask 255.255.255.0; Gateway 172.18.48.1)
- **B1**: 172.18.49.11 (Subnet mask 255.255.255.0; Gateway 172.18.49.1)

The preceding configuration could survive two errors: loss of routing on one network and loss of a single SP.

The following is how a simple network topology should be achieved:

- The iSCSI host and storage ports should be on dedicated switches or on a dedicated VLAN on shared switches.
- Network conditions and latency affects bandwidth and throughput rates.
- iSCSI performance is commonly affected by network contentions, routing, and so on. Look at your MTU configuration and if possible use jumbo frames.

Remember, if you use jumbo frames, an MTU of 9,000 must be set to the host, storage, and all the switches in between.

- Routed iSCSI traffic increases latency. In an ideal configuration, you should put the host and the iSCSI frontend port on the same subnet, and there should not be any gateways defined on the iSCSI ports. If they are not on the same subnet, users should define static routes.
- iSCSI-based storage system performance gets affected largely by latency in the storage network.

For a balanced bandwidth configuration, follow these points:

- A balanced bandwidth iSCSI configuration is when the host iSCSI initiator's bandwidth is greater than or equal to the bandwidth of its connected storage system's ports. One storage system port should be configured as active/active wherever supported.
- Network settings also affect performance. Follow these points to mitigate it:
    - Use jumbo frames
    - Disable pause frames
    - Disable the TCP-delayed Ack

Designing a highly available and high-performance FC storage

Availability refers to the storage system's ability to provide user access to data in the case of a hardware or software fault. Midrange systems are classified as highly available because they provide access to data without any single point of failure. However, the following configuration settings can improve performance under degraded mode scenarios.

Single **Disk Array Enclosure** (**DAE**) provisioning, which is a disk storage system that contains multiple disk drives, is the practice of restricting the placement of a RAID group within a single enclosure. This is sometimes called horizontal provisioning. Single DAE provisioning is the default method of provisioning RAID groups, and because of its convenience and high availability attributes, it is the most commonly used method. However, you may need to check the vendor configuration for this.

In multiple DAE provisioning, two or more enclosures are used. An example of multiple DAE provisioning requirements is where drives are selected from one or more additional DAEs because there are not enough drives remaining in one enclosure to fully configure the desired RAID group. Another example is SAS backend port balancing. The resulting configuration may or may not span backend ports depending on the storage system model and the drive to enclosure placement.

The following is a typical configuration for multiple DAEs connected to Storage Processors that reside in **Disk Processor Enclosure (DPE)**:

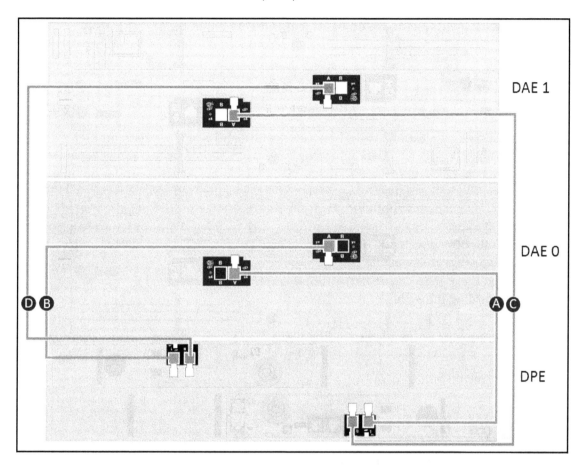

The preceding configuration is considered highly available because if path **A** fails due to a port, card, or cable failure, the storage processor is still able to talk to the disks in **DAE 0** using path **B**.

If vertical provisioning was used for compelling performance reasons, provision drives within RAID groups to take advantage of request forwarding. This is done as follows:

- **RAID 5**: At least two (2) drives per SAS backend port in the same DAE
- **RAID 6**: At least three (3) drives per backend port in the same DAE
- **RAID 1/0**: Both drives of a mirrored pair on separate backend ports

Getting ready

To step through this recipe, you will need a couple of ESXi Servers, an HBA card, and a Fibre Channel storage system. No other prerequisites are required.

How to do it...

Follow these guidelines to ensure high availability:

1. Maintain at least two paths between the host and storage system for high availability. Ideally, the cabling for these paths should be physically separated.
2. Make sure that these paths are handled by separate switching if it is not directly connecting hosts and storage systems. This includes redundant, separate HBAs and attachment to both the storage system's storage processors.
3. Make sure path management software, such as PowerPath, and dynamic multipathing software on hosts (to enable failover to alternate paths and load balancing) are available.
4. Run the `# esxcli storage core path` list to get detailed information regarding the paths.
5. Run `# esxcli storage core path list -d <naa.ID>` to list detailed information of the corresponding paths for a specific device.
6. Run `# esxcli storage nmp device list` to lists of LUN multipathing information.

How it works...

If you use EMC Storage, then all the LUNs bound within a virtual provisioning pool will have data loss because of a complete failure of a component pool RAID group.

The larger the number of private RAID groups within the pool, the bigger the failure domain would be.

The trade-off factors in choosing a RAID level are:

- Availability
- Performance
- Capacity utilization

RAID level data protection

There are three levels of data protection available for pools, using nothing but RAID levels; these three levels are as follows:

- **RAID 5** has good data protection capability and has excellent read performance. However, it does not have much write performance and that is due to parity calculations. As it uses parity, if one drive of a private RAID group fails, no data is lost. RAID 5 is appropriate for small- to medium-sized pools. If capacity utilization or performance is a priority and we have a solid design for data protection in place (backups, replication, hot spares, and so on), then having RAID level 5 is a sound decision:

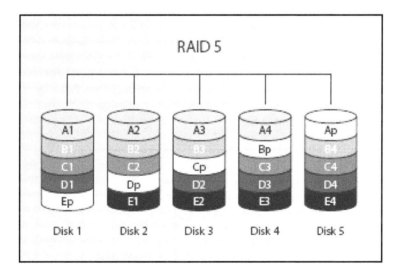

- **RAID 6** provides the highest data availability. It is similar to RAID 5; however, it uses striping with parity and uses two parity drives. With the second parity drive, up to two drives may fail in a private RAID group and result in no data loss. RAID 6 is appropriate for any size pool, including the largest possible. The downside is that you get less usable space than RAID 5. If the priority is absolutely on availability, then RAID 6 is recommended at the cost of performance. It is generally used for larger, slower disk drives:

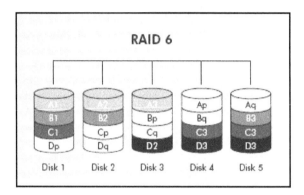

- **RAID 1/0** or **RAID 10** has high data availability. In this RAID, two drives are mirrored together and then striped. Because of this design, you can achieve high I/O rates (especially small random write I/Os). A single disk failure in a private RAID group results in no data loss. However, if a primary and its mirror fail together, then data will be lost. RAID 10 is inefficient as half the available space is taken by copies of the data. If you need faster storage performance, RAID 10 is a simple, relatively cheaper fix:

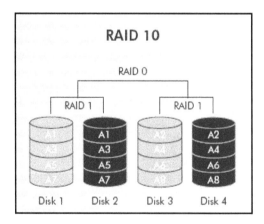

Performance impact of queuing on the storage array and host

There are several storage queues:

- Device driver queue
- Kernel queue
- Storage array queue

The device driver queue is used for low-level interaction with the storage device. This queue controls the number of active commands that can be on an LUN at the same time. This number is effectively the concurrency of the storage stack. If you set the device queue to 1, then each storage command becomes sequential.

The kernel queue is an overflow queue for the device driver queues. This queue enables features that optimize storage (it doesn't include them; they are built using the queue). These features include multipathing for failover and load balancing, prioritization of storage activities, which is based on VM and cluster shares, and optimizations to improve the efficiency of long sequential operations.

Here's an example of this: batching several incoming read requests and doing 1, 4-7, and 14 hashes together because they're all on nearby parts of the disk, then doing hash 2.

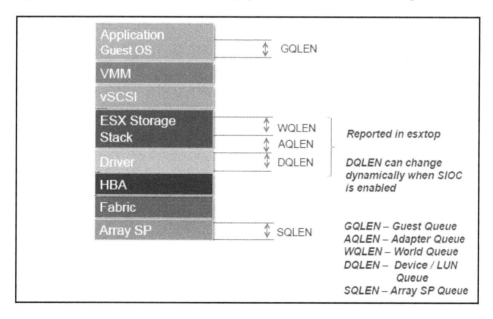

SCSI device drivers have a configurable parameter called the LUN queue depth that determines how many commands can be active at one time in a given LUN. The default value is 64. If the total number of outstanding commands of all VMs exceeds the LUN queue depth, the excess commands are queued in the ESXi kernel, which increases latency:

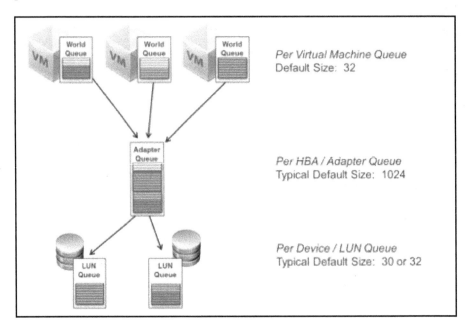

Getting ready

To step through this recipe, you will need one or more running ESXi Servers, a vCenter Server, and vSphere Web Client. No other prerequisites are required.

How to do it...

If the performance of your **hardware bus adapters** (**HBAs**) is unsatisfactory or your SAN storage processors are overutilized, you can adjust your ESXi hosts' maximum queue depth value. The maximum value refers to the queue depths reported for various paths to the LUN. When you lower this value, it throttles the ESXi host's throughput and alleviates SAN contention concerns if multiple hosts overutilize the storage and fill its command queue.

In a way, this solves the problem, but on the other hand, it just pushes the problem closer to the demand. Now, instead of the SP failing to deliver all of the I/O power that is required, it's the hosts that are failing to deliver I/O as fast as the VMs want. Tweaking queue depths is mostly just an easy thing to do that doesn't actually deliver better performance overall. You should consider rearchitecting the storage infrastructure to meet higher demand (for example, using faster drives, more spindles, or higher performing RAID); alternatively, you can investigate whether you can lower the demand by tuning the applications or moving VMs to other storage arrays.

To adjust the queue depth for an HBA, perform the following steps:

1. Verify which HBA module is currently loaded by entering one of these commands:

   - For QLogic:

     ```
     # esxcli system module list | grep qla
     ```

   - For Emulex:

     ```
     # esxcli system module list | grep lpfc
     ```

   - For Brocade:

     ```
     # esxcli system module list | grep bfa
     ```

2. Run one of these commands:

The examples show the QLogic qla2xxx and Emulex lpfc820 modules. Use the appropriate module based on the outcome of the previous step.

- For QLogic:

      # esxcli system module parameters set -p ql2xmaxqdepth=64 -
      m qla2xxx

- For Emulex:

      # esxcli system module parameters set -p
      lpfc0_lun_queue_depth=64 -m lpfc820

- For Brocade:

      # esxcli system module parameters set -p
      bfa_lun_queue_depth=64 -m bfa

3. In this case, the HBAs represented by `ql2x` and `lpfc0` have their LUN queue depths set to `64`. If all the Emulex cards on the host need to be updated, apply the global parameter `lpfc_lun_queue_depth` instead.

4. Reboot your host.

5. Run this command to confirm that your changes have been applied:

       # esxcli system module parameters list -m driver

   Here, the `driver` is your QLogic, Emulex, or Brocade adapter driver module, such as `lpfc820`, `qla2xxx`, or `bfa`.

The output appears similar to this:

```
Name                            Type Value Description
------------------------------- ---- ----- -----------------------------------
-
..... ql2xmaxqdepth              int   64    Maximum queue depth to
report for target devices.
.....
```

When one VM is active on an LUN, you only need to set the maximum queue depth. When multiple VMs are active on an LUN, the `Disk.SchedNumReqOutstanding` value is also relevant. The queue depth value, in this case, is equal to whichever value is the lowest of the two settings, namely adapter queue depth or `Disk.SchedNumReqOutstanding`:

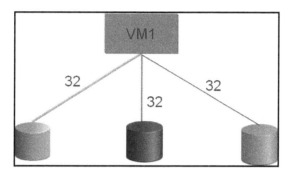

In this example, you have **32**. It is the sum total of all commands. And this is where you need `Disk.ShedNumReqOutstanding`:

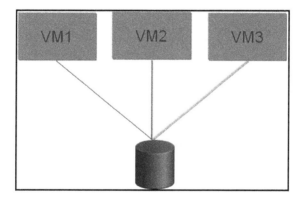

But you will still have only **32** Active if you do not change the LUN queue depth as well.

 For more information on `Disk.SchedNumReqOutstanding`, refer to `http://www.yellow-bricks.com/2011/06/23/disk-schednumreqoutstanding-the-story/`.

The following procedures only apply to the ESXi/ESX host that the parameters are changed on. You must make the same changes to all the other ESXi/ESX hosts that have the datastore/LUN presented to them. In vSphere 5.5 and above, the parameter is set per device.

To set the VMkernel limit per device, perform the following steps:

1. SSH to the ESXi host.
2. Run the following command to list all the devices:

```
# esxcli storage core device list
```

3. Find the device you want to change. It will start with naa.
4. Run the following command with the correct naa value:

```
# esxcli storage core device set -d naa.xxx -O value
```

5. The – is a capital **O**, not a zero. The value parameter is the number of outstanding disk requests.
6. Run the following command to see the value:

```
# esxcli storage core device list -d naa.xxx
```

7. The number of outstanding disk requests is shown as 'No of outstanding IOs with competing worlds:'.

How it works...

To understand the effect of queuing on the storage array, take the situation where the VMs on an ESXi host are generating a constant number of SCSI commands equal to the LUN queue depth, which means that the LUN queue buffer is constantly full (# commands in the LUN queue buffer = LUN queue depth). This is an example of the device driver queue. If multiple ESXi hosts share the same LUN, SCSI commands to that LUN from all the hosts are processed by the storage processor on the storage array, which means multiple commands begin queuing up, resulting in high latencies.

When you use a shared LUN to place all your VMs, then the total number of outstanding commands permitted from all VMs on a host to that LUN is governed by the Maximum Outstanding Disk Requests configuration parameter, which is set at the host level.

If you want to reduce latency, make sure that the sum of the active commands in all VMs does not consistently exceed the LUN queue depth. If you are using vSphere **Storage I/O Control** (**SIOC**), then that takes care of any manual queue depth configuration. However, SIOC is only available with the vSphere Enterprise Plus license. SIOC has been covered in Chapter 4, *DRS, SDRS, and Resource Control Design* already.

However, if you want to know the calculation of queue depth, note that it is the result of a combination of a number of host paths and the execution throttle value; the number of presented LUNs through the host port must be less than the target port's queue depth. This means it is $T = P * q * L$ where:

T = Target port queue depth

P = Paths connected to the target port

Q = Queue depth

L = Number of LUNs presented to the host through this port

However, in a vSphere infrastructure, multiple ESXi hosts communicate with the storage port; therefore, the queue depth should be calculated by the following formula:

$T = ESX\ Host\ 1\ (P * Q * L) + ESX\ Host\ 2\ (P * Q * L) \ldots.. + ESX\ Host\ n\ (P * Q * L)$

Factors that affect storage performance

Storage performance is affected by many factors; however, some of them are really important. These are:

- VMFS partition alignment
- Spanned VMFS volumes
- SCSI reservation

Getting ready

To step through this recipe, you will need one or more running ESXi Servers, a vCenter Server, and vSphere Web Client. No other prerequisites are required.

How to do it...

The first thing you have to counter is the VMFS partition alignment, as follows:

1. The alignment of your VMFS partitions can affect performance, and it happens only if you create the datastore using CLI since vSphere Web Client is not impacted by misalignment. Like other disk-based file systems, VMFS suffers a penalty when the partition is unaligned. Using VMware vSphere Web Client to create VMFS datastores avoids this problem because it automatically aligns the datastores along the 1 MB boundary:

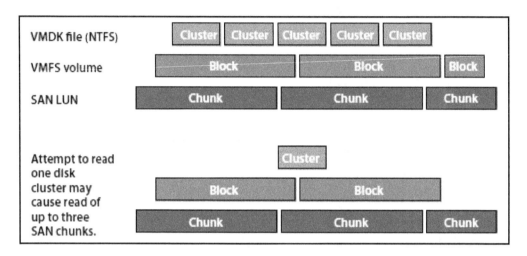

If you are using Windows 2008 or later in your guest OS, then it automatically aligns partitions using a default starting offset of 1 MB; however, prior to Windows 2008, manual alignment is required using `Diskpart.exe` (or `diskpar.exe`).

To manually align your VMFS partitions, check your storage vendor's recommendations for the partition starting block. If your storage vendor makes no specific recommendation, use a starting block that is a multiple of 8 KB.

 To align your VMFS filesystem, refer to `http://www.vmware.com/pdf/esx 3_partition_align.pdf`.

Once you have aligned your VMFS volume and guest OS disk, your alignment will look like this:

2. Before performing an alignment, carefully evaluate the performance effect of the unaligned VMFS partition on your particular workload. The degree of improvement through alignment is highly dependent on workloads and array types. You might want to refer to the alignment recommendations from your array vendor for further information:

   If a VMFS3 partition was created using an earlier version of ESXi that aligned along the 64 KB boundary and that filesystem is then upgraded to VMFS5, it will retain its 64 KB alignment. 1 MB alignment can be obtained by deleting the partition and recreating it using vSphere Client and an ESXi host.

3. Now you need to take care of spanned VMFS volumes:

   A spanned VMFS volume includes multiple extents (part or an entire LUN). Spanning is a good feature to use if you need to add more storage to a VMFS volume while it is in use. Predicting performance with spanned volumes is not straightforward because the user does not have control over how the data from the various VMs is laid out on the different LUNs that form the spanned VMFS volume.

For example, consider a spanned VMFS volume with two 100 GB LUNs. Two VMs are on this spanned VMFS and the sum total of their sizes is 150 GB. The user cannot determine the contents of each LUN in the spanned volume directly. Hence, determining the performance properties of this configuration is not straightforward.

Mixing storage devices of different performance characteristics on the same spanned volume could cause an imbalance in VM performance. This imbalance might occur if a VM's blocks are allocated across device boundaries, and each device might have a different queue depth.

4. Last, but not least part is SCSI reservation:

VMFS is a clustered filesystem and uses SCSI reservations as part of its distributed locking algorithms. Administrative operations, such as creating or deleting a virtual disk, extending a VMFS volume, or creating or deleting snapshots, result in metadata updates to the filesystem using locks and thus result in SCSI reservations. A reservation causes the LUN to be available exclusively to a single ESXi host for a brief period of time. Although an acceptable practice is to perform a limited number of administrative tasks during peak hours, postponing major maintenance to off-peak hours in order to minimize the effect on the VM performance is better.

The impact of SCSI reservations depends on the number and nature of storage or VMFS administrative tasks being performed, as follows:

- The longer an administrative task runs (for example, creating a VM with a larger disk or cloning from a template that resides on a slow NFS share), the longer the VMs are affected. Also, the time to reserve and release an LUN is highly hardware-dependent and vendor-dependent.
- Running administrative tasks from a particular ESXi host does not have much effect on the I/O-intensive VMs running on the same ESXi host.

SCSI reservation conflicts used to be a big problem in a lot of real cases in ESX 2.x days, but it is not a problem in the recent releases of VMware vSphere ESXi, especially with VMFS5 (atomic test and set, opportunistic locking/preallocating sectors in metadata). Also, VAAI plays a major role there. We have countered VAAI in a different recipe in this chapter.

Using VAAI or VASA to boost storage performance

Various storage functions, such as cloning and snapshots, are performed more efficiently by the storage array (target) than by a host (initiator). In a virtualized environment, since virtual disks are files on VMFS and disk, arrays cannot interpret the VMFS on-disk data layout; you cannot leverage hardware functions on a per-VM or per virtual disk (file) basis.

vStorage APIs for Array Integration (**VAAI**) are a set of new protocol interfaces between ESXi and storage arrays and new application programming interfaces in VMkernel. Using a small set of primitives (fundamental operations) that can be issued to the array using these interfaces, ESXi is able to improve its offering of storage services.

The fundamental operations are:

- **Atomic test & set** (**ATS**)--new locking mechanism
- Clone blocks/full copy/XCOPY
- Zero blocks/write same

The goal of VAAI is to help storage vendors provide hardware assistance to speed up VMware I/O operations that are more efficiently accomplished in the storage hardware. VAAI plugins can improve the performance of data transfer and are transparent to the end user.

Atomic test and set

ATS is a mechanism to modify a disk sector to improve the performance of the ESXi host when doing metadata updates.

Clone blocks/full copy/XCOPY

This does a full copy of blocks and the ESXi host is guaranteed to have full space access to the blocks. Default offloaded clone size is 4 MB.

Zero blocks/write same

This basically writes zeroes. This will address the issue of time falling behind in a VM when the guest operating system writes to the previously unwritten regions of its virtual disk. This primitive will improve your MSCS in virtualization environment solutions where we need to zero out the virtual disk. Default zeroing size is 1 MB.

Getting ready

To step through this recipe, you will need one or more running ESXi servers, a vCenter Server, and vSphere Web Client. You also need a VAAI-supported storage array connected to these ESXi Servers and an SSH client (PuTTY). No other prerequisites are required.

How to do it...

VAAI is a storage-compatible feature. So first check with your vendor whether your storage is VAAI supported or look at VMware HCL for that.

However, you also need to check the vSphere side to see if it is enabled there as well. By default, it is enabled on the ESXi host:

1. Open VMware vSphere Web Client.
2. In the **Inventory** pane, navigate to the ESXi host.
3. Click on the **Configure** tab.
4. Under **System**, click on **Advanced System Settings**.
5. Search for **DataMover.Hardware**.
6. Check the value of the **DataMover.HardwareAcceleratedMove** setting and that should be **1**.

7. Check the value of the **DataMover.HardwareAcceleratedInit** setting and that should be **1**:

8. Click on **Edit** to change these values if required.
9. Search for **VMFS3.Hardware.**

10. Check the value of the **VMFS3.HardwareAcceleratedLocking** setting and that should be 1:

11. Click on **Edit** to change these values if required.
12. Repeat this process for all the ESXi hosts connected to the storage.
13. If you are using VAAI-capable/supported storage, then you can see this status in vSphere Client by following the proceeding steps:
    1. Log in to vCenter Web Client.
    2. Select **Hosts and Clusters** on the home screen.
    3. Navigate to an ESXI host.
    4. Click on the **Configure** tab.
    5. Navigate to **Datastores** in the **Storage** section.
    6. Check **Hardware Acceleration Status**. It should be **Supported**. If the Hardware Acceleration column is not shown, right-click on the column header, select **show/hide columns**, then check **Hardware Acceleration**:

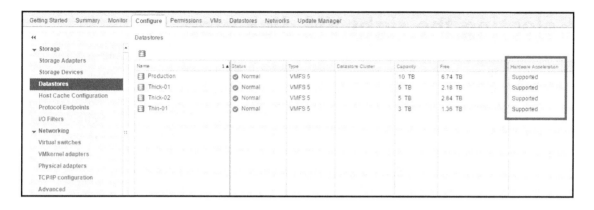

How it works…

The VMkernel core data mover has traditionally done software data movement. Now, with the hardware primitives in place, the data mover can use these primitives to offload certain operations to the array. When a data movement operation is invoked and the corresponding hardware offload operation is enabled, the data mover will first attempt to use the hardware offload. If the hardware offload operation fails, the data mover will fall back to the traditional software method of data movement.

If using the hardware offload does succeed, the hardware data movement should perform significantly better than the software data movement. It should consume fewer CPU cycles and less bandwidth on the fabric. Improvements in performance can be observed by timing operations that use these primitives and `esxtop` to track values such as CMDS/s, READS/s, WRITES/s, MBREAD/s, and MBWRTN/s of storage adapters during the operation.

VMFS uses the data mover to handle certain data operations. One application that invokes these operations is `disklib`. It is in turn used by utilities such as `vmkfstools` and `hostd` to manipulate the VM disks.

Now you may ask what those operations are where it will be leveraged. The following functionality leverages VMFS data movement services:

- Creating a full clone of a VM
- Importing a VMDK using `vmkfstools -i`
- Importing a VM or provisioning a VM of a VM template in vSphere Client
- Creating `eagerzeroedthick` disks via `vmkfstools` or by provisioning a VM
- Storage VMotion of a VM
- Committing redo logs or when snapshots and linked, clones are deleted

Selecting the right VM disk type

When you create a virtual disk, you can specify disk properties, such as size, format, clustering features, and more. However, the most important property is the format.

The type of virtual disk used by your VM can have an effect on the I/O performance; thus, it plays a vital role in maintaining disk performance. The type of disks that are available today are:

- Thick provision eager zeroed
- Thick provision lazy zeroed
- Thin provision

You need to carefully evaluate the workload and the performance factors of each disk before you choose one.

Getting ready

To step through this recipe, you will need one or more running ESXi Servers, a vCenter Server, and vSphere Web Client. No other prerequisites are required.

How to do it...

When you create a disk inside a VM, you have the option to select the type of disk, as follows:

1. Open up vSphere Web Client and log in to the vCenter Server.
2. Select **Hosts and Clusters** on the **Home** screen.
3. Navigate to the ESXi host where you want to create a new VM.
4. Right-click on the host and select **New Virtual Machine**.
5. Select **Create a new virtual machine** and click on **Next**.
6. Specify the name of the VM and the folder where it should be created. Click on **Next**.
7. Select **compute resource** and click on **Next**.
8. Select the datastore you want to put it in and click on **Next**.

9. Select the compatibility level (which sets the hardware version) and click on **Next**.

10. Select the guest OS's family and version. Click on **Next**.

11. Edit **CPU**, **Memory**, **Network**, and **SCSI controller**.

12. In the **New Hard Disk** section, select the size of the VM hard disk.

13. At this point, you have to select one of the mentioned types of disk. By default, **Thick Provision Lazy Zeroed** is selected. However, you have the option to select any one of the three types:

14. Once you have customized the hardware, click on **Next**.

15. Review the configuration and click on **Finish**.

How it works...

Let's look at the different types of disks:

- **Eager zeroed thick**: Disk space is allocated and zeroed out at the time of creation. Although this extends the time it takes to create the disk, using this disk type results in more consistent performance, even the first time we write to each block. The primary use of this disk type is for quorum drives in an MSCS cluster. You can create eager zeroed thick disks on the Command Prompt with vmkfstools. As per VMware, there is no statistical difference between eager or lazy once all the blocks have been zeroed. It is the zeroing process that creates an inconsistent performance on the lazy filesystem, and this is where eager benefits.

- **Lazy zeroed thick**: Disk space is allocated at the time of creation, but each block is zeroed only on the first write. This disk type results in shorter creation time but reduced performance the first time a block is written to the disk. Subsequent writes, however, have the same performance as an eager zeroed thick disk. This disk type is the default type used to create virtual disks using vSphere Client and is good for most cases.

- **Thin**: Disk space is allocated and zeroed upon demand, instead of upon creation. Using this disk type results in a shorter creation time but reduced performance the first time a block is written to the disk. Subsequent writes have the same performance as an eager zeroed thick disk. Use this disk type when space usage is the main concern of all types of applications.

> Thin and lazy zeroed thick disks deliver virtually the same performance. It's the writing zeros, not the allocation, that is expensive. Only eager zeroed provides any real performance improvement. And even that is usually not tremendous. There's a really good white paper on this at `http://www.vmware.com/pdf/vsp_4_thinprov_perf.pdf`.

Monitoring command queuing

There are metrics for monitoring the number of active `disk` commands and the number of `disk` commands that are queued. These metrics provide information about your disk performance. They are often used to further interpret the latency values that you might be observing.

The number of active commands: This metric represents the number of I/O operations that are currently active. This includes operations for which the host is processing. This metric can serve as a quick view of storage activity. If the value of this metric is close to or zero, the storage subsystem is not used. If the value is a non-zero number, sustained over time, then constant interaction with the storage subsystem takes place.

The number of commands queued: This metric represents the number of I/O operations that require processing but have not yet been addressed. Commands are queued and waiting to be managed by the kernel when the driver's active command buffer is full. Occasionally, a queue will form and result in a small, non-zero value for **QUED**. However, any significant average of queued commands means that the storage hardware is unable to keep up with the host's needs.

Getting ready

To step through this recipe, you will need one or more running ESXi Servers, a couple of storage I/O-hungry VMs, a vCenter Server, and vSphere Web Client, and an SSH Client (PuTTY). No other prerequisites are required.

How to do it...

To monitor command queuing in VMkernel, follow these steps:

1. Open up the SSH Client and log in to ESXi.
2. Run the `esxtop` command there.
3. On the screen, select *D* to monitor the adapter's queue.
4. Check the `KAVG/cmd` column and monitor the value there:

```
 10.          - PuTTY

10:00:37am up 25 days 19:57, 494 worlds, 17 VMs, 52 vCPUs; CPU load average: 0.19, 0.18, 0.17

ADAPTR PATH            NPTH   CMDS/s  READS/s WRITES/s MBREAD/s MBWRTN/s DAVG/cmd KAVG/cmd GAVG/cmd QAVG/cmd
  vmhba0  -               1     0.38     0.38     0.00     0.00     0.00     0.22     0.02     0.25     0.00
vmhba32 -               0     0.00     0.00     0.00     0.00     0.00     0.00     0.00     0.00     0.00
vmhba33 -               0     0.00     0.00     0.00     0.00     0.00     0.00     0.00     0.00     0.00
vmhba34 -               0     0.00     0.00     0.00     0.00     0.00     0.00     0.00     0.00     0.00
vmhba35 -               0     0.00     0.00     0.00     0.00     0.00     0.00     0.00     0.00     0.00
vmhba36 -               0     0.00     0.00     0.00     0.00     0.00     0.00     0.00     0.00     0.00
```

To monitor queuing at the device level, follow these steps:

5. Open up the SSH Client and log in to the ESXi.
6. Run the `esxtop` command there.
7. On the screen, select *U* to monitor the disk device's queue.
8. Check the `ACTV` and `QUED` columns and monitor the value there:

How it works...

Here is an example of monitoring the kernel latency value, that is, `KAVG/cmd`. This value is being monitored for the `vmhba0` device. In the first `resxtop` screen, the kernel latency value is `0.02` milliseconds (average per I/O command in the monitoring period). This is a good value because it is nearly zero.

In the second **resxtop** screen (type *U* in the window), where we have the NFS datastore attached to the ESXi host, we can see there are 18 active I/Os (`ACTV`) and 0 being queued (`QUED`). This means that there are some active I/Os, but queuing is not happening at the VMkernel level.

Queuing happens if there is excessive I/O on the device and the LUN queue depth setting is not sufficient. The default LUN queue depth is 64. However, if there are too many (more than 64) to handle simultaneously, the device will get bottlenecked to only 64 outstanding I/Os at a time. To resolve this, you would change the queue depth of the device driver.

Also, look at what `esxtop` vCenter for device latency per I/O command. This is the average delay in milliseconds per I/O from the time an ESXi host sends the command out until the time the host hears back that the array has completed the I/O.

Identifying a severely overloaded storage

When storage is severely overloaded, commands are aborted because the storage subsystem takes far too long to respond to the commands. The storage subsystem doesn't respond within an acceptable amount of time, as defined by the guest operating system or application. Aborted commands are a sign that the storage hardware is overloaded and unable to handle the requests in line with the host's expectations.

The number of aborted commands can be monitored using either vSphere Web Client or resxtop, as follows:

- From vSphere Web Client, monitor the `disk` command aborts
- From esxtop, monitor ABRTS/s

Getting ready

To step through this recipe, you will need one or more running ESXi Servers, a vCenter Server, vSphere Web Client, and an SSH Client (such as PuTTY). No other prerequisites are required.

How to do it...

To monitor the `disk` command aborts using vSphere Client, follow these steps:

1. Open up vSphere Web Client.
2. Log in to the vCenter Server.
3. Navigate to the **Hosts and Clusters** section.
4. Select the host where you want to monitor the disk aborts.
5. Now click on the **Monitor** tab, then the **Performance** tab.
6. Select **Advanced** and **Switch to Disk** from the drop-down menu window.
7. Click on **Chart Options** and select the **Commands aborted** counter.
8. Click on **OK**, and now you can see the metric in the performance chart.

To monitor the `disk` command aborts using an SSH client such as PuTTY, follow these steps:

1. Open up SSH client and log in to the ESXi Server.
2. Run `esxtop` there.
3. For the disk device error, type *U*.
4. Now type *F* to change the settings and type *1* to select **Error Stats**. Hit *Enter* to return.

Once this is done, you can see the `ABRTS/s` field there. Monitor this field for the `disk` command aborts:

This counter tracks the SCSI aborts. Aborts generally occur because the array is taking far too long to respond to commands.

Setting up VVols

Virtual Volumes (**VVols**) were introduced in vSphere 6.0. Normally, when using iSCSI, NFS, or Fibre Channel storage, the VMware administrator creates a small number of large LUNs that hold many VMs. Administrators are forced to manage these datastores and decide which VMs reside in them. Policy-based metrics, such as QoS, can only be applied at the datastore level so all the VMs in the datastore get the same service level. Furthermore, LUNs and datastore sizes are over-provisioned, which wastes space on the storage array. Creating a new datastore often involves both the storage administrator to create the LUN and the VMware administrator to turn that LUN into a datastore.

All of these issues are solved by VVols. When you create a VM and target VVol storage, each component of the VM that requires storage is given a VVol on the storage array. vCenter and the storage array use a VASA provider in order to communicate.

On the storage array, compatibility profiles are created and tagged by the storage administrator. These tags can be used by the VMware administrator to place the VM on the correct storage.

Getting ready

To step through this recipe, you will need one or more running ESXi Servers, a vCenter Server, vSphere Web Client, and a VVol-compliant storage array. No other prerequisites are required.

How to do it...

In this recipe, we will be connecting vSphere to an EMC Unity. The first step is to add the storage system as a VASA provider:

1. Open up vSphere Web Client.
2. Log in to the vCenter Server.
3. Click on **vCenter Server**, then go to the **Configure** tab.
4. Under the **More** section, click on **Storage Providers**.
5. Click on **Register a new storage provider**.
6. Enter the storage details and click on **OK**:

7. If successful, the storage provider will appear as a storage provider.

8. On the storage array, create the protocol endpoint, the storage container(s). Be sure to allow your ESXi host access to the storage container.

9. In vCenter, go to the **Hosts and Clusters** section, select a host, then go to the **Datastores** tab.

10. Click on **Create a New Datastore**.

11. Select a location and click on **Next**.

12. For the type, select **VVol** and click on **Next**.

13. The next screen should display the storage container you created on the storage array. Enter a datastore name and click on **Next** and then **Finish**:

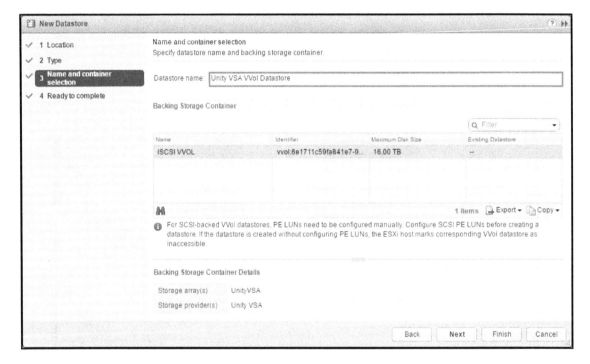

14. Repeat steps 9-13 on other hosts.

15. Create a VM and select the **VVol** datastore as the storage location.

In the following screenshot, you can see the results of creating a VM called **VM on a VVol** with two 40 GB hard disks. On Unity VSA, we can see that this caused three files to be created--one configuration file and two hard disk files:

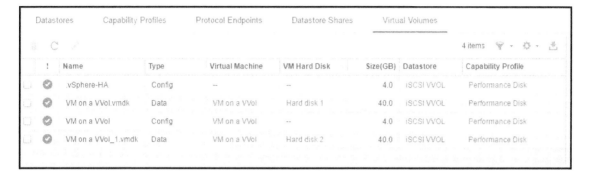

!	Name	Type	Virtual Machine	VM Hard Disk	Size(GB)	Datastore	Capability Profile
	.vSphere-HA	Config	--	--	4.0	iSCSI VVOL	Performance Disk
	VM on a VVol.vmdk	Data	VM on a VVol	Hard disk 1	40.0	iSCSI VVOL	Performance Disk
	VM on a VVol	Config	VM on a VVol	--	4.0	iSCSI VVOL	Performance Disk
	VM on a VVol_1.vmdk	Data	VM on a VVol	Hard disk 2	40.0	iSCSI VVOL	Performance Disk

Introduction to vSAN

VMware **Virtual Storage Area Network** (vSAN), was introduced in vSphere 5.5. vSAN is VMware's solution for customers that want software-defined, hyper-converged storage. By installing local drives in your ESXi hosts and purchasing vSAN licensing, you can create a highly available VMware solution that doesn't rely on an external storage array.

vSAN is a very interesting technology and would require a dedicated book to fully explore, so we will just cover the basics here. Hardware-wise, vSAN requires at least one flash disk for caching and at least one storage disk per ESXi host. In a hybrid vSAN, the storage disk will be a spinning disk. In an all flash vSAN, the storage disk will be a flash disk.

vSAN also requires an independent vSAN license, either Standard, Advanced, or Enterprise. If you want to run vSAN with deduplication, compression, and erasure coding, you must have an Advanced or Enterprise license.

Once you have configured vSAN, you will have a datastore presented to each ESXi host in the cluster. The capacity for this datastore comes from the sum of all the storage disks on all ESXi hosts in the vSAN cluster. When you provision a VM and it is stored on the vSAN datastore, you assign it a storage policy that determines its level of protection. If your storage policy is set such that the VM can tolerate one host failure, the VM disks will be spread across the storage disks of two ESXi hosts. The result of this is that if your VM is 100 GB in size, it will actually take up 200 GB of space on your vSAN.

vSAN data is passed between ESXi hosts using a dedicated VMkernel that runs the vSAN service. It is strongly recommended that you have 10 G network for hybrid workloads. For all flash vSANs, a 10 G network is required. ESXi hosts that do not have vSAN disks can still access the vSAN datastore as long as they have a vSAN VMkernel configured and have a vSAN license.

 To learn more about vSAN, visit Duncan Epping's fantastic blog at `http://ww w.yellow-bricks.com/virtual-san/` or VMware's vSAN product page at `ht tp://www.vmware.com/products/virtual-san.html`.

Getting ready

To step through this recipe, you will need three or more running ESXi Servers (licensed with VSAN) in a cluster that each have one available flash drive and at least one other available disk. You will also need a vCenter Server and vSphere Web Client. No other prerequisites are required.

How to do it...

First, configure the vSAN network:

1. Open up vSphere Web Client.
2. Log in to the vCenter Server.
3. Click on the ESXi host where you want to add the vSAN network and go to the **Configure** tab, then click on **VMkernel adapters** under **Networking.**
4. Click on **Add host networking**.
5. Select **VMkernel Network Adapter** and click on **Next**.
6. You can either select an existing vSwitch or create a new vSwitch. We will select an existing vSwitch. Click **on Next**.
7. Enter a network label, a VLAN, and the Virtual SAN service. Click on **Next**.
8. Enter an IP address for VMkernel or use DHCP. Click on **Next**, then on **Finish**.
9. Repeat steps 3-8 on all ESXi hosts.

In this screenshot, we have **VMkernel port** called **vSAN network** on **vSwitch1** that has an IP address and is connected to one 1 G port:

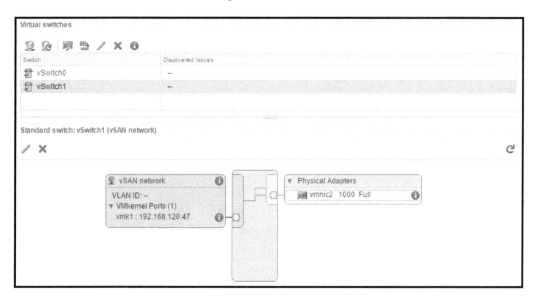

The next step is to enable vSAN and configure the drives. Before we can do this, we must temporarily disable vSphere HA. We will turn to vSphere HA when we are done configuring vSAN:

1. In the **Hosts and Clusters** view, click on **your cluster**, then on the **Configure** tab and then on **vSphere Availability** under **Services**.
2. Click on **Edit** in the top-right corner.
3. Uncheck **Turn ON** vSphere HA, then click on **OK**.
4. In the **Hosts and Clusters** view, click on **your cluster**, then on the **Configure** tab, and then on **General** under **Virtual SAN**.
5. Click on **Configure** in the top-right corner.
6. If you want vSAN to automatically claim all the unused disks on your ESXi host, set **Add disks to storage** to **Automatic**. We will use **Manual**.
7. If you have an all flash vSAN, you can enable deduplication and compression.
8. Click on **Next**.
9. In the **Network validation** screen, all the hosts should show **vSAN** enabled as **Yes**. Click on **Next**.
10. In the **Claim disks** screen, assign your cache tier disks and your storage tier disks. Click on **next**, then on **Finish**.

11. Give the system a few minutes to apply the configuration.

12. Click on **Disk Management** under **Virtual SAN** to see the hosts and their disk configurations. In this example, we have three hosts, and each host has one 223 GB cache drive and three 5.46 TB storage drives:

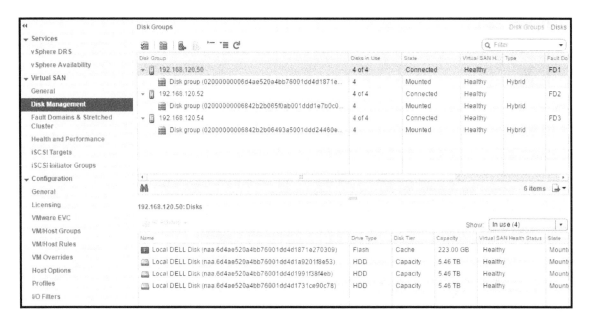

13. In the **Hosts and Clusters** view, click on **your cluster**, then on the **Configure** tab, and then on **vSphere Availability** under **Services**.

14. Click on **Edit** in the top-right corner.

15. Check **Turn ON vSphere HA** then click **OK**.

The preceding steps will automatically create a vSAN datastore called **vsanDatastore** that is visible on the **Storage** tab. In this example, we have three hosts each with three disks at 5.46 TB. So, 3*3*5.46 = our **vsanDatastore** capacity:

If we place a VM on our new **vsanDatastore** using the default storage policy of "Number of failures to tolerate = 1," then vSphere will place the VMDK file on one of the hosts' disks and a copy of the VMDK on another host's disks. We can see this by clicking on the cluster, then going to the **Monitor** tab and then the **Virtual SAN** tab. If we expand our VM that is on **vsanDatastore** and click on the hard disk, vSphere will create **RAID 1** (mirror) of the data on two hosts with the third host acting as the witness:

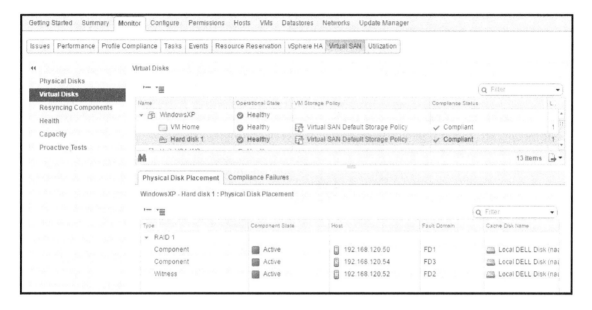

Health check for vSAN

If you run vSAN in your production environment, it will be a mission-critical component and thus must be monitored closely. Fortunately, VMware has some tools to help you validate your configuration. The health check is only compatible with vSAN version 6.0 and higher. We will explore the following three health check items:

- Installing the health check plug on the vCenter server.
- Checking the health of the vSAN configuration.
- Running the vSAN Proactive tests.

Getting ready

To step through this recipe, you will need three or more running ESXi Servers in a cluster that has vSAN enabled. You will also need a vCenter Server and vSphere Web Client. No other prerequisites are required.

How to do it…

First, install the vCenter health check plugin on your vCenter server. For this installation, we assume that you are running the vCenter appliance. We will install the plugin on the vCenter server, then enable the plugin that will require a reboot of all hosts. If DRS is enabled on your cluster, a rolling reboot of the hosts will be performed:

1. Log in to https://www.vmware.com/download.
2. Click on **Download Product** in the **VMware vSAN** section.
3. Select your version of vSAN from the drop-down menu.
4. Go to the **Drivers & Tools** tab, then expand the VMware Virtual SAN Tools, **Plug-ins and Appliances** section.
5. Click on **Go to downloads** for the VMware Virtual SAN Health Check Plugin item.
6. Download the .rpm file for the health check plugin.
7. Upload this file to the appliance.
8. From the vCenter appliance command line, install the RPM file with the following command. Change the name of the RPM file to match the file you downloaded:

```
# rpm -Uvh VMware-vsan-health-6.0.1-2937162.x86_64.rpm
```

9. Now, run the post-installation script to restart vCenter services. Note that this will disrupt all the current vCenter sessions:

```
# /usr/lib/vmware-vpx/vsan-health/health-rpm-post-install.sh
```

10. Once the post-installation script is done, go to **Web Client**, then the **Hosts and Clusters** view and click on your cluster. Go to the **Configure** tab, then **Health and Performance** under **Virtual SAN**.

11. Click on **Enable** in the top-right corner and then on **OK** to enable the health service.

12. The process deploys a VIB file to each one of your ESXi hosts. The ESXi hosts need to be restarted in order to use the health check plugin. If DRS is enabled, a rolling reboot of your hosts will be performed. If DRS is disabled, you will need to perform the reboots manually.

13. Once all the hosts have been restarted, go back to **Health and Performance** under **Virtual SAN**.

14. The **Health service** should be **Enabled**:

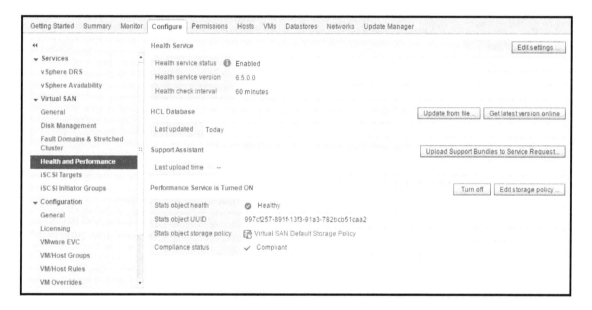

It is a good idea to click on **Update from file...** in the **HCL Database** section. This will update the hardware compatibility list that the health check runs against.

Now that the health check components are installed, let's run a health check:

1. In the **Hosts and Clusters** view of vSphere Web Client, click on your cluster.
2. Go to the **Monitor** tab, then the **Virtual SAN** subtab and click on **Health**.
3. Click on the **Retest** button to refresh the test results.
4. Ideally, all the tests should pass:

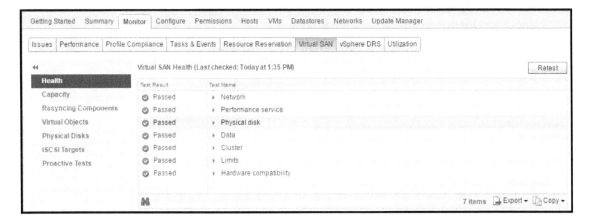

5. If there are any tests that warnings or have failed, expand that test name and click on the test with an issue. There will be a description of the problem and an **Ask VMware** button that will take you to a VMware KB page that explains the health check in detail and why it might report a warning or error.

The last health-related item we are going to look at is running the vSAN Proactive tests:

1. In the **Hosts and Clusters** view of vSphere Web Client, click on **your cluster**.
2. Go to the **Monitor** tab, then the **Virtual SAN** subtab and click on **Proactive tests**.
3. There are three tests: **VM creation test**, **Multicast performance test**, and **Storage performance test**.
4. For each test, click on it and click on the green play button. The results should look similar to this:

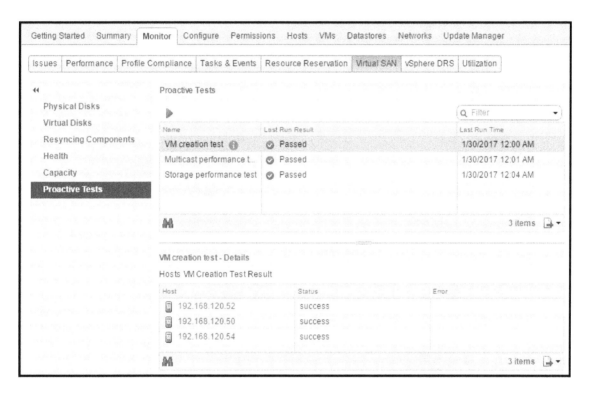

7
Designing vCenter on Windows for Best Performance

In this chapter, we will cover the tasks related to designing vCenter on Windows for best performance. You will learn the following aspects of vCenter design:

- Things to bear in mind while designing the vCenter platform
- Deploying Platform Services Controller
- Deploying the vCenter server components
- Designing vCenter server for redundancy
- Designing a highly available vCenter database
- vCenter database size and location affects performance
- Using vSphere 6.x Certificate Manager for certificates
- Designing vCenter server for Auto Deploy

Introduction

vCenter server is vSphere's virtualization platform that provides the necessary management framework to deliver the needs of today's virtualization administrators. So you need to be very careful about taking decisions while designing your vCenter and management platform, which will have performance factors integrated as well. vCenter can be installed in two ways: on top of a Windows server or as a virtual appliance.

In this chapter, we will talk about vCenter running on Windows. In vSphere 6.x, there are two components to the vCenter server installation: vCenter server itself and **Platform Services Controller** (**PSC**). For small vSphere installations, both the components can be installed on the same VM. For large-scale deployments, vCenter components will be installed on a VM and PSC will be installed on one or more different VMs. For these recipes, we will install PSC on its own VM.

Things to bear in mind while designing the vCenter platform

There are three main decisions you need to make when designing your vCenter system.

The first decision is whether you are going to install vCenter on Windows or install **vCenter server Appliance** (**VCSA**). In vSphere Version 6.5, VCSA's capabilities are identical to the Windows version. Unlike the previous version, the 6.5 VCSA supports Update Manager. VCSA also supports the same number of ESXi hosts and VMs using its embedded PostgreSQL database. If you decide to use VCSA, you can skip this chapter and go to Chapter 8, *Designing VCSA for Best Performance*; if you want to install vCenter on Windows, read on.

The second decision is whether you are going to install the vCenter server on physical or virtual hardware. If you are going to install VCSA, the decision is already made—your vCenter will be virtual. One could argue that installing vCenter on a VM that runs on the same hardware that it is managing could be an issue. If the VMware host that runs vCenter fails, then the vCenter VM fails too. However, in VMware vSphere, you can easily mitigate that risk by putting your vCenter server on a vSphere HA Cluster. If the VMware host that runs the vCenter VM fails, then HA will restart the vCenter VM on another host. Running vCenter server on a VM has several benefits as well:

- It can be easily backed up and restored as a whole unit, unlike a physical machine.
- It can be moved to another ESXi host using vMotion for planned maintenance.
- It can be load balanced across hosts using the vSphere Distributed Resource Scheduler cluster.
- It can also be protected using vSphere HA.
- It can be protected more easily for disaster recovery, using SRM or other ways of replicating and failing over to the recovery site.
- For every other reason, you're already using VMs over physical machines.

The third decision you need to make is whether you are going to run the embedded PostgreSQL database or use an external database. If you are running VCSA, the only database option is the embedded PostgreSQL database. If you run vCenter on Windows, your external database can be Oracle or Microsoft SQL.

How to do it...

The requirements for your vCenter installation are different, depending on the size of your environment. When sizing the vCenter server, the requirements are the same if you have an embedded PSC or an external PSC. The following requirements are the same if you are running vCenter on Windows or VCSA:

	Number of CPUs	RAM (GBs)	Default Storage Size	Large Storage Size	X-Large Storage Size
Platform Services Controller	2	4	30 GB	30 GB	30 GB
Tiny vCenter with up to 10 Hosts and 100 VMs	2	10	250 GB	775 GB	1,650 GB
Small vCenter with up to 100 Hosts and 1,000 VMs	4	16	290 GB	820 GB	1,700 GB
Medium vCenter with up to 400 Hosts and 4,000 VMs	8	24	425 GB	925 GB	1,805 GB
Large vCenter with up to 1,000 Hosts and 10,000 VMs	16	32	640 GB	990 GB	1,870 GB
XLarge vCenter with up to 2,000 Hosts and 35,000 VMs	24	48	980 GB	1,030 GB	1910 GB

Deploying Platform Services Controller

PSC must be installed before installing the vCenter server. If you are installing PSC and the vCenter software on the same VM, then you can install them at the same time. PSC runs three services: vCenter Single Sign-On, vSphere License Service, and VMware Certificate Authority. You can deploy a single PSC or multiple instances of PSC that are joined to the same **Single Sign-On** (**SSO**) domain. In this recipe, we will install PSC on an existing Windows 2012 R2 VM.

Getting ready

To step through this recipe, you will need a fresh installation of Windows 2012 R2 server with at least two CPUs and 4 GB of RAM free. No other prerequisites are required.

How to do it...

These instructions are specific to the vSphere 6.5 vCenter installation. Here are the steps to install PSC on an existing Windows 2012 R2 server:

1. Download VMware vCenter server and modules for the Windows ISO file from: http://www.vmware.com/download.
2. Mount the ISO file once it is downloaded.
3. Launch the **Autorun** application in the root folder.
4. Click on **vCenter server for Windows** and then the **Install** button.
5. Click on **Next**.
6. Accept EULA, then click **Next**.
7. For the deployment type, click on **Platform Services Controller** under **External Deployment**:

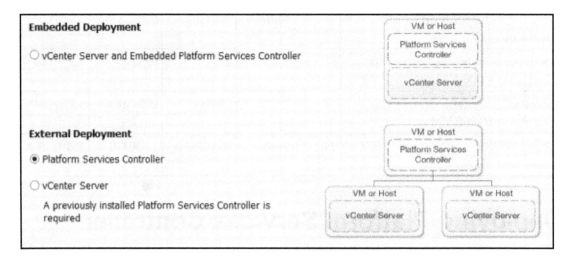

8. Verify the system name and click **Next**.
9. Choose your SSO domain name, user, and password. Click on **Next**.
10. Change the default ports if needed. Click on **Next**.
11. Change the destination directory if needed. Click on **Next**.
12. Choose whether to join CEIP or not and click **Next**.
13. Review the settings and click on **Install**.
14. When the installation is done, click **Finish**.

Deploying the vCenter server components

The vCenter software can be installed on either a physical server or a VM. In either case, the steps are the same. The vCenter server requires a database that can either be the PostgreSQL database included with the installer or an external Oracle or Microsoft database. In this example, we will use the PostgreSQL database.

Getting ready

To step through this recipe, you will need a fresh installation of Windows 2012 R2 VM with at least two CPUs and 10 GB of RAM. No other prerequisites are required.

How to do it...

To deploy the vCenter server, perform the following steps:

1. Download VMware vCenter server and the modules for the Windows ISO file from `http://www.vmware.com/download`.
2. Mount the ISO file once it is downloaded.
3. Launch the autorun application in the root folder.
4. Click on the **vCenter server for Windows** and then the **Install** button.
5. Click on **Next**.
6. Accept EULA, then click on **Next**.

7. For the deployment type, click on the **vCenter server** under **External Deployment**. These steps assume that you have an external PSC instance; if you want to install the vCenter server with PSC, select the **Embedded Deployment** option:

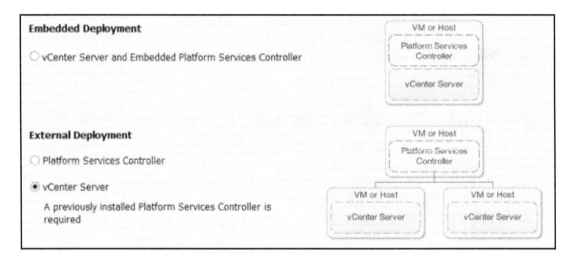

8. Verify the system name and click on **Next**.
9. Enter the PSC FQDN and SSO administrator password of your PSC instance. Click on **Next**.
10. Enter the vCenter server service account you want to use, then click on **Next**.
11. Enter your database settings. We will be using the embedded PostgreSQL database. Click on **Next**.
12. Verify the default ports and click on **Next**.
13. Change the destination directories if desired and click on **Next**.
14. Click on **Install**.
15. This installation will take several minutes. When it is done, click on **Finish**.

Designing vCenter server for redundancy

For a better performing vSphere infrastructure, you need to think about the redundancy of your vCenter server. So, the question is how would you provide redundancy for your vCenter server?

Well, this decision can be taken based on certain criteria:

1. How much downtime can you tolerate?
2. What is your desired level of failover automation for vCenter server?
3. What is your budget for maintaining the availability method?

There are a couple of redundancy methods that are available for both your Windows-based vCenter server. You can use VMware HA or FT to protect a Windows vCenter VM. If you choose a physical Windows-based vCenter server, then you can use third-party clustering software, such as Microsoft Cluster Service, to provide redundancy.

 VMware does not certify these third-party solutions. VMware will offer the best support for any issues encountered with an environment that uses third-party solutions for protecting against VMware VirtualCenter downtime.

You can also choose a manual configuration and manual failover for your vCenter server system. However, it can take much longer than your automated solution using vSphere HA, vCenter Server Heartbeat, or any other third-party clustering software. Not only does it take time to set up the initial configuration of your vCenter server, but also to synchronize these two systems and ensure there would be failover at the time of service disruption.

How to do it...

Follow these steps to design a redundant vCenter server:

1. Make sure that you put this vCenter server on a vSphere-HA-enabled cluster for automated redundancy. Although vSphere HA does protect against operating system and hardware failures, it does not protect against vCenter server service failure.
2. For a faster and automated solution for the redundant vCenter server, choose vCenter Server Heartbeat or a third-party solution, such as Microsoft Cluster Services. One advantage of using vCenter Server Heartbeat is that it monitors for vCenter server service failures in addition to the overall operating system failure.

3. If your vCenter server is physical, consider the following options to provide redundancy:

   - Configure Microsoft Cluster Services between two physical vCenter servers.
   - Use P2V software to create a backup of your physical vCenter server to a VM.
   - Use P2P software to image your physical vCenter server to another physical machine

Other advantages are that vCenter Server Heartbeat can protect the database server, work with either the physical machine or VM, and automatically maintain the synchronization between the primary and backup servers.

However, the main disadvantages of these solutions are they need to be purchased and maintained over a period of time.

They are also more difficult to configure than merely running a VM in a vSphere cluster with HA enabled. For many environments, HA provides good enough availability with minimal configuration cost or hassle.

 It is important to understand that ESXi hosts can do HA restarts even when the vCenter server is down. The vCenter server is needed to configure HA, but not for it to run. HA will restart the VM that runs vCenter in case there is a host failure.

Designing a highly available vCenter database

It does not really matter which platform or flavor of vCenter server you are using, but you must protect your vCenter server database. All configuration information about vSphere inventory objects, such as objects, roles, alarms, performance data, host profiles, and so on, are kept in the vCenter server database.

In case there are database failures, such as lost data or corrupted data, all this information may get lost and should be restored from a backup; alternatively, the entire inventory should be reconfigured manually. If you do not have a backup copy of your vCenter server database, then at the time of failure, you will lose the history of your tasks, events, and performance information apart from those already mentioned previously.

So, in a nutshell, you should use any of the available methods to maintain a backup copy of your vCenter server database. Some options are listed in the next section.

How to do it...

You can choose a number of solutions for maintaining a highly available vCenter server database:

1. Use any available and supported vendor-supplied availability and maintenance solutions.
2. If you are using a vCenter server database in a VM, then protect it using vSphere HA.
3. If you cannot use any vendor-specific tools to maintain the availability of the vCenter database, then use vCenter Server Heartbeat to protect the database server; it works for both the physical machine and VM. However, it comes at an additional cost. For environments that require highly available management components (VDI environments, which constantly deploy new desktops in an automated fashion, or vCloud/self-service/service provider environments), this solution should be investigated.

4. You still need to take regular backups of the vCenter server database to protect the actual database information.

vCenter database size and location affects performance

For any kind of vCenter platform, you need to have a vCenter database, but the question is how does your database size affect your vCenter performance.

If adequate resources are available for your vCenter database, then the supported versions of vCenter databases, such as Oracle and SQL, perform very well. However, you need to understand that a vCenter server task retention policy and higher performance statistics collection settings can increase the database size dramatically, which in turn will affect your vCenter server performance. But, the bundled database of either the vCenter server system or VCSA is a separate matter. The bundled database is intended for the evaluation of the vSphere software or supporting a small infrastructure of up to 20 hosts and 200 VMs. In this case, the vCenter database is collocated with the vCenter server instance. Logging level also affects the performance and size of the vCenter database.

Now when this is over, the next question is, should you place the vCenter server database in the same vCenter Management Server computer or on some other VM?

If you think your environment will grow beyond 20 hosts or 200 VMs, VMware recommends not to place the vCenter server database on the same system as the vCenter server.

It is not a matter of whether your vCenter server is physical or virtual, but removing the database from being collocated removes any possibility of resource contention between these two, except for network latency. If the vCenter server and database systems are virtual, separation means that either VM can be easily resized to accommodate current performance needs.

VMware bundled with the vCenter database is for supporting test systems or a small infrastructure. The built-in database is a PostgreSQL database for vCenter on Windows and VCSA 6.0 and above.

How to do it...

To choose a location and size of the vCenter server database, perform the following:

1. Choose the logging level (this logging level is a vCenter setting and not a database log file setting) carefully so that your vCenter server database will not grow too much and affect the performance in turn.

   Use the knowledge base article at `http://kb.vmware.com/selfservice/m icrosites/search.do?language=en_US&cmd=displayKC&externalId =1004795` to change the logging level for vCenter server.

2. Consider the vCenter server task and event retention policy, which will increase the size of the vCenter server database.
3. Also, choose the performance statistics collection settings carefully, which will also increase the database size and affect your vCenter server database performance.
4. If you are deploying vCenter for a large environment, then do not collocate the vCenter database with the vCenter server system. It will help you avoid any possibility of CPU and memory resource contention.

5. Preferably, choose a vCenter server database on a VM if does not already exist in the environment. Having a vCenter server database on a virtual platform has many benefits as follows:
    - If needed, it can be easily backed up and recreated.
    - During planned maintenance, it can be moved to other hosts using vMotion.
    - It can be load balanced using vSphere DRS across hosts.
    - You can easily protect it by vSphere HA without extra cost and maintenance. Check with your database vendor for details.
    - You can take a snapshot of it as well for business continuity and testing.

Using vSphere 6.x Certificate Manager for certificates

Security for vCenter server is really important. However, it is an organization's security policy and architecture decision whether to use certificates or not.

If your organization's policy requires a certificate, then you must use one. Also, if there is a potential possibility of man-in-the-middle attacks when using management interfaces, such as vSphere Web Client, then using certificates is a must.

VMware products use standard X.509 Version 3 certificates to encrypt session information sent over the **Secure Socket Layer** (**SSL**) protocol connections between components. However, by default, vSphere includes self-signed certificates. It is an organization's policy that will decide whether to use self-signed certificates or the internally signed or externally signed certificates. You need to purchase externally signed certificates unless you use the other two.

You need to keep a backup of those certificates to protect them from being lost or getting corrupt. Also, you need to consider using certificates when you are going to employ vSphere FT or vCenter in linked mode.

With the release of vSphere 6.0, VMware released the vSphere Certificate Manager utility, which is intended to enable performing most certificate management tasks interactively from the command line. vSphere Certificate Manager allows you to select which task to perform and will insert certificates in appropriate locations, stopping and restarting services as needed.

vSphere Certificate Manager is intended to replace the need to manually perform the steps listed previously; however, those steps can still be performed, and historically, they have been tried-and-true. So, this was intended to educate and show you how you can use the vSphere Certificate Manager utility to perform these tasks; however, if you still need to perform actions manually, those steps and guidance will still be available.

Getting ready

To step through this recipe, you will need one or more vCenter servers, either self-signed certificates or internally or externally signed certificates, and a working installation of the vSphere Certificate Manager utility. No other prerequisites are required.

 VMware does not support the use of Wildcard certificates.

How to do it...

When using Certificate Manager, the following formerly manual tasks are now automated by the utility:

- Certificates are automatically placed in **VMware Endpoint Certificate Store (VECS)**
- Regeneration of VMCA root certificates
- Stopping and restarting of services

To get started, launch the vSphere 6.x Certificate Manager utility using the Command Prompt:

- Windows vCenter server: `C:\Program Files\VMware\vCenter server\vmcad\certificate-manager`
- vCenter server Appliance: `/usr/lib/vmware-vmca/bin/certificate-manager`

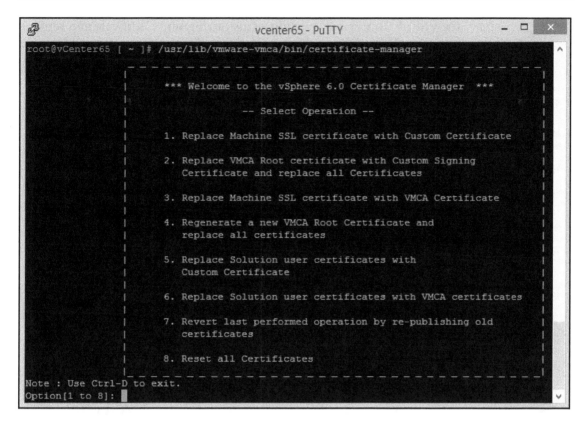

When you launch the vSphere Certificate Manager utility, you're presented with the following eight options to choose from. The requirements, configuration, and use of those options are listed now:

1. Replace the Machine SSL certificate with a custom certificate. This option generates Certificate Signing Requests and keys for the Machine SSL certificate and requires the following information:
   - The `administrator@vsphere.local` password or the equivalent administrator account
   - The path to a custom certificate and key for the Machine certificate are installed
   - The path to a custom certificate for the VMCA Root certificate

2. Replace the VMCA Root certificate with a Custom Signing Certificate and replace all the certificates. This option generates Certificate Signing Requests and keys for the VMCA Root Signing certificate and requires the following:
    - The `administrator@vsphere.local` password or equivalent administrator account
    - The `certool.cfg` file configured (this is used by VMCA when generating certificates)
    - Root Signing certificate
    - Root

3. Replace the Machine SSL certificate with a VMCA-generated certificate. This option replaces the Machine SSL certificate with a VMCA-generated certificate and requires the following:
    - The `administrator@vsphere.local` password or equivalent administrator account
    - The `certool.cfg` file configured (this is used by VMCA when generating certificates)

4. Regenerate a new default VMCA Root certificate and replace all the certificates. This option regenerates a new default VMCA Root certificate and replaces all the certificates. It requires the following:
    - The `administrator@vsphere.local` password or equivalent administrator account.
    - The `certool.cfg` file configured (this is used by VMCA when generating certificates)

5. Replace the Solution User Certificates with Custom CA certificates. This option replaces the Solution User Certificates with custom CA certificates and requires the following:
    - The `administrator@vsphere.local` password or equivalent administrator account.
    - The path to the custom Root CA certificate.
    - The path to the custom certificate and key for the vpxd Solution User.
    - The path to the custom certificate and key for the vpxd-extension Solution User.
    - The path to the custom certificate and key for the vSphere-webclient Solution User.
    - The path to the custom certificate and key for the machine Solution User.

6. Replace the Machine SSL certificate and Solution User certificates with the VMCA-generated certificate. This option replaces the Machine SSL certificate and Solution User certificates with the VMCA-generated certificate and requires the following:
    - The `administrator@vsphere.local` password or equivalent administrator account.

7. Revert to the last performed operation by republishing old certificates. This option reverts the last performed operation by republishing old certificates. vSphere Certificate Manager only supports one level of a revert. Running vSphere Certificate Manager Utility a second time will not allow you to revert the first of the two runs.

8. Reset all the certificates. This option resets all the certificates and requires the following:
    - The `administrator@vsphere.local` password or equivalent administrator account.
    - The `certool.cfg` file configured (this is used by VMCA when generating certificates)

See also

For more information on generating certificate requests and certificates, additional notes, and optional configurations using the vSphere Certificate Manager utility, refer to the following:

- *How to use vSphere 6.x (2097936)*
- *Configuring the vSphere 6.0 U1b or later VMware Certificate Authority as a Subordinate Certificate Authority (2147542)*
- *Replacing default certificates with CA-signed SSL certificates in vSphere 6.x (2111219)*
- *How to download and install vCenter server root certificates to avoid web browser certificate warnings (2108294)*

Designing vCenter server for Auto Deploy

If you are looking at provisioning 100s of ESXi hosts in your datacenter and don't know how to rapidly provision those, then Auto Deploy is your answer. With Auto Deploy, you can specify the image that will be used to provision the ESXi hosts. Also, you can specify/configure host profiles that will help you get those hosts configured if you need them to be identical and add them to a vCenter .

Auto Deploy uses a PXE boot infrastructure in conjunction with vSphere host profiles to provision and customize that host. An ESXi host does not store any state information; Auto Deploy manages that state information. Auto Deploy stores this state information of each ESXi host in different locations. When a host boots for the first time, the vCenter server system creates a corresponding host object and stores the information in the database. However, since ESXi 5.1, VMware introduced two different features along with stateless ESXi; they are called stateless caching and stateful installs:

- In stateless caching, the host boots from Auto Deploy but will fall back to the cached image in the event the DHCP/TFTP/Auto Deploy server is not available.
- In stateful installs, the host does the initial boot from the Auto Deploy server, which installs an ESXi image on the local disk. All subsequent boots are from the ESXi image saved on the local disk.

Getting ready

To step through this recipe, you will need one or more ESXi Servers (licensed with Enterprise Plus) not deployed with Auto Deploy, a vCenter server, and the Auto Deploy server installed. No other prerequisites are required.

How to do it...

vCenter is a necessary component in Auto Deploy.

If you configure the hosts provisioned with Auto Deploy with a vSphere Distributed Switch or if you have VMs configured with the autostart manager, then you need to deploy the vCenter server system and maintain its availability that matches the availability of the Auto Deploy server. But now, the question is how do you do that or what are the approaches you can take to make it happen? Well, there are several approaches that you can choose from:

- You can deploy your Auto Deploy server on the same machine where your vCenter server is running.
- You can choose vCenter Server Heartbeat which delivers high availability by protecting virtual and cloud infrastructure from an application, configuration, operating system, or hardware-related outages.
- You can deploy the vCenter server in a VM, then you can put this VM on a vSphere-HA-protected cluster. Also, you can set Restart Priority as High for this VM.
- Do not use any ESXi hosts that are managed or deployed by Auto Deploy for hosting Auto Deploy or the vCenter server system. This is because if there are any outages, then none of your hosts will be able to boot from Auto Deploy. Take two locally deployed ESXi boxes and create a cluster and put your Auto Deploy components there.

However, this approach is not suitable if you use the Auto Start as it is not supported in a cluster enabled for vSphere HA.

8
Designing VCSA for Best Performance

As discussed in the previous chapter, there are two ways to deploy a vCenter Server: vCenter running on Windows and **vCenter Server Appliance** (**VCSA**). In this chapter, we will discuss VCSA as a virtual appliance. We will cover the following topics:

- Deploying Platform Services Controller
- Deploying VCSA server components
- Setting up vCenter Server High Availability
- Adding VCSA to your Windows domain and adding users
- Checking VCSA performance using vimtop
- Checking VCSA performance using the GUI

Introduction

Since it was introduced, VCSA has lagged behind the vCenter deployment on Windows in terms of functionality and scalability. In vSphere 6.5, however, VCSA has all the features of the Windows version, including Update Manager, and can scale to the same size in terms of supported hosts and VMs. It is also quicker to deploy and it doesn't use a costly Windows license.

It also includes native replication and backup that you don't get with the Windows version. With all these improvements in vSphere 6.5, is there any reason to use vCenter on Windows? The only downside to running VCSA is that it is Linux-based, and therefore, troubleshooting takes a little Linux knowledge. If you want to keep a strictly Windows environment, then go with vCenter on Windows; otherwise, use VCSA.

The table indicates the recommended sizes for CPUs, RAM, and storage for your VCSA, depending on the number of hosts and VMs that will be in your environment:

VCSA platforms	Number of CPUs	RAM (GBs)	Default storage size	Large storage size	X-Large storage size
VCSA **Platform Services Controller** (**PSC**) only	2	4	30 GB	30 GB	30 GB
Tiny VCSA with up to 10 hosts and 100 VMs	2	10	250 GB	775 GB	1,650 GB
Small VCSA with up to 100 hosts and 1,000 VMs	4	16	290 GB	820 GB	1,700 GB
Medium VCSA with up to 400 hosts and 4,000 VMs	8	24	425 GB	925 GB	1,805 GB
Large VCSA with up to 1,000 hosts and 10,000 VMs	16	32	640 GB	990 GB	1,870 GB
XLarge VCSA with up to 2,000 hosts and 35,000 VMs	24	48	980 GB	1,030 GB	1910 GB

Deploying Platform Services Controller

As with the Windows version, VCSA can be deployed with either an embedded or external PSC. In this recipe, we will install just the VCSA PSC.

Getting ready

To step through this recipe, you will need an ESXi host with at least 2 CPUs and 4 GB of RAM free. You will also need a Windows, Linux, or Mac where you can run the installer. We will be running the installer from Windows. No other prerequisites are required.

How to do it...

These instructions are specific to the vSphere 6.5 VCSA installation. The 6.0 installation is done through a web page, but the steps are similar. Here are the steps to install PSC on your ESXi host:

1. Download the VCSA ISO file from `http://www.vmware.com/download`.
2. Mount the ISO file once it is downloaded.
3. Using the CD, open the `vcsa-ui-installer` folder.
4. Open the subfolder called `win32`. If you are running the installer on Linux or Mac, open the appropriate folder.
5. Double-click on **installer.exe**.
6. Click on **Install**.
7. Click on **Next**, then read and accept EULA and click **Next**.
8. Select the deployment type, click on **Platform Services Controller** under **External Platform Services Controller**. Click on **Next**.
9. Enter the FQDN, login, and password details of the ESXi host where you want to deploy PSC. Click on **Next**.
10. Enter the name and root password of your PSC and click **Next**.
11. Choose the datastore where you want this VM to be stored. Enable thin disk mode if desired. Click on **Next**.
12. Enter networking information and click **Next**.
13. Review the settings and click **Finish**.
14. When the installation is done, click **Finish**.

The PSC appliance installation will take 10-15 minutes. Once it is done, follow these instructions to continue the setup:

1. Open a web browser and navigate to `https://<PSC IP address>:5480`.
2. Click on the **Setup Platform Services Controller Appliance** link.
3. Enter the root password from the preceding setup and click on **Log in**.
4. Verify that stage 1 has completed and click **Next**.
5. Enter NTP server(s). Review the network settings and change if necessary. Click on **Next**.
6. Decide whether you want to join an SSO domain or create a new one. Fill out the SSO information. Click on **Next**.

7. Decide whether you want to join **Customer Experience Improvement Program** (**CEIP**) and click **Next**.

8. Review the settings and click **Finish**.

This step will take another 5-10 minutes to complete. Once done, you will receive a notification and the appliance management page:

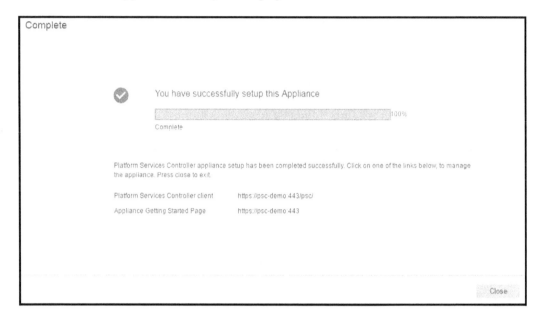

When you log into the appliance page, all the health statuses should be green and the SSO domain should be running:

Deploying VCSA server components

In this recipe, we will install just the vCenter portion of VCSA and then connect it to the PSC that we created earlier. This installation uses the same download process as that of the PSC.

Getting ready

To step through this recipe, you will need an ESXi host with at least 2 CPUs and 4 GB of RAM free. You will also need a Windows, Linux, or Mac where you can run the installer. We will be running the installer from Windows. No other prerequisites are required.

How to do it...

These instructions are specific to the vSphere 6.5 VCSA installation. The 6.0 installation is done through a web page, but the steps are similar. Here are the steps to install PSC on your ESXi host:

1. Download the VCSA ISO file from `http://www.vmware.com/download`.
2. Mount the ISO file once it is downloaded.
3. Using the CD, open the `vcsa-ui-installer` folder.
4. Open the subfolder called `win32`. If you are running the installer on Linux or Mac, open the appropriate folder.
5. Double-click on **installer.exe**.
6. Click on **Install**.
7. Click on **Next**, then read and accept EULA and click **Next**.
8. Select the deployment type and click on **vCenter Server** under **External Platform Services Controller**. Then click on **Next**.
9. Select the deployment and storage size. Click on **Next**.
10. Choose the datastore where you want this VM to be stored. Enable thin disk mode if desired. Click on **Next**.
11. Enter networking information and click **Next**.
12. Review the settings and click **Finish**.
13. When the installation is done, click **Finish**.

The VCSA appliance installation will take 10-15 minutes. Once it is done, follow these instructions to continue the setup:

1. Open a web browser and navigate to `https://<VCSA address>:5480`.
2. Click on Set up vCenter Server Appliance.
3. Enter the root password from the preceding setup and click on **Log in**.
4. Verify that stage 1 has completed and click **Next**.
5. Enter the NTP server(s). Review the network settings and change if necessary. Click on **Next**.
6. Enter the PSC information for your PSC and click **Next**.
7. Validate the settings and click **Finish**.
8. The configuration will take about 10 minutes. When done, log in to `https://<VCSA IP>:5480` and wait for the services to start.
9. All the services should be started:

Note that the **Single Sign-On** status says **Not applicable** because we are using an external PSC instance.

Setting up vCenter Server High Availability

High availability is an important feature of any mission-critical system, and VCSA is no exception. Since your VCSA system manages your entire virtualized environment, it needs to be able to recover from hardware and software failures. When using VCSA in vSphere 6.5, you can configure **vCenter Server High Availability** (**VCHA**). If VCSA fails, VCHA is designed to carry out the failover and be back up and running in less than 5 minutes. VCHA is only available with VCSA and is not available for vCenter running in Windows.

VCHA consists of an active and passive VCSA and a witness. The active VCSA does synchronous vPostgres DB replication and file replication to the passive VCSA. There is also a floating management IP address that is tied to the active VCSA. If the active VCSA goes offline, the passive VCSA and the witness will create a quorum, take over the floating IP address, and become the active VCSA. If the offline VCSA comes back online, it becomes the passive VCSA and begins syncing with the active VCSA.

Implementing VCHA requires a few extra components. First, you must have a VCHA network for your two VCSA nodes and the witness to communicate. This network does not require 10 Gbps speed, but latency should be 10 ms or less. You must also have three additional IPs allocated: one for each VCSA and one for the witness. These IPs need to be on a different subnet than the floating management IP of the active VCSA. In addition, your VCSA should be at least a *small* configuration with 4 vCPUs and 16 GB of RAM.

There are two ways to deploy VCHA: basic and advanced. Basic deployment is automated via a wizard, and advanced is a manual process. We will configure VCHA using the basic option.

Getting ready

To step through this recipe, you will need a running VCSA and vSphere Web Client. No other prerequisites are required.

How to do it…

The following are the steps to create VCHA. First, create the VCHA network. This is a VM port group that the active VCSA, the passive VCSA, and the witness communicate and replicate on. They can be attached to your existing vSwitch or an independent vSwitch:

1. Log in to your VCSA using vSphere Web Client.
2. Click on your host, then go to the **Configure** tab. Click on **Virtual switches** under **Networking**.
3. Click on the **Add host networking** button.
4. Select Virtual Machine Port Group and click **Next**.
5. Select the existing switch and click **Next**.
6. Enter the VCHA network for the Network label and click **Next**.
7. Review the settings and click **Finish**.
8. Repeat steps 2-7 for your other hosts:

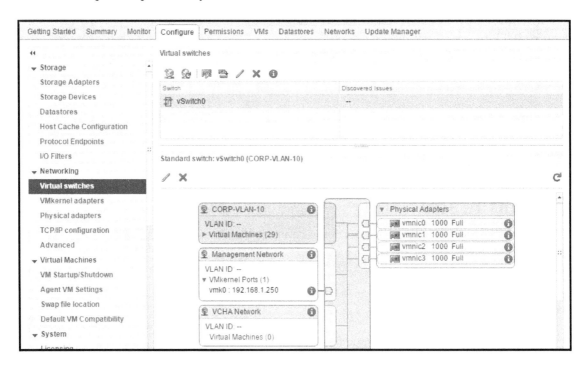

Now that we have created the VCHA network port group on all hosts, we can run the Basic configuration of VCHA.

> As of VCSA Version 6.5.0.5200, the basic VCHA wizard will fail if your VCSA has capital letters in its name. If the name contains capital letters, follow the instructions in this post to change the `/etc/vmware/systemname_info.json` file to have all lowercase letters, then reboot VCSA before running `https://communities.vmware.com/th read/547117`.

1. Log in to your VCSA using vSphere Web Client. Log in using the `administrator@vsphere.local` (or your PSC domain) account as the wizard may fail if you use another account.
2. Click on **VCSA**, then click on the **Configure** tab, and then **vCenter HA** under **Settings**.
3. Click on the **Configure** button:

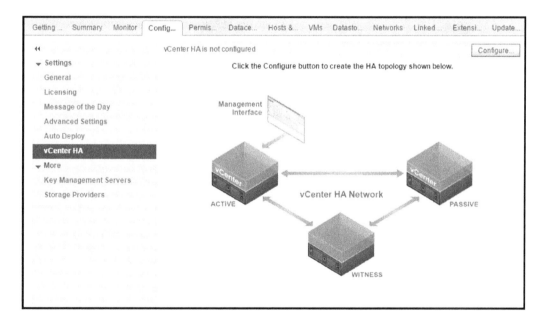

4. Select the **Basic** option, then click **Next**.
5. Enter and IP address and subnet mask for the existing VCSA server on the VCHA network. This IP address needs to be on a different subnet than the main VCSA management IP. Click on the **browse** button and select the VCHA network that we created previously. Click on **Next**.

6. Enter the IP address for the passive VCSA node and the witness node on the VCHA network. Click on **Next**.

7. Next, you can specify the properties the VCSA peer and witness.

It is best practice to put all three VMs on different datastores and on different hosts.

8. Click on the **Edit** button to walk through the configuration of the VCSA peer and witness and make these changes. If you are successful, compatibility checks will succeed. Click on **Next**.

9. Review the settings and click on **Finish**.

10. Wait for about 5 minutes for the system to configure the second VCSA and the witness. To name the VMs, the wizard will append the peer to the secondary VCSA and witness to the VCSA witness.

11. When the process has completed, go back to the **Configure** tab and click on **vCenter HA**. You should see that **vCenter HA** is enabled and your active, passive, and witness VMs are up:

12. Now go to the **Monitor** tab and click on **vCenter HA** to check the status of the replication. Everything should be in sync:

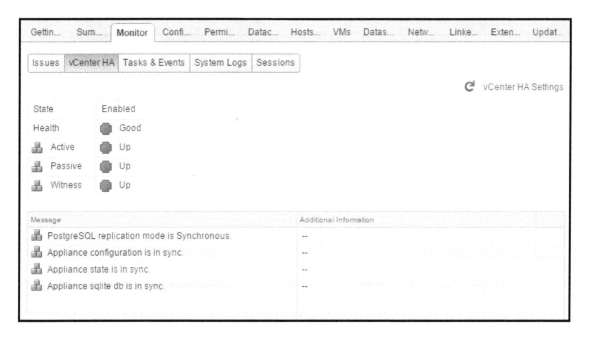

Finally, we will test the failover of VCSA. To do this, we will simply power off the active VCSA and watch the failover process:

1. With vCenter HA enabled, right-click on the active VCSA VM and select **Power**, then **Power off**.
2. Depending on the size of your environment, failover may take up to 5 minutes.
3. Log out of the web client and refresh the web page.
4. When you connect to the web client again, you may see a Failover in progress screen. If you see this, wait for a couple more minutes.

5. After you log back in to the VCHA IP address, click on VCHA and go to the **Configure** tab and then **vCenter HA** under **Settings**. You should see that the VM that was originally in the **Active** role is now down and in the passive role:

6. Now go to the **Monitor** tab and click on **vCenter HA** to check the status of the replication. Since the passive VCSA is down, all of the replication will be out of sync:

At this point, we can simply power on the first VCSA and wait for a few minutes, and replication will start to sync and the health status will go back to green. The system will not trigger a failback automatically, so the second VCSA will continue in the role of the active VCSA until another failure occurs. To trigger a failback manually, click on the **Initiate Failover** button:

If the active VCSA does ever have an actual failure and cannot be repaired, go to the **Configure** tab and click on **vCenter HA** under the **Settings** section, then click on the **Redeploy** button to recreate a secondary VCSA.

Adding VCSA to your Windows domain and adding users

If your company runs on a Microsoft **Active Directory** (**AD**) domain, then allowing administrators to use their AD credentials to access the VCSA is critical to the security of the VCSA as well as simplifying admin access. When you add your VCSA to the AD domain, you can give permissions to AD groups, then manage the membership in AD instead of the VCSA.

When running the vCenter Server on Windows, this process is very straightforward as the vCenter Server is most likely already joined to the AD domain. Since the VCSA is Linux-based, it most likely will not be joined to the AD domain.

If you are running an external PSC, then the PSC will be added to the AD domain instead of the VCSA. In this recipe, we will join the PSC to the AD domain, then set up user authentication to the AD domain.

Getting ready

To step through this recipe, you will need a running VCSA that has network access to an AD domain and vSphere Web Client. No other prerequisites are required.

How to do it...

First, we will join the VCSA to the AD domain:

1. Open a web browser and go to the address of the VCSA.
2. Log in using `administrator@vsphere.local` (or your SSO domain) and the correct password.
3. From the VCSA home screen, go to **Administration**, then **System configuration** under **Deployment**.
4. Click on **Nodes** and then on the name of your PSC. If you are running an embedded PSC, click on **VCSA** instead.
5. Now click on the **Manage** tab, then **Active Directory** under **Advanced**.
6. Click on the **Join** button.
7. Enter the domain name, username (without domain prefix), and password. Then click **OK**. The **Organizational unit** field is not required. Click on **OK**.
8. A screen will flash but nothing will appear to change. This is OK.
9. Right-click on the PSC (or VCSA) and select **Reboot**. Enter a reason, then click **OK**.
10. Wait for about 5 minutes for the system to reboot.

11. Log back in and go to the same location; the AD domain should now be filled in:

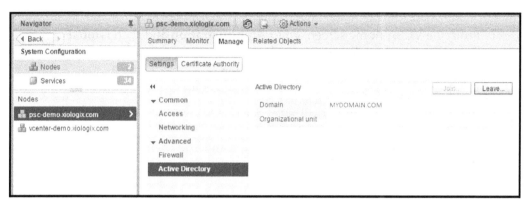

Now we will add an identity source so that the VCSA can authenticate against the AD domain:

1. From the VCSA home screen, go to **Administration** and then **Configuration** under **Single Sign-On**.
2. Go to the **Identity Sources** tab, then click on the + sign to add an identity source.
3. To connect to the AD, select the **Active Directory (Integrated Windows Authentication)** option. Click on **Next**.
4. The next screen should have the domain that you entered in the preceding step 7. You can use the machine account or choose to specify an account. Click on **Next**.
5. Review the summary, then click **Finish**.
6. Your domain name should appear as a new item in the **Identity Sources** screen.
7. To verify that everything is working, go back and click on **Users and Groups** under **Single Sign-On**. Then click on the **Users** tab and select your domain. After a few seconds, all the domain accounts should be listed:

Now that we have joined the AD domain and have added the domain as an identity source, we can follow the normal process to give users and groups permissions to vCenter:

1. From the VCSA home screen, go to **Administration** and then **Global Permissions** under **Access Control**.
2. Click on the **Manage** tab, then on the + icon.
3. In the **Add Permission** window, click on the **Add** button.
4. In the **Select User/Groups** window, select your domain from the drop-down menu.
5. Now you can search for users and groups and add them to the list at the bottom.
6. Click on **OK** to add these users and groups.

In this example, I have added my domain administrator's group as administrator-level users:

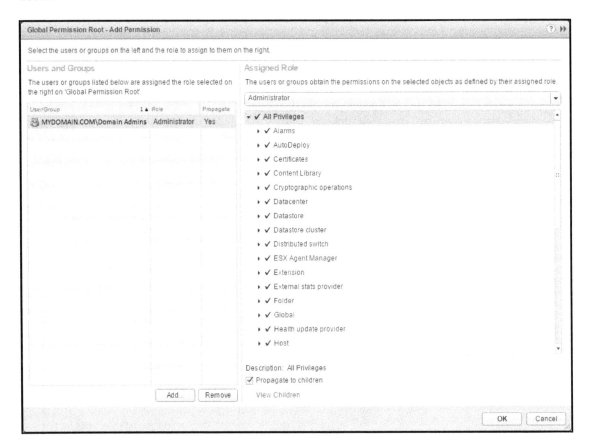

Now anyone that is a member of the **Domain Admins** group can log in to vSphere Web Client using their AD domain credentials:

Note that in order for users to log in to vSphere Web Client using their Windows session credentials, they will need to install Enhanced Authentication Plugin on their system.

Checking VCSA performance using vimtop

Monitoring the performance of your VCSA is a critical part of managing your virtual environment. If your VCSA is not performing well, vSphere admins will experience lag in vSphere Web Client and system processes, such as vMotion, HA, and DRS, will not perform as well as expected.

In this recipe, we'll check the performance of your VCSA using vimtop.

Getting ready

To step through this recipe you must have a running VCSA and an SSH Client (Putty). No other prerequisites are required.

How to do it...

To look at vimtop, we will connect to your VCSA via SSH:

1. Open the VCSA CLI in Putty.
2. Log in as the root with the root password.
3. Once logged in, you will be presented with the Command prompt.
4. Type shell and hit *Enter*. This will launch Bash and get you to a # prompt.
5. Now type vimtop and hit *Enter*:

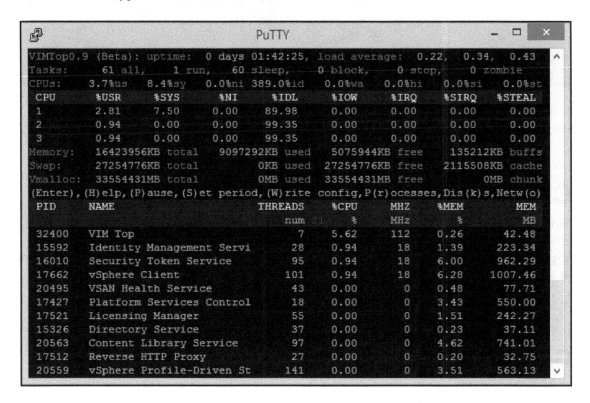

Vimtop is similar to esxtop but has some advanced features. First of all, you will notice that vimtop uses colors to make it more readable. By default, we can see the VCSA uptime, the load average, CPU usage, memory usage, and the top processes. The processes are sorted in descending order based on **%CPU**. Let's say that our VCSA is running low on RAM and we want to sort the processes in descending order by **%MEM**. To do this, use the right arrow key to move to the right until the **%MEM** column is highlighted, then use the z key to clear the current sort, and finally, use the d key to sort in descending order:

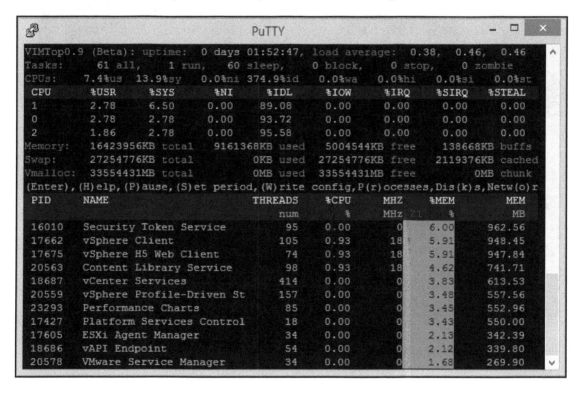

Now let's say that our CPU usage is high and we suspect that performance charts are causing slowness. We can hit the left arrow until the **%CPU** column is highlighted, then hit *z* and *d* to clear the sort and sort the **%CPU** column in descending order. Then we can use the down arrow key to highlight the **Performance Charts** process:

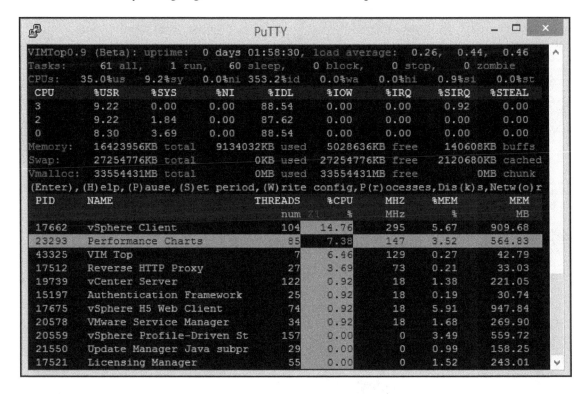

The nice thing about highlighting a certain process is that the process will stay highlighted as it moves up and down the screen, allowing you to easily follow it.

To view all the keyboard options, hit the *H* key.

Checking VCSA performance using the GUI

We have seen that we can monitor performance from the VCSA command line using vimtop. For a more graphical view, we can log into the VCSA GUI and look at the performance graphs.

Getting ready

To step through this recipe you must have a running VCSA and access to the VCSA web client. No other prerequisites are required.

How to do it...

We will now log in to the VCSA management page to look at its performance:

1. Open a web browser and go to `https://<VCSA management IP>:5480`.
2. Log in as the root with the root password.
3. Click on **CPU and Memory**.
4. These graphs give a **CPU and Memory** graph based on the intervals of 1 day, 1 week, 1 month, or 1 quarter. The graphs are not customizable but should give you an overview of the performance of your VCSA:

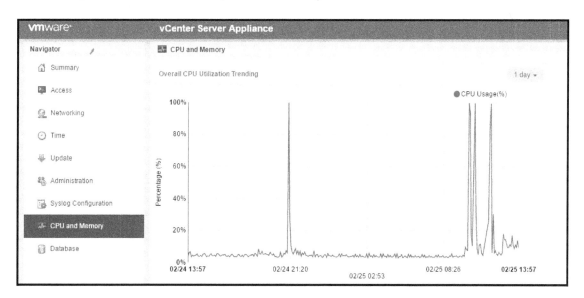

5. Now click on the **Database** tab on the left.

This page will show the amount of database usage for **Alarms**, **Events**, **Tasks**, and **Stats,** as well as the remaining free space:

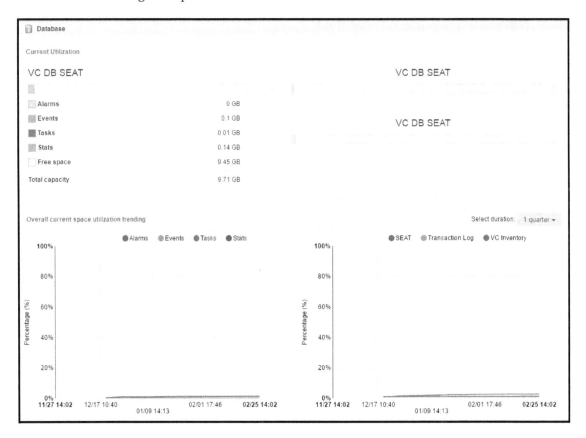

The page also has graphs for estimating when your database will be at capacity.

9

Virtual Machine and Virtual Environment Performance Design

In this chapter, we will cover the tasks related to VM and application performance design. You will learn the following aspects of VM and application performance design:

- Setting the right time in Guest OS
- Virtual NUMA considerations
- Choosing the SCSI controller for storage
- Impact of VM swap file placement
- Using large pages in VMs
- Guest OS networking considerations
- When you should or should not virtualize an application
- Measuring the environment's performance

Introduction

Proper configuration of a VM can reduce the possibility of performance problems occurring during a normal operation.

In this chapter, we will discuss the guidelines for creating an optimal VM configuration.

You can maintain and even improve the performance of your applications by ensuring that your VM is optimally configured. Follow the guidelines when configuring your VM for optimal performance. These guidelines pertain to the guest operating system, VMware Tools, and virtual hardware resources (CPU, memory, storage, and networking).

Setting the right time in Guest OS

Keeping accurate time is very important for any operating system. Unfortunately, the methods that operating systems use to keep track of time on physical machines do not work well in a virtual environment. Many OSes use a method called **tick counting** to keep accurate time. This method uses hardware interrupts at a known frequency, then the OS counts the ticks to come up with the current time. In a virtual environment, the hardware is virtualized and shared among many VMs. Because of this, VMs may lose ticks and cause the time to become inaccurate.

Newer operating systems use a tickless timekeeping method, which is easier to support in a virtual environment. In this method, a hardware device keeps track of the number of time units since the system booted, then the operating system reads this counter as needed. This method causes less CPU overhead than tick counting. In order to use tickless timekeeping, the VM must be alerted so that the OS is using tickless timekeeping. If this is not done, the VM will default back to tick counting.

There are several clock synchronization services available on VMs:

- NTP for Linux
- Windows Time service for Windows
- VMware Tools for supported OS

For Linux guests, VMware recommends NTP instead of VMware Tools for time synchronization.

The main reason behind recommending this is sync in VMware Tools will only correct the time that falls behind, so if it ever gets ahead for some reason, it won't fix that; however, NTP will, and most customers already have Guest OS builds that sync time with NTP or **Active Directory** (**AD**) anyway (and having Guest OS time synced in two ways could lead to conflicts).

Despite these potential problems, NTP behaves fairly well in a VM when configured correctly. NTP accounts for some of its readings to be anomalous due to network delays, scheduling delays on the localhost, and other factors, and it will filter out such readings.

For further information, refer to `http://www.vmware.com/files/pdf/tec hpaper/Timekeeping-In-VirtualMachines.pdf`(white paper).

Generally, it is best to use only one clock synchronization service at a time in a given VM. This avoids the situation where multiple services attempt to make conflicting changes to the clock. So, if you are using NTP or the Windows Time service, it is best to turn VMware Tools's periodic clock synchronization off.

If you are using an ESXi host with AD Integration, then it is extremely important to synchronize the time between the ESXi and AD so that it can serve the Kerberos security protocol. If the time skew is greater than 300 seconds, then a server may not be able to authenticate to the domain. VMware ESXi supports the synchronization of time by using an external NTP server as well. You can configure NTP on the ESXi host via Configure | System | Time Configuration.

AD depends on accurate timekeeping, and the risk you must mitigate is how to prevent clock drift. A successful AD implementation requires planning of time services.

Microsoft uses Kerberos v5 as the authentication protocol, and for Kerberos to work properly, it requires time synchronization. The timestamped authentication tickets generated by Kerberos are based on the workstation's time. This ticket remains alive for only 5 minutes. If your clock drifts significantly, the authentication tickets will not be issued, become outdated, or simply expire. This will result in authentication denial or an inability to log in to the domain to access network resources.

So if you are planning for an AD implementation, you should consider the most effective way of providing an accurate time to domain controllers.

The domain controller that holds the PDC Emulator role for the forest root domain is the *master* timeserver for the forest. This is the root time server for synchronizing the clocks of all Windows computers in the forest. You can configure PDC to either use an external source or an internal source to set its time. So, if you modify the defaults of this domain controller's role to synchronize with an alternative external time source, then you can ensure that all other DCs and workstations within the domain are accurate.

For further information, refer to the following two KB articles: Timekeeping best practices for Windows, including NTP(1318) at `http ://kb.vmware.com/kb/1318` and Timekeeping best practices for Linux guests(1006427) at `http://kb.vmware.com/kb/1006427`.

Getting ready

To step through this recipe, you will need a couple of ESXi Servers, a Windows VM running AD services, an instance of installed vCenter Server, and vSphere Web Client. No other prerequisites are required.

How to do it…

To configure the ESXi NTP, follow these steps. Configure ESXi to synchronize the time with the Windows Server AD domain controller:

1. Connect to the ESXi host or vCenter Server using vSphere Web Client.
2. Select the ESXi host from the inventory.
3. Click on the **Configure** tab, then click on **Time Configuration** under **System**:

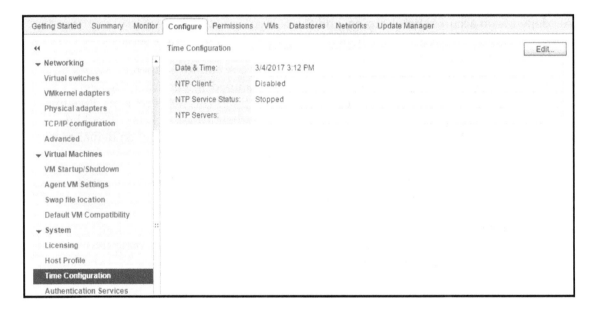

4. Click on **Edit….**
5. Click on **Use Network Time Protocol (Enable NTP client)**.
6. Click on **Start** if NTP Service Status says.
7. Select **Start and stop with host**.

8. For the **NTP Servers**, specify the fully qualified domain name or IP address of the Windows Server domain controller(s) separated by commas:

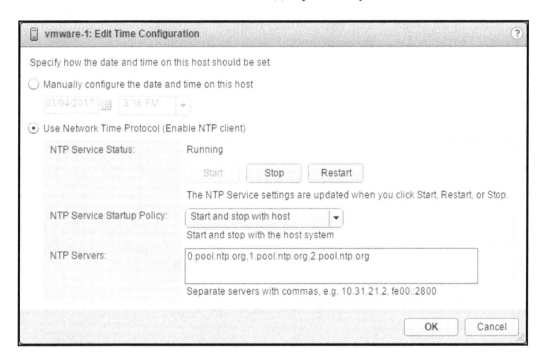

9. Click on **OK**.
10. The system will attempt to synchronize with the NTP servers specified. Give the system a couple of minutes to do this, then check the date and time to make sure it is accurate.

Virtual NUMA considerations

Non-uniform memory access, also known as **NUMA**, is designed with memory locality in mind so that pools of adjacent memory are placed in islands called NUMA nodes. Here, memory is divided between physical CPUs into NUMA nodes. In a dual CPU server, half the memory is on NUMA node 0 along with CPU 0, and the other half of memory is on NUMA node 1 with CPU 1. The CPU in NUMA node 0 considers the memory in NUMA node 0 to be local (fast) and the memory in NUMA node 1 to be remote (slower). Because of this, the more memory we can give a VM within a NUMA node, the more efficiently that VM can access its memory.

vSphere 6.5 has made changes to its CPU scheduler to optimize the virtual NUMA topology. In vSphere 6.0, if you were to create a VM with 16 CPUs and two cores per socket, eight Virtual Proximity Domains would be created. If you create a VM with the same configuration in vSphere 6.5, only two Virtual Proximity Domains are created, which match the Physical Proximity Domains of the host.

What if your VM needs to be bigger than a NUMA node? One of the features originally introduced in vSphere 5 is **Virtual NUMA (vNUMA)** or the ability of NUMA inside a VM to be presented to the guest OS.

vNUMA is designed for modern OSes that are NUMA-aware and can make intelligent page management decisions based on locality. A characteristic aspect of vNUMA is that it incorporates **distributed shared memory** (**DSM**) inside the hypervisor, which is in contrast to the more traditional approach of providing it in the middleware.

When creating a VM, you have the option to specify the number of virtual sockets and cores per virtual socket. If the number of cores per virtual socket on a vNUMA-enabled VM is set to any value other than the default of one and that value doesn't align with the underlying physical host topology, performance might be slightly reduced.

Therefore, for best performance, if a VM is to be configured with a non-default number of cores per virtual socket, that number should be an integer multiple or integer divisor of the physical NUMA node size.

Getting ready

To step through this recipe, you will need a couple of ESXi Servers, a couple of working VMs that have more than eight vCPUs, some VMs with smaller vCPUs, an instance of installed vCenter Server, and vSphere Web Client. No other prerequisites are required.

How to do it...

The following recipe will show you the NUMA configuration of your VM:

1. Enable SSH access to the host where your VM is running.
2. SSH to the host and log in as the root.
3. Find the path to the VM's log file using this command:

```
# vmdumper -l | grep <VM name>
```

4. This will output the path to the `.vmx` file for the VM you specified.

5. Now look for the information in the `vmware.log` for that VM (not the `.vmx` file),
   ```
   # cat /vmfs/volumes/5390c2da-
   b6859d14-2d39-90b11c097755/Demo/vmware.log | grep numa:
   ```

In this case, we have 16 vCPUs that are in two Virtual Proximity Domains. These correlate correctly to the two Physical Proximity Domains available on the host ESXi server.

See also

For more information on vNUMA, consult the following sources:

- http://frankdenneman.nl/2016/12/12/decoupling-cores-per-socket-virtual-numa-topology-vsphere-6-5/
- http://www.davidklee.net/2016/11/29/vmware-vsphere-6-5-breaks-your-sql-server-vnuma-settings/

Choosing the SCSI controller for storage

In vSphere 6.x, there are four types of SCSI controllers for a VM. They are:

- BusLogic Parallel
- LSI Logic Parallel
- LSI Logic SAS
- VMware Paravirtual

In order to successfully boot a VM, the guest OS must support the type of SCSI HBA you choose for your VM hardware.

BusLogic Parallel is there to support your old Guest OS; an example is Microsoft Windows 2000 Server.

LSI Logic Parallel is there to support most guest operating systems. There is not much difference in I/O performance between Bus Logic and LSI Logic; however, there is a slight difference in the way the hardware represents itself inside the guest. VMware recommends picking up LSI Logic for your Linux.

LSI Logic SAS has been built to support even newer Guest Operating Systems with advanced feature support, for example, clustering support in Windows 2008 and newer. As it is a specially built controller, it boosts the I/O performance slightly than your legacy controller. You need to use VM hardware version 7 and above to get the ability to use it.

VMware Paravirtual is VMware's virtualization-aware controller for high-performing VMs. It is built to reduce CPU overhead while still increasing I/O throughput. This driver coalesces interrupts to reduce the amount of CPU processing required.

This controller also requires hardware version 7 and above. As a best practice, you can still use a default controller for the OS to come up, and for the high I/O load VM, you can use the VMware Paravirtual controller for the data disk. In this way, operational complexity is reduced.

In some cases, large I/O requests issued by applications in a VM can be split by the guest storage driver. Changing the guest operating system's registry settings to issue larger block sizes can eliminate this splitting, thus enhancing performance.

Getting ready

To step through this recipe, you will need one or more running ESXi Servers, a fully functioning vCenter Server, and vSphere Web Client. No other prerequisites are required.

How to do it...

SCSI Controller selection can be made in the following:

1. During the VM creation.
2. After the creation, using **Edit Settings**.

When creating a VM, choose the type of OS you want and then on the **SCSI Controller** screen, select the controller you want for this VM. A default choice will be populated, based on your Guest OS selection:

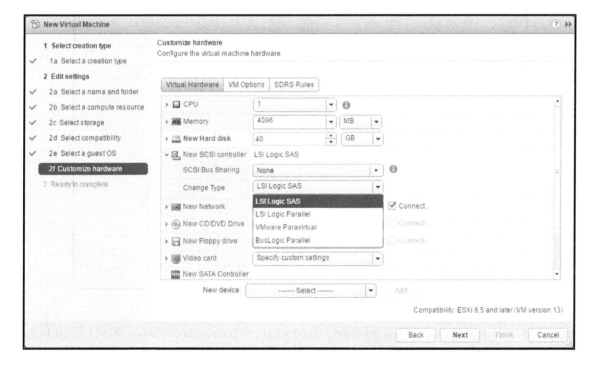

The SCSI Controller selection can also be changed using the **Edit Settings** menu item (available by right-clicking on the VM in the inventory panel) under **vSphere Web Client**. The VM must be powered down to change the SCSI Controller type:

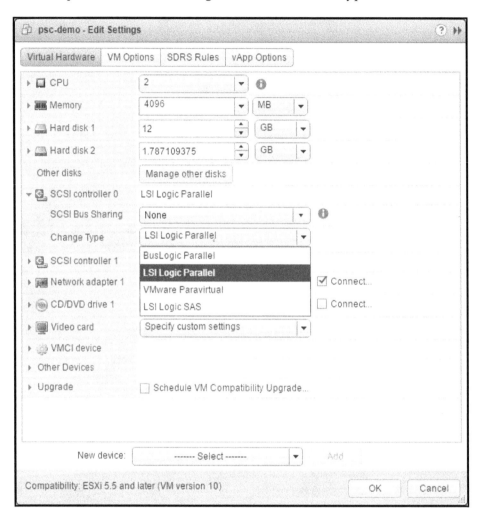

Once a VM has been powered on, it must still boot its operating system. It won't boot if the guest operating system does not include a driver for the configured virtual SCSI Controller.

Impact of VM swap file placement

The creation of a VM's swap file is automatic. By default, this file is created in the VM's working directory, but a different location can be set.

Swap file contains swapped memory pages and its size is determined as allocated RAM size—reservation. If performance is important in the design, 100 percent memory reservations should be created, causing no need to swap to disk.

You can optionally configure a special host cache on an SSD (if one is installed) to be used for the swap to host cache feature. This swap cache is shared by all the VMs running on the host. In addition, host-level swapping of the VMs' most active pages benefits from the low latency of SSD. The swap to host cache feature makes the best use of potentially limited SSD space. This feature is also optimized for large block sizes where some SSDs work best.

If a host does not use the swap to host cache feature, place the VM swap files on low latency, high bandwidth storage systems. The best choice is usually local SSD. If the host does not have local SSD, the second choice would be remote SSD. Remote SSD would still provide low latencies of SSD, though with the added latency of remote access.

Other than SSD storage, place the VM's swap file on the fastest available datastore. This datastore might be on a Fiber Channel SAN array or a fast local disk. Do not store swap files on thin provisioned LUNs. Running a VM with a swap file that is stored on a thin provisioned LUN can cause swap file growth to fail if no space is available on the LUN. This failure can lead to the termination of the VM.

This also has some impact on the vMotion operation too. Placing your VM swap file in a local datastore will increase the vMotion time for that VM because the destination ESXi host cannot connect to the local datastore; the file has to be placed on a datastore that is available for the new ESXi host running the incoming VM. Because of this reason, the destination host needs to create a new swap file in its swap file destination. As a new file has to be created and swapped, memory pages potentially need to be copied; this increases vMotion time.

In addition, placing your swap file on a replicated datastore increases vMotion time. When moving the contents of a swap file to a replicated datastore, the swap file and its contents need to be replicated to the replica datastore as well; each block is copied from the source datastore to the destination datastore if synchronous replication is used.

Getting ready

To step through this recipe, you will need one or more running ESXi Servers, a couple of datastores attached (Local SSD and Remote SSD) to these ESXi Servers, a vCenter Server, and vSphere Web Client. No other prerequisites are required.

How to do it…

You can define an alternate swap file location at the cluster level and the VM level.

To define an alternate swap file location at the cluster level, follow these steps:

1. Click on the cluster in the inventory and go to the **Configure** tab.
2. Click on **General** under **Configuration**.
3. Click on **Edit** in the **General** section.
4. Choose the option to store the swap file in the datastore specified by the host and click **OK**:

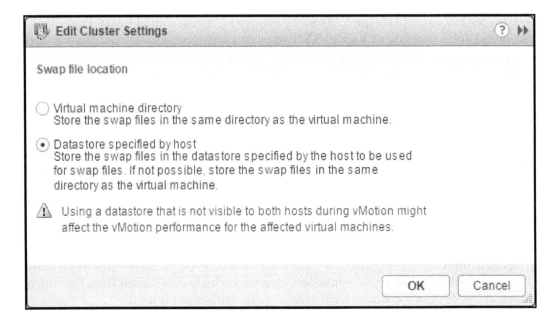

5. Now, select the ESXi host from the inventory and click on the **Configure** tab.
6. Click on **Swap file location** under the **Virtual Machines** section.
7. Click on the **Edit** link and select the datastore to use as that swap file location. Click **OK**:

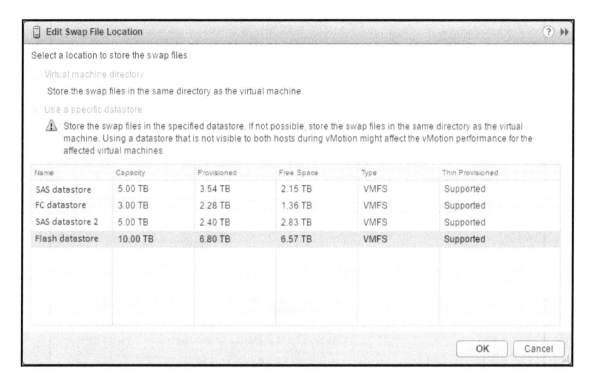

8. Repeat this step for your other ESXi hosts.

To define an alternate **Swap file location** at the VM level, the VM must be powered off, then follow these steps:

1. Right-click on the VM in the inventory and select **Edit Settings**.
2. In the **Virtual Machine Properties** dialog box, click on the **VM Options** tab.
3. Expand the **Advanced** section and select **Datastore specified by host** under the Swap file location.

4. Click on **OK**.

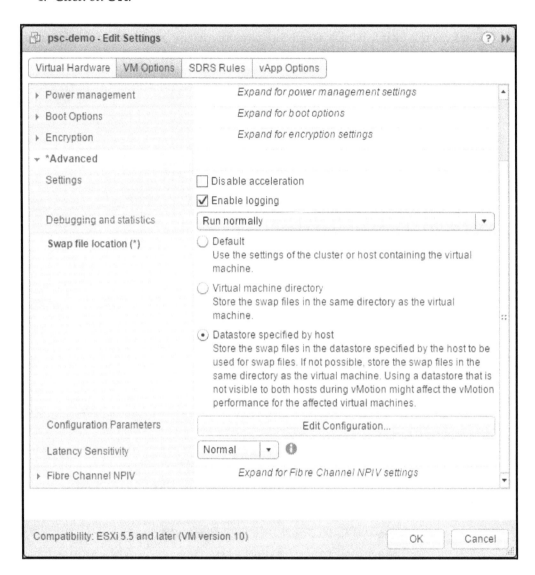

Using large pages in VMs

VMware ESXi provides 2 MB memory pages, commonly referred to as **large pages**, along with usual 4 KB memory pages. ESXi will always try to allocate 2 M pages for main memory and only on failure try for a 4 or small page. VMs are large pages if 2 M sequences of contiguous are available. The idea is to reduce the amount of page sharing and also increase the memory footprint of the VMs. The biggest benefit is of mitigating **TLB**-miss (short for **Translation Lookaside Buffer**), which costs as much as possible for Nested Page Table-enabled servers running ESXi.

However, allocating memory in 2 M chunks may cause the memory allocated to the VM to become fragmented. But as small pages are allocated by a guest and VM, these larger sequences need to be broken up.

So if defragmentation occurs, there could be enough memory to satisfy a large page request even when there is no 2 M contiguous Memory Page Number available. The defragmenter's job is to remap the existing allocated small pages in a 2 M region to allow that range to be mapped with a large page.

Transparent Page Sharing (**TPS**) runs across a host's VMs periodically (every 60 minutes by default) and reclaims identical 4 KB pages. However, this only happens when there are no large pages (2 MB pages). If you use large pages (2 MB), TPS does not come into the picture because of the **cost** of comparing these much larger pages. This is until there is memory contention, at which point the large pages are broken down into 4 KB blocks and identical pages are shared.

Large pages offer performance improvements. Reclamation of large pages does not happen if there is not enough physical memory to back all of the VMs' memory requests.

Memory saving happens due to TPS kick in when you run lots of VMs with very similar memory usage on a host. You will not see any memory saving until your host thinks it is under pressure, which will happen if large pages don't get shared. The host will wait until it hits 94 percent memory usage (6 percent free) before it deems itself under memory contention and starts to break those large pages into smaller 4 KB ones.

In a typical environment where you have many similar VMs, you are consistently going to run your host at around 94 percent memory used. All those identical memory pages can still be reclaimed, just as before, and you are gaining performance gain of large pages.

Getting ready

To step through this recipe, you will need one or more running ESXi Servers, a fully functioning vCenter Server, and vSphere Web Client. No other prerequisites are required.

How to do it...

The configuration of large pages in the operating system and the application are outside the scope of this article. See the vendor documentation for details on how to adjust these settings. The instructions on where to adjust large page settings for the ESXi 6.x host to align with the needs of your guest operating system and applications are as follows:

1. From vSphere Web Client, open the **Hosts and Clusters** view.
2. Select a host and go to the **Configure** tab.
3. Under the **System** section, click on **Advanced System Settings**.
4. Click on the **Edit** button.
5. In the filter box, enter Mem and hit *Enter*.
6. Double-click on the **Mem.AllocGuestLargePage** setting
7. Click **OK** when complete.

Set the **Mem.AllocGuestLargePage** option to **1** to enable the backing of guest large pages with host large pages. This reduces TLB misses and improves performance in server workloads that use guest large pages.

The default setting is **Mem.AllocGuestLargePage=1** in vSphere 5.1 and above:

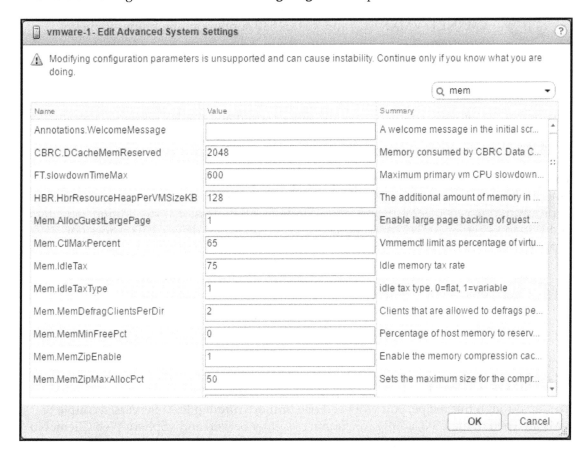

Guest OS networking considerations

Refer to `Chapter 3`, *Networking Performance Design*, where the *Selecting the correct virtual network adapter* recipe talks about the trade-off factors in choosing the correct adapter.

For the best performance, use the VMXNET3 network adapter for operating systems in which it is supported. The VM must use a virtual hardware of version 7 or later, and VMware Tools must be installed in the guest operating system.

If VMXNET3 is not supported in your guest operating system, use the enhanced VMXNET (which requires VMware Tools). Both the enhanced VMXNET (VMXNET2) and VMXNET3 support jumbo frames for better performance.

For the best networking performance, use network adapters that support hardware features, such as TCP checksum offload, TCP segmentation offload, and jumbo frames.

Ensure that the network adapters have the proper speed and duplex settings. Typically, for 10/100 NICs, set the speed and duplex. Make sure that the duplex is set to full duplex. For NICS, Gigabit Ethernet, or higher, set the speed and duplex to the auto-negotiate.

You can also choose E1000, which is an emulated version of the Intel 82545 EM Gigabit Ethernet NIC. A driver for this NIC is not included with all guest operating systems. Typically, Linux versions 2.4.19 and later, Windows XP Professional x64 Edition and later, and Windows Server 2003 (32-bit) and later include the E1000 driver. E1000 does not support jumbo frames prior to ESXi/ESX 4.1.

 Refer to `http://kb.vmware.com/kb/1001805` for more information on other known issues related to vNIC selection and OS support.

Getting ready

To step through this recipe, you will need one or more running ESXi Servers, a couple of VMs attached to the ESXi, a fully functioning vCenter Server, and vSphere Web Client. No other prerequisites are required.

How to do it...

Choosing a network adapter based on your performance requirement can be done in two ways. One is when you are creating a VM and the other is by using **Edit Settings** of the existing VM.

1. Open up vSphere Client and log in to the vCenter Server.
2. In the **Home** screen, select any ESXi Server, go to **File**, and select **New Virtual Machine**.

3. Now, after selecting the other entire configuration, go to the **Network** section.

4. Here, select the type of **Network Adapter** you want and choose which **Network Portgroup** you want to connect it to:

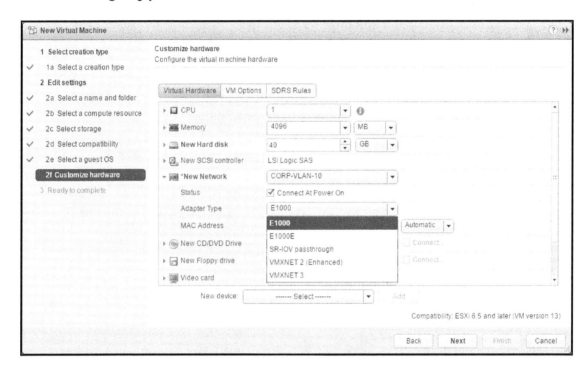

5. Finish the other configuration and select **Finish**.

See also

For other advanced configurations, refer to the following links:

- *Configuring Flow Control on VMware ESXi and ESX(1013413)* at `http://kb.vmware.com/kb/1013413`

- *Enabling Jumbo Frames on virtual distributed switches(1038827)* at `http://kb.vmware.com/kb/1038827`

- *Modifying the rc.local or sh.local file in ESX/ESXi to execute commands while booting(2043564)* at `http://kb.vmware.com/kb/2043564`

When you should or should not virtualize an application

Applications can be categorized into three basic groups:

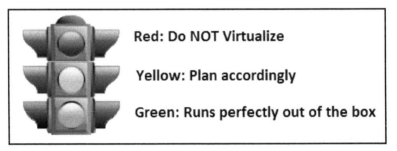

- **Green**: In this group, applications can be virtualized right out of the box. They have great performance with no tuning required.
- **Yellow**: In this group, applications have good performance but require some tuning and attention for optimal performance.
- **Red**: In this group, applications exceed the capabilities of the virtual platform and should not be virtualized. Also, it includes applications in which the software vendor does not support virtualization.

The vast majority of applications are green, which means that no performance tuning is required. Yellow applications are smaller but still a significant group. There are very few red applications (that is, applications that do not virtualize).

Getting ready

To step through this recipe, you will need one or more running ESXi Servers, more than one datastore attached to the ESXi, a couple of VMs on those datastores, a vCenter Server, and vSphere Web Client. No other prerequisites are required.

How to do it...

To determine which group (green, yellow, or red) your application belongs to, you need to pay attention to CPU, memory, network bandwidth, and storage:

1. Regarding your VM configuration, a VM scales to 128 vCPUs. Therefore, if your enterprise application uses more than 128 CPUs or if your application requires more than 6 TB of memory, you should not run the application in a VM.

2. A variety of tools provides the information that you need to characterize a native application. For example, the Linux top command gives you CPU usage and the memory size of an application. The iostat and netstat commands give you I/O bandwidth information. On a Windows system, Perfmon provides you with similar counters.

Use the resource requirements of your application and the following table to determine if your application is a good fit for virtualization (green), a good fit for virtualization but may need tuning (yellow) or not a good fit for virtualization (red).

Resource	Application	Category
CPU	CPU-intensive, more than 128 CPUs	Green (with latest HW Technology), red
Memory	Memory-intensive, greater than 6TB RAM	Green (with latest HW Technology), red
Network Bandwidth	1-27 Gb/S greater than 27 Gb/S	Yellow, red
Storage Bandwidth	10-250K IOPs (consider I/O size) greater than 250K IOPs (consider I/O size)	Yellow, red

Measuring the environment's performance

To monitor performance, users look at the application itself. Various tools exist for monitoring application performance. However, in this recipe, we will use **VMware vRealize Operations Manager** (**VROPS**).

Tuning an enterprise application for performance is challenging because, to begin with, the host running the VMs in which these applications run might be dealing with workloads of varying characteristics. As a result, the root cause of a performance problem might end up being a combination of problems that are CPU-related, memory-related, networking-related, and storage-related.

As a system administrator, you measure performance in terms of resource utilization. From the perspective of the user, the best measurement of performance is the response time of the application itself. In addition to resource utilization metrics, there are two performance measurements that can help an application owner determine whether or not an application's performance is acceptable:

- Throughput
- Latency

Throughput refers to the number of transactions that can execute in a given amount of time. There are various ways to measure throughput: megabytes per second, IOPS, transactions per second, or instructions per second.

Latency is the measurement of how much time it takes to do a specific job. Examples are instruction completion latency, network latency, disk I/O latency, and response time. Throughput and latency are often interrelated.

Application performance issues are not always related to resource utilization problems. They can be caused by the application itself, such as malformed queries or lengthy SQL coding. In addition, application performance issues remain the same whether you are using physical hardware or virtual hardware.

VROPS provides visibility from the application to the storage and provides administrators with an overall picture of the health of the environment.

Getting ready

To step through this recipe, you will need one or more running ESXi Servers, a set of applications running within VMs (such as SharePoint, Spring Source, Postgres SQL, and Python), a fully functioning vCenter Server, and vSphere Web Client. No other prerequisites are required.

How to do it...

There is a **vRealize Operations Manager** icon in the **Administration** section of the vSphere 6.5 home screen. We will use this icon to start the installation of VROPS:

1. Go to `http://www.vmware.com/download`and download vRealize Operations Manager - Appliance installation OVF file.

2. Click on the **vRealize Operations Manager** button from the home screen of the web client:

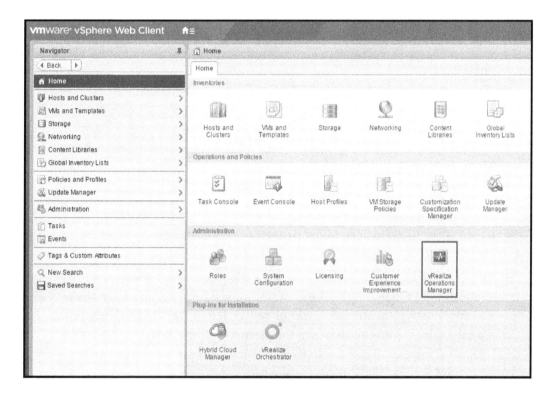

3. Click on the link in the **Basic Tasks** section.

4. Browse to find the vRealize Operations Manager - Appliance installation OVF file you downloaded from step 1. Click on **Next**.

5. Enter a name for the VROPS VM and specify a datacenter or folder. Click on **Next**.

6. Select the host that will run the VM. Click on **Next**.

7. Review the template details and click on **Next**.

8. Read and accept the license agreement. Click on **Next**.
9. Choose the size of appliance you want to create based on the number of VMs you have. Click on **Next**.
10. Pick the datastore that will hold the VM. Click on **Next**.
11. Click on the network where the VM will be connected. Click on **Next**.
12. Enter the network information for the VM and click on **Next**.
13. Review all the settings for the VM and click on **Finish**.

The VROPS VM will take several minutes to create and boot. When it is done, browse to the IP address you specified in step 12.

14. You will be presented with a **Get Started** screen with three options. Click on **New Installation**.
15. This wizard will create a new VROPS cluster. Click on **Next**.
16. Enter a password for the admin user, confirm, and then click on **Next**.
17. Use the default certificate or install a certificate if you have one. Click on **Next**.
18. Enter a name for the master node of the VROPS cluster and add an NTP server. Click on **Next**.
19. Review the next steps, then click on **Finish**.

You will be presented with the vRealize Operations Manager Administration screen. The cluster will be in the process of being configured; wait until it is done. Then follow these steps:

19. When the first node appears in the **Nodes** section, click on **Start vRealize Operations Manager** in the **System Status** section. This will take several minutes to start. When it finishes, you will be redirected to the VROPS login page.
20. Log in using the admin user and the password from step 16.
21. The configuration wizard will appear. Click on **Next**.
22. Read and accept EULA. Click on **Next**.
23. Enter a product key or choose Product Evaluation. Click on **Next**.
24. Either join the CEIP or do not join, then click on **Next**.
25. Click on **Finish**.
26. You will be logged into the **vRealize Operations Manager** screen.
27. In the **Solutions** section, click on **VMware vSphere** and click on **cogs** to configure the connection to your vCenter server.
28. In the **wizard**, enter your vCenter information and click on **Save Settings**.

At this point, the screen should look similar to the following, with the collection state indicating:

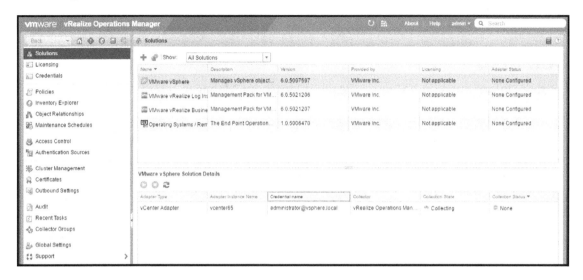

Once VROPS has completed processing the objects in the environment, you can log into the IP address of the VROPS VM and view the results:

In this case, most of our VMs are healthy (green), but we have a few with warnings (yellow) and errors (red). You can click on the yellow or red squares to drill down to the VM to see the details of the issue.

See also

For more information on VMware vRealize Operations Manager, refer to these links:

- *VMware's vRealize Operations product page* at `http://kb.vmware.com/kb/1013413`
- *VMware vRealize Operations Documentation* at `https://www.vmware.com/support/pubs/vmware-vrops-suite-pubs.html`
- *VMware's Cloud Management blog* at `https://blogs.vmware.com/management`

10
Performance Tools

In this chapter, we will cover topics related to performance tools and how they can help us test and improve the performance of our VMware environment. You will learn about the following performance tools:

- PowerCLI - introduction
- PowerCLI scripts
- PowerCLI for Docker
- HCIBench
- Runecast
- Iometer
- VMware IOInsight

Introduction

VMware is anything if not complete with tools, scripts, and third-party products that enable you to take advantage of your investment and infrastructure at their finest. In this chapter, we will discuss some of these items in brief and others in detail—how you could go deeper into using and exploring a virtualization environment and improving its performance.

PowerCLI - introduction

VMware first introduced PowerCLI in September 2008 as a way to manage ESX 3.0 and vCenter 2.5, using a Shell by leveraging the scripting capabilities of PowerShell. In these nearly 10 years, VMware PowerCLI has grown to become a very powerful management and automation tool for vSphere, vCloud, vRealize Operations Manager, and VMware Horizon, with over 500 cmdlets.

There are many tasks, for example, finding snapshots for VMs, that are very tedious in vSphere Web Client but can be easily performed using a single line with the PowerCLI script. Whether you're installing a native instance of PowerCLI on your Windows workstation or server or running an instance of PowerCLI Core using Docker, managing a VMware infrastructure has never been easier.

In the following recipe, we will install PowerCLI on a Windows 10 workstation and connect it to our vCenter server.

Getting ready

To step through this recipe, you will need at least one ESXi Server, an instance of vCenter Server, and a Windows workstation. No other prerequisites are required.

How to do it…

First, download and install PowerCLI, then perform the following steps:

1. Open your favorite browser and go to `https://www.vmware.com/downloads`.
2. Click on the **VMware vSphere**.
3. Go to the **Drivers & Tools** tab.
4. Expand the **Automation Tools and SDK(s)** section.
5. Click on the **VMware PowerCLI 6.5 Release 1** link.
6. Click on the **Download** link and log in to begin the download.
7. Once downloaded, start the installer.
8. Take the default installation options or adjust as required.

Now that you have installed PowerCLI, run it and connect it to your vCenter server:

1. Run the VMware PowerCLI shortcut from your desktop.
2. If you get an error about scripts being disabled on the system, follow the instructions at `http://go.microsoft.com/fwlink/?LinkID=135170` to fix the issue.
3. Close PowerCLI and reopen it. Say **Always run to the Initialize-PowerCLIEnvironment.ps1 script**.

> If you get a message similar to `Unable to find type [VMware.VimAutomation.sdk.Util10.ProductInfo]`, restart your system and run PowerCLI again.

4. Now that you have PowerCLI started, run the following script to connect to your vCenter Server:

```
Connect-VIServer <vCenter server name>
```

5. This script will automatically use your local Windows credentials to connect to the vCenter Server. If your local Windows credentials don't have permissions to log in to it, you will be prompted for a username and password.
6. The output should be similar to the following:

7. Now that you are connected to vCenter, run a simple script to list your hosts:

```
Get-VMHost
```

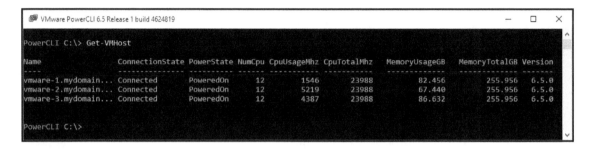

This is the expected output of the command. In the next recipe, we will explore more PowerCLI scripts.

See also

- The PowerCLI poster at https://blogs.vmware.com/PowerCLI/2017/02/powerc li-65-poster.html is a good reference for all things PowerCLI
- The PowerCLI blog at https://blogs.vmware.com/PowerCLI/ is a good place to start looking for more information

PowerCLI scripts

VMware PowerCLI is an extremely powerful tool, and there are countless blogs, forums, and conversations in VMware communities that provide complex scripts and one-liners to better serve and manage your infrastructure. In this recipe, we'll discuss a few samples and syntaxes of some very powerful one-liners that are useful when managing as small as a single VMware vCenter with three ESXi hosts or as complex as thousands of vCenter systems with hundreds of thousands of hosts.

How it works…

This recipe is divided into two sections: one-line scripts and multiline scripts. One-line scripts can be entered in the PowerCLI window itself. For multiline scripts, it is a good idea to write the script in the PowerShell ISE, then run it in the PowerCLI window.

PowerCLI Scripts – one-liner

The one-liners and scripts that will follow touch specifically on items that can often have a direct impact on your virtual environment or VM performance, so they should be used appropriately to identify any challenges to be corrected.

- The following command will dump a list of VMs and provide their names, the names of their snapshots, when they were created, and their size:

    ```
    Get-VM | Get-Snapshot | Select VM, Name, Created, SizeMB
    ```

- The following command will dump your VMware Tools version, which is helpful to determine whether there are any dated VMs:

    ```
    Get-VM | Get-View | Select Name,
    @{N="ToolsVersion";E={$_.config.tools.toolsVersion}}
    ```

- The following command will dump all the datastores and their respective multipath policies:

    ```
    Get-VMhost | Get-SCSILun | Select VMHost, Vendor, MultipathPolicy
    ```

- The following command goes a step further than the preceding ones and identifies all the datastores that have a fixed multipath policy:

    ```
    Get-VMhost | Get-SCSILun | Where {$_.MultipathPolicy -EQ "Fixed"} |
    Select VMHost, Vendor, MultipathPolicy
    ```

- The following command goes one step further and identifies only the datastores by Pure Storage, where the multipath policy is fixed:

    ```
    Get-VMhost | Get-SCSILun | Where {$_.Vendor -EQ "PURE"} | Where
    {$_.MultipathPolicy -EQ "Fixed"} | Select VMHost, Vendor,
    MultipathPolicy
    ```

    PowerCLI can be used to query information but can also be used to set parameters.

Be very careful when making changes using a script. Running a script that doesn't perform as expected can cause serious damage to your infrastructure.

- The following command will identify Pure Storage disks that are currently set to fix and change them to `RoundRobin`:

```
Get-VMhost | Get-SCSILun | Where {$_.Vendor -EQ "PURE"} | Where
{$_.MultipathPolicy -EQ "Fixed"} | Set-SCSILun -MultipathPolicy
"RoundRobin"
```

There are obviously millions of other iterations of one-liner-type capabilities you can use to support and manage your environment. The preceding list is by no means the end-all list of things you're capable of; though, this list is a useful set of commands you should run at least once, if not multiple times, while managing your VMware vSphere environment.

PowerCLI Scripts – multiline

Just as VMware, PowerCLI is considered a very powerful tool to enable your environment, and its ability to do things with a single line can be very powerful. However, some things are better done in multiline scripts in order to be successful..

Multi-line scripts can be either typed in the PowerCLI command screen or entered in a separate file and called from the command line. To make use of a separate script file, create a file with the `.ps1` extension, then right-click on it and select **Edit**. This will open the script in Windows PowerShell ISE. You can now enter the script. The following script lists the number of paths per datastore per host:

Save the script, then go back to the PowerCLI command line and simply call the name of the script. Be sure to use the full path of the script location, or use . \ if the script is in the current path. You may need to adjust your PowerShell security parameters to allow remote scripts to run from the command line:

```
Select VMware PowerCLI 6.5 Release 1 build 4624819                                          —  □  ×

PowerCLI C:\> .\myScript.ps1

VMHost                    Datastore        LUN                                      Active Paths
------                    ---------        ---                                      ------------
vmware-1.mydomain.com Thick-01        naa.6006016009103900585beeb7e1ece311              2
vmware-1.mydomain.com Thin-01         naa.6006016009103900920eb6d0e1ece311              2
vmware-1.mydomain.com Thick-02        naa.6006016009103900ecb324f12ede311               2
vmware-2.mydomain.com Thick-01        naa.6006016009103900585beeb7e1ece311              2
vmware-2.mydomain.com Thin-01         naa.6006016009103900920eb6d0e1ece311              2
vmware-2.mydomain.com Thick-02        naa.6006016009103900ecb324f12ede311               2
vmware-3.mydomain.com Thick-01        naa.6006016009103900585beeb7e1ece311              2
vmware-3.mydomain.com Thin-01         naa.6006016009103900920eb6d0e1ece311              2
vmware-3.mydomain.com Thick-02        naa.6006016009103900ecb324f12ede311               2

PowerCLI C:\> _
```

A small sample of multi-line scripts is included in the following list to leverage the understanding of this tool:

- This script lets you shut down a VM, change it's memory and CPU requirements and power on the system:

  ```
  $vm_name = Get-VM "VMware vCenter Log Insight 1.0.4" ForEach ($vm
  in $vm_name){ $vm_name | Shutdown-VMGuest -Confirm:$False Sleep 60
  $vm_name | Set-VM -MemoryGB 8 -NumCpu 2 -Confirm:$False $vm_name |
  Start-VM }
  ```

- This script will let you know whether a datastore had been upgraded from VMFS v3 to v5 or has been recreated:

  ```
  foreach ($myHost in get-VMHost)
  {
      Write-Host '$myHost = ' $myHost
      $esxcli = Get-EsxCli -VMHost $myHost
      $esxcli.storage.core.device.partition.list() |
      Where {$_.StartSector -eq "128"} |
      Select Device, StartSector
  }
  ```

This is just a small sample; an average VMware PowerCLI script will have dozens of lines, if not hundreds, of text and would be prohibitive to include here. Do take advantage of the community and blogs that are ripe with wonderful, detailed, and complex scripts ready for you to use with PowerCLI.

PowerCLI for Docker

Although as powerful a tool and environment both PowerCLI and PowerShell have been, for years they have been overwhelmingly restricted solely to a Microsoft Windows platform, which limited management and interaction coming from Linux and Mac-based platforms. Over time, this was resolved with alternate solutions for supporting and managing your VMware vSphere environment on those platforms; these solutions include the PowerCLI tool natively running within a containerized Docker environment.

In the following recipe, we will install PowerCLI into a Docker environment and connect it to our vCenter server.

Getting ready

To step through this recipe, you will need at least one ESXi Server, an instance of vCenter Server, and a Windows or Mac workstation. No other prerequisites are required.

How to do it...

First, download and install Docker and perform the following steps:

1. Open your favorite browser and download the instance of Docker Community Edition that applies to your OS:
   - Windows: `https://www.docker.com/docker-windows`
   - Mac: `https://www.docker.com/docker-mac`
2. Once downloaded, start the installer.
3. Take the default install options or adjust as required.

Now that you have installed Docker CE, download and use the PowerCLI Core:

1. Run the Terminal or Command Prompt to access your Docker instance.
2. Pull the PowerCLI Core image from DockerHub by running the following command:

```
docker pull vmware/powerclicore
```

```
[C:\>
[C:\>docker pull vmware/powerclicore
Using default tag: latest
latest: Pulling from vmware/powerclicore
93b3dcee11d6: Already exists
d6641ceee635: Pull complete
62bbcce52faa: Pull complete
e86aa7a78685: Pull complete
db20fbdf24c0: Pull complete
37379feb8f29: Pull complete
8abb449d1e29: Pull complete
a9cd6d9452e7: Pull complete
50886ff01a73: Pull complete
74af7eaa49c1: Pull complete
878c611eaf2c: Pull complete
39b1b7978191: Pull complete
98e632013bea: Pull complete
4362432cb5ea: Pull complete
19f5f892ae79: Pull complete
29b0b093b159: Pull complete
913ad6409b89: Pull complete
ad5db0a55033: Pull complete
Digest: sha256:d33ac26c0c704a7aa48f5c7c66cb76ec3959beda2962ccd6a41a96351055b5d0
Status: Downloaded newer image for vmware/powerclicore:latest
C:\>
```

Now that the Docker PowerCLI Core environment is loaded, initialize it with the following command:

```
docker run --rm -it --entrypoint='/usr/bin/powershell' vmware/powerclicore
```

```
[C:\>
[C:\>docker run --rm -it --entrypoint='/usr/bin/powershell' vmware/powerclicore
PowerShell
Copyright (C) 2016 Microsoft Corporation. All rights reserved.


        Welcome to VMware vSphere PowerCLI!


Log in to a vCenter Server or ESX host:              Connect-VIServer
To find out what commands are available, type:       Get-VICommand
Once you've connected, display all virtual machines: Get-VM


        Copyright (C) VMware, Inc. All rights reserved.



Loading personal and system profiles took 1262ms.
PS /powershell>
```

At this point, PowerCLI is initialized; connect to vCenter and run scripts/commands as usual.

See also

William Lam's blog has very useful information on working with PowerCLI and Docker; check out his blogs on initializing and scripting here:

- PowerCLI with Docker: `http://www.virtuallyghetto.com/2016/10/powercli-core-is-now-available-on-docker-hub.html`
- PowerCLI with Docker and Scripts: `http://www.virtuallyghetto.com/2016/10/5-different-ways-to-run-powercli-script-using-powercli-core-docker-container.html`

HCIBench

HCIBench is a tool from VMware that is designed to test the performance of vSAN datastores, but it can also be used to test the performance of non-vSAN datastores. You can use this tool to benchmark your existing storage performance or use it when evaluating a new storage platform.

There are two components to HCIBench: the controller VM and the Vdbench guest VM(s). The controller VM is an appliance that deploys the guest VMs, runs the tests, and collects the results. The Vdbench guests provide the I/O traffic to the storage.

Getting ready

To step through this recipe, you will need at least one ESXi Server, an instance of installed vCenter Server, and vSphere Web Client. You will also need one IP address for the controller and one IP address for each guest. No other prerequisites are required.

How to do it...

The first step is to download the HCIBench software:

1. Go to `https://labs.vmware.com/flings/hcibench`.
2. Download the `HCIBench<version>.ova` file.

Now, deploy the controller VM and perform the following steps:

1. Log in to vSphere Web Client.
2. Navigate to the **Hosts and Clusters** view, then right-click on your cluster and select **Deploy OVF Template**.
3. In the wizard, browse and select the `HCIBench<version>.ova` file we downloaded earlier. Click on **Next**.
4. Enter the name of the new VM and select the desired datacenter. Click on **Next**.
5. Select the desired host or cluster. Click on **Next**.
6. Review the details and click on **Next**.
7. Read the license agreement and click on **Accept**. Click on **Next**.
8. Select thin provisioning for the disk format. Select the desired storage location. Click on **Next**.

9. In the **Select Networks** screen, HCIBench will be accessed via the public network. Vdbench guests will be deployed and will require DHCP in the private network. Both Public Network and Private Network can be mapped to the same network if you like. Click on **Next**.

10. In the **Customize Template** screen, expand the root credentials at the bottom and enter the root password. Click on **Next**.

11. Review the configuration, then click on **Finish**.

The HCIBench VM will be deployed. Once this is done, power on the VM. When the VM is running, follow these steps to configure your test:

1. Click on the **HCIBench VM** and find its IP address under the **Summary** tab:

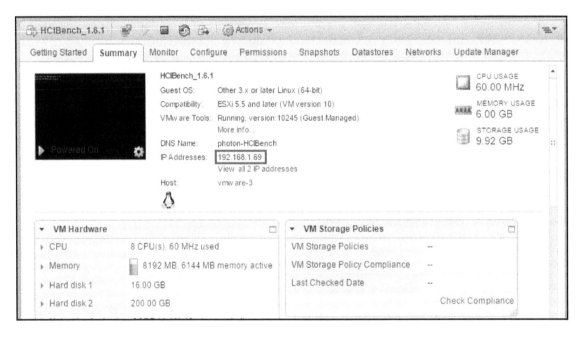

2. Go to `http://<IP address>:8080`.

3. Log in with the root and the password specified during the deployment.

4. You will be presented with a page with a large number of parameters:

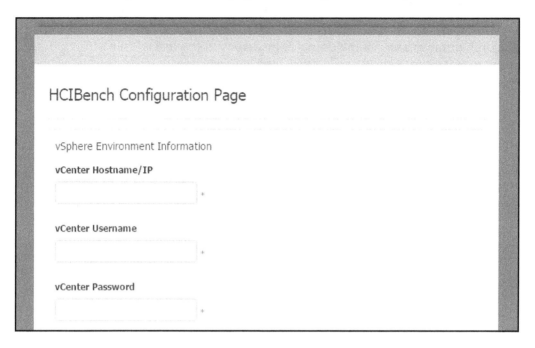

5. Enter the **vCenter Hostname/IP**, **vCenter Username**, and **vCenter Password** of the vCenter system where you want to run the tests.
6. Enter the **Datacenter Name**, **Cluster Name**, and **Network Name** where the Vdbench guests will be deployed. The **Network Name** is optional and will default to the VM network if left blank.
7. Click on the checkbox for **Enable DHCP Service** on the network if the mapped Private Network does not have a DHCP server already.
8. Enter the datastore name that you will be testing against. If you enter multiple datastores, the Vdbench guests will be deployed evenly on the datastores.
9. Click on the checkbox for **Clear Read/Write Cache Before Each Testing** if you are testing a vSAN datastore and want to clear the cache tier before the test.
10. If you would like to specify the hosts where the guests will be deployed, click on the **Deploy on Hosts** checkbox and enter one or more hostnames.

 If you do not specify the hosts, the guests will be deployed evenly across all the hosts. If a distributed switch port group is used as the client VM network, Deploy on Hosts must be unchecked.

11. If you are testing against vSAN, check the **Easy Run** checkbox. If you are running this test against non-vSAN storage, leave this box unchecked.

12. Enter the number of VMs to be deployed.

13. Enter the number of data disks to be deployed on each guest VM.

14. Enter the size of each data disk in GB.

15. Click on **Re-Use The Existing VMs If Possible** if you have run the test previously and want to reuse the existing VMs.

16. Give the test a name.

17. Select an existing Vdbench parameter file or click on **Generate** to create one:

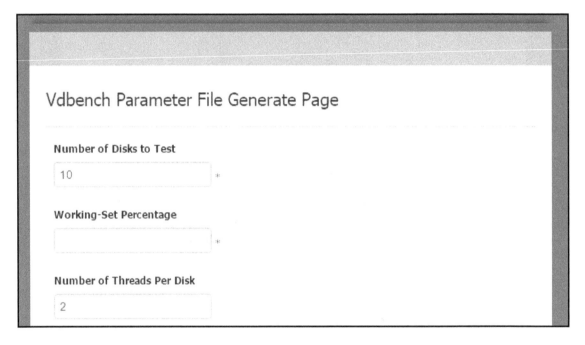

18. The number of disks to test must match the number of data disks in the previous screen. Once you have generated the Vdbench parameter file, close the page, go back to the main page, and click on **Refresh**. Your parameter file will appear in the drop-down list:

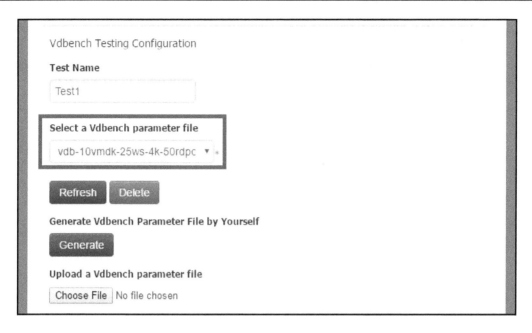

19. In the **Prepare Virtual Disk Before Testing** drop-down list, select **Random** if your storage has deduplication enabled. Otherwise, select **Zero**.
20. Enter a value in the **Testing Duration** field if you want to override the elapsed value to the Vdbench parameter file.
21. Check the **Clean up VMs after testing** checkbox if you want the guest VMs to be deleted after the test.
22. Click on **Download** to download the Vdbench file from the Oracle website. Once it has been downloaded, click on **Choose File** to upload the ZIP file. Then, click on **Upload Vdbench**. This is a one-time operation, and these options will disappear after you upload the Vdbench file:

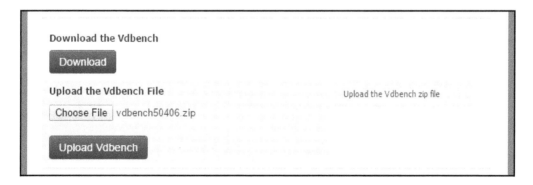

23. Click on the **Save Configuration** button. Any issues will be reported so you can fix them.

24. Click on the **Validate** button and fix any issues that are reported. If any issues are found, fix the issue, save the configuration, then run the validation again:

Information   ×

2017-04-06 16:11:27 -0700: Validating VC IP and Crendetial...

2017-04-06 16:11:32 -0700: VC IP and Credential Validated

2017-04-06 16:11:32 -0700: Validating Datacenter MyDatacenter...

2017-04-06 16:11:36 -0700: Datacenter MyDatacenter Validated

2017-04-06 16:11:36 -0700: Validating Cluster Production...

2017-04-06 16:11:39 -0700: Cluster Production Validated

2017-04-06 16:11:42 -0700: Cluster Production has DRS mode: fullyAutomated

2017-04-06 16:11:42 -0700: Validating If Hosts in Cluster Production Could be Connected...

2017-04-06 16:11:56 -0700: All Hosts could be Connected

2017-04-06 16:11:56 -0700: Validating Network VM Network...

2017-04-06 16:12:02 -0700: Network VM Network Validated

2017-04-06 16:12:02 -0700: Checking If Network VM Network is accessible from all the hosts of Production...

2017-04-06 16:12:06 -0700: Network VM Network is accessible from host vmware-1

2017-04-06 16:12:10 -0700: Network VM Network is accessible from host vmware-2

2017-04-06 16:12:13 -0700: Network VM Network is accessible from host vmware-3

2017-04-06 16:12:13 -0700: Network VM Network is accessible from all the hosts of Production

2017-04-06 16:12:13 -0700: Validating Type of Network VM Network...

2017-04-06 16:12:17 -0700: Network VM Network Type is Network

2017-04-06 16:12:17 -0700: Validating Datastore Thick-01...

2017-04-06 16:12:20 -0700: Datastore Thick-01 Validated

2017-04-06 16:12:20 -0700: Checking Datastore Thick-01 type...

2017-04-06 16:12:23 -0700: Datastore Thick-01 type is VMFS

2017-04-06 16:12:23 -0700: Checking If Datastore Thick-01 is accessible from all the hosts of Production...

2017-04-06 16:12:27 -0700: Datastore Thick-01 is accessible from host vmware-1

2017-04-06 16:12:27 -0700: Datastore Thick-01 is accessible from host vmware-2

2017-04-06 16:12:27 -0700: Datastore Thick-01 is accessible from host vmware-3

2017-04-06 16:12:27 -0700: Datastore Thick-01 is accessible from all the hosts of Production

2017-04-06 16:12:30 -0700: Deploy on hosts: False. Skip validating hosts...

2017-04-06 16:12:45 -0700: All the config has been validated, please go ahead to kick off testing

---

25. Click on **Test** to start running the tests. The controller VM will connect to vCenter and deploy the test VMs:

In vCenter, you will see several tasks as the guest VMs are being created. Eventually, you will see the guest VMs in your inventory. They will be located in a new folder called `vdb-<cluster name>-vms`:

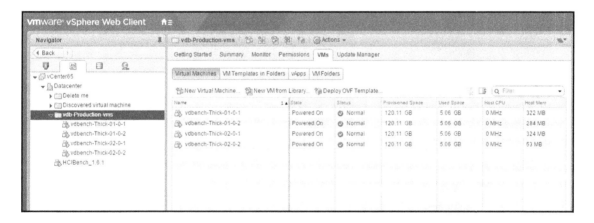

After the system has finished preparing the guest VMs and their disks, the testing will begin:

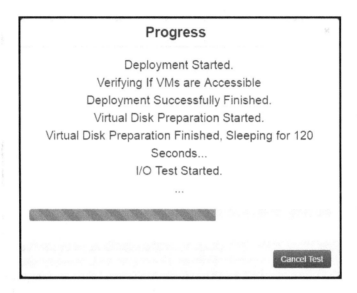

Once the test has finished, close the progress screen and click on the **Result** button to browse the results page. Open the folder with your test name, then open the text file to view the results. This will show IOPS, throughput, and latency of each datastore specified.

Runecast

Up to 90 percent of the issues that occur in VMware environments have already been documented in VMware KB articles. Runecast compares your specific VMware environment against the VMware knowledge base and tells you which issues you are likely to run into. You can then follow the VMware KB to proactively fix the issue. Runecast is a licensed software product, but it has a fully functional 30-day free trial service that is easy to deploy. Runecast deploys on a virtual appliance, and downloading the software to receiving your results should take less than 15 minutes.

Getting ready

To step through this recipe, you will need at least one ESXi Server, an instance of installed vCenter Server, and vSphere Web Client. You will also need an IP address for the Runecast appliance. No other prerequisites are required.

How to do it...

The first step is to download the Runecast software:

1. Go to `https://www.runecast.biz`.
2. Click on **Free Trial** on the main page.
3. Fill in your information and click on **Create Account**.
4. Once you are logged in, download the Runecast Analyzer (`.ova`).
5. Log in to vSphere Web Client and go to the **Hosts and Clusters** view.
6. Right-click on your cluster and select **Deploy OVF Template...**.
7. In the **Deploy OVF Template** wizard, select the **.ovf** file you downloaded. Click on **Next**.
8. Enter a name and select a datacenter. Click on **Next**.
9. Select a host or cluster. Click on **Next**.
10. Review the details. Click on **Next**.
11. Read and accept EULA. Click on **Next**.
12. Choose your configuration based on the size of your environment. Click on **next**.
13. Pick your datastore. Click on **Next**.
14. Choose the network you want to use. Click on **Next**.
15. Enter your network details. Click on **Next**.
16. Review the settings. Click on **Finish**.

17. The wizard will deploy the OVF and configure the appliance. This will take a few minutes. When it is done, power on the appliance and go to the IP address you assigned. Log in with the `rcuser` username and the password as **Runecast!**:

Now that you have deployed the appliance, connect it to your vCenter and run the analysis:

1. Click on the cog at the top-right corner.
2. Click on the vCenter Connection tab, then click on **Add vCenter**.
3. Enter the FQDN or IP of your vCenter Server, the port, and the username and password. Click on **Save**.
4. The system will connect to your vCenter server and show it in the list.
5. Go back to **Dashboard** and click on the **Analyze Now** button at the top of the screen.

6. After a couple of minutes, the screen should show the results of the analysis:

As you can see, Runecast has scanned 70 inventory objects, performed over 20 thousand checks, and has identified multiple issues. You can click on **Inventory** on the left-hand side to see the issues associated with each host or VM:

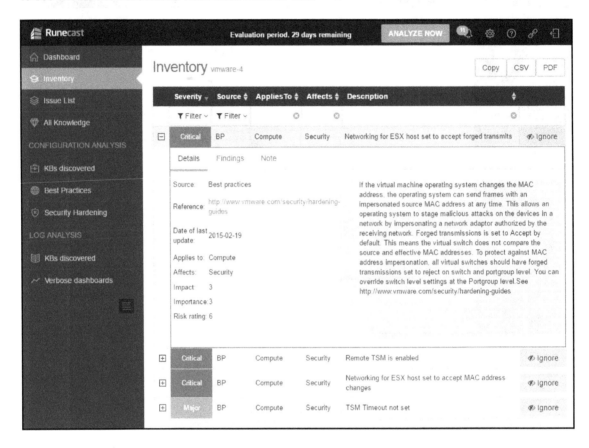

Clicking on an issue shows a summary of the issue and the reference link you can use to solve the issue. You can also click on the **Ignore** button to tell Runecast that you don't want to see this alert again.

You can also view where your configuration settings are in a VMware KB or check whether they are consistent with VMware **Best Practices** or the Security Hardening Recommendations:

Runecast also searches through the ESXi logs to find applicable KBs to your environment. You can click on the KBs discovered tab to see these results:

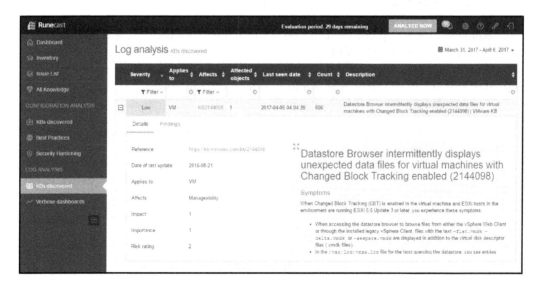

Iometer

Iometer is a piece of software that is both a workload generator and a measurement tool. It can be run on a local system, or it can generate and measure loads on multiple network systems. As the name implies, Iometer works by generating I/O to a disk target and measuring the IOPS, latency, CPU utilization, and errors. It can be set to generate different I/O sizes, read/write distributions, random/sequential distribution, burstiness, and I/O alignment. Changing these parameters will show how the storage subsystem can handle, say, 4k IOPS versus 32k IOPS.

Getting ready

To step through this recipe, you will need at least one ESXi Server, an instance of installed vCenter Server, and vSphere Web Client. You will also need a VM where you can run Iometer. No other prerequisites are required.

How to do it...

The first step is to download Iometer to the VM where we want to run the tests:

1. Download the appropriate executable from `http://www.iometer.org/doc/downloads.html`.
2. Once downloaded, run the `Iometer.exe file`.

Iometer requires some setup before it can be started. For these tests, I created a second 10 GB hard drive labeled `E:` on the VM where the Iometer tests will be performed. By default, Iometer creates one manager (with the same name as your VM) and four workers (Worker 1 through 4). We will run the tests with the defaults, but you can create additional managers and workers depending on your testing needs:

1. Click on the plus sign next to the manager to see the four default workers.
2. You can add or remove workers as required.

3. For each of the workers, do the following:
   1. Click on the worker.
   2. Click on the **Disk Targets** tab and select the drive you want to target:

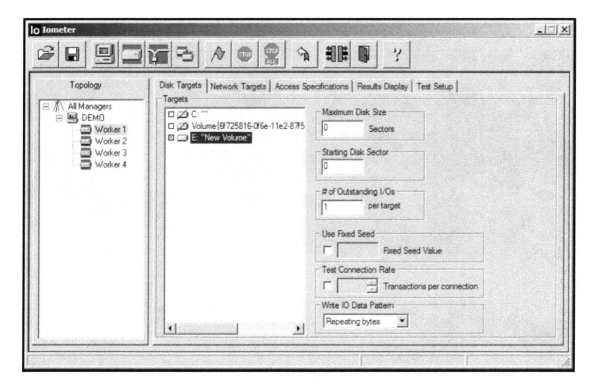

3. Click on the **Access Specifications** tab and add the All in one (at the bottom) option to **Assigned Access Specifications**. If you have a specific block size, read/write ratio, or randomness that you want to test, select one of the specifications from the list. You can also click on **New** to create your own custom specification:

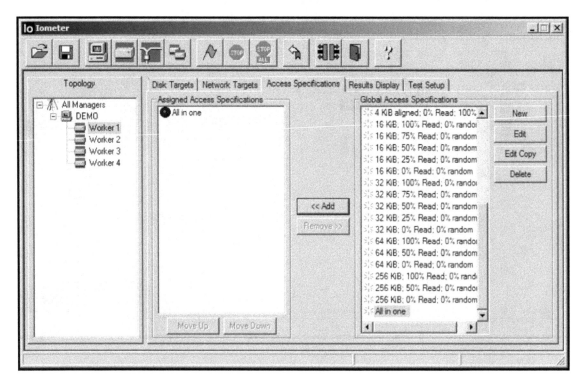

4. Click back on the manager in the **Topology** section.
5. Click on the **Results Display** tab and change Update Frequency to 5.
6. Click on the **Start Tests** button with the green flag icon.
7. Select a location for the results file from the pop-up window.
8. Wait for the test files to be created.
9. When the test is run, you will see the results in the **Results Display** tab.

When the test is running, Iometer will look something like this:

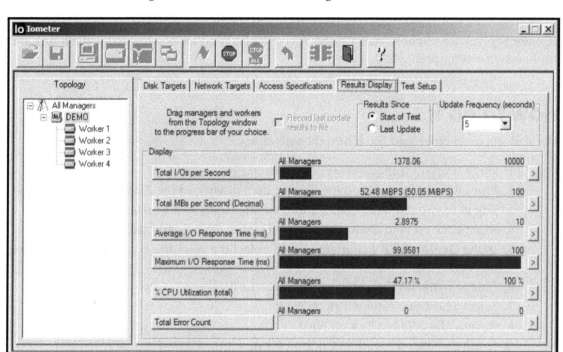

See also...

For more information on using Iometer, refer to the Users Guide section at `http://www.iom eter.org/doc/documents.html`.

VMware IOInsight

VMware IOInsight is a tool that was developed by the VMware Performance Group to help customers understand their storage I/O behavior. You can use this information to tune your storage. IOInsight is a virtual appliance that captures I/O traces from ESXi and displays the results in a web-based interface. In this recipe, we will download, install, and run an analysis using VMware IOInsight.

Getting ready

To step through this recipe, you will need at least one ESXi Server, an instance of installed vCenter Server, and vSphere Web Client. You will also need an IP address for the IOInsight appliance. No other prerequisites are required.

How to do it...

The first step is to download the IOInsight software:

1. Go to `https://labs.vmware.com/flings/ioinsight`.
2. From the main page, read the license, then download the ZIP file. Unzip the file.
3. Log in to vSphere Web Client and go to the **Hosts and Clusters** view.
4. Right-click on your cluster and select **Deploy OVF Template....**
5. In the **Deploy OVF Template** wizard, select the `.ova` file you downloaded. Click on **Next**.
6. Enter a name for the appliance and select a datacenter. Click on **Next**.
7. Select a host or cluster. Click on **Next**.
8. Review the details. Click on **Next**.
9. Select the storage location. Click on **Next**.
10. Select the destination network. Click on **Next**.
11. Review the settings and click on **Finish**.
12. Once the VM has been created, power it on.

Now that the IOInsight appliance is created and running, log in and run a test:

1. Click on the IOInsight VM in vSphere Web Client, then go to the **Summary** tab. Find the IP address for the appliance, then browse to `https://<VM_IP>` using Chrome or Safari:

2. Enter the hostname or IP of your vCenter Server and login credentials. Click on **Login**.
3. On the left-hand side, you will see the hosts attached to vCenter. Click on the + next to a host that contains the VM you want to analyze and enter the root password.
4. This will show the VMs running on that host. Expand the VM you want to analyze, then select the drive(s) you want to analyze.
5. It is recommended that you select eight or less VMDK files to reduce overhead.
6. On the right-hand side of the web page, enter a name for the test and select a duration.

7. Select Basic I/O Analyzer, then click on **Start**. This will take you to the results page. The screen will show the graphs after a few seconds:

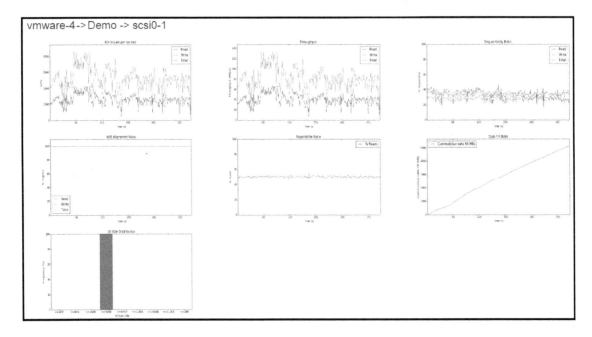

On this particular VM, I was running Iometer with a 32 k test with 50 percent reads. We can see that IOInsight correctly identified the Read/Write ratio and I/O Size Distribution.

Index

www.ingramcontent.com/pod-product-compliance
Lightning Source LLC
Chambersburg PA
CBHW062059050326
40690CB00016B/3153